Roman Empire
at War

To Joy, Autumn, Ian and Corrender.

Roman Empire at War

A Compendium of Battles from 31 BC to AD 565

Donathan Taylor

Pen & Sword
MILITARY

First published in Great Britain in 2016 by
PEN & SWORD MILITARY
An imprint of
Pen & Sword Books Ltd
47 Church Street
Barnsley
South Yorkshire
S70 2AS

ISBN 978-1-47386-908-0

Typeset by Concept, Huddersfield, West Yorkshire.
Printed and bound in England by CPI Group (UK) Ltd, Croydon, CR0 4YY.

Pen & Sword Books Ltd incorporates the imprints of Pen & Sword Archaeology, Atlas, Aviation, Battleground, Discovery, Family History, History, Maritime, Military, Naval, Politics, Railways, Select, Social History, Transport, True Crime, and Claymore Press, Frontline Books, Leo Cooper, Praetorian Press, Remember When, Seaforth Publishing and Wharncliffe.

For a complete list of Pen & Sword titles please contact
PEN & SWORD BOOKS LIMITED
47 Church Street, Barnsley, South Yorkshire, S70 2AS, England
E-mail: enquiries@pen-and-sword.co.uk
Website: www.pen-and-sword.co.uk

Contents

Acknowledgements

I am indebted to staff of the Rupert and Pauline Richardson Library for their unfailing support of my work. The director, Mrs. Alice Specht, was very gracious in permitting me the opportunity to personally retain ample portions of the library's collection of Loeb Classics for months at a time, and the acquisitions department is second-to-none in its ability to garner rare published materials from various special collections. I am likewise grateful to the staff of the British Library for their kind and patient assistance, as well as to Mr Ian Taylor for drafting the maps.

The author also wishes to thank William Heinemann Ltd and Harvard University Press, and the Loeb Classical Library. Special thanks must go to Philip Sidnell, Matt Jones and the firm of Pen & Sword Books for their generous guidance throughout this project. Also, a very grateful word of appreciation to Tony Walton, whose editorial talents have allowed this author to retain ample portions of his personal and professional dignity; any errors are mine.

Also, a heartfelt word of gratitude to my mentors Donald Engels, Robert Fink, Ira Taylor and Thomas Kennedy. Thanks also to Colin Wells for fondly remembered words of encouragement years ago.

I wish to offer very special appreciation to B.W. Aston, Kenneth Jacobs and Paul Madden, colleagues who, as senior scholars, encouraged a young historian to tackle what then seemed a monumental task. Sadly, they did not live to see the publication of this work. They were friends with whom I shared many laughs and much serious conversation over countless cups of coffee, and I miss them.

Finally, to my wife Joy – friend, soul mate, best critic, encourager, inspiration. There are no words sufficient to express the debt of gratitude I owe her. Suffice to say, you're still the one.

Preface

The primary purpose of this compendium is to provide readers with a basic, one-volume reference of the most significant battles in Roman Imperial history. The information in each entry is drawn exclusively from ancient, late antique and early medieval texts, in order to offer a brief description of each battle based solely on the information provided by the earliest surviving sources which chronicle the event. Such an approach will provide the reader with a concise foundation of information to which they can then confidently apply later scholarly interpretation presented in secondary sources in order to achieve a more accurate understanding of the most likely battlefield scenario.

In writing the battlefield descriptions I have not sought to subject the evidence contained in the original sources to intense analysis, nor have I attempted to embellish upon the surviving accounts, beyond that which was necessary to provide clarity to the modern reader. In essence, I've allowed the original writers to speak for themselves. My task was simply to harmonize the disparate information in order to provide a better appreciation of what the ancients describe as occurring on the field of battle.

A task of this nature cannot be truly and properly addressed unless one is willing to undertake an exhaustive reading of the ancient authors. Otherwise, one runs the risk of overlooking any number of battles to which the classical writers will in many cases devote only a few lines in their texts. The names of battles included in this work are typically derived from one or more of the extant sources consulted, and so in many cases may not bear the name perhaps more commonly used to identify a specific engagement in general or popular studies of Late Roman history. When an exact name is not given in the sources, the battle is identified by the nearest community (Rome, Carthage, Nisibis, etc.) or recognizable geographical feature (Severn River, Ponte Salario, Actium Promontory, etc.).

I cannot claim emphatically that this work includes every single Roman battlefield contest mentioned in the original sources that might be deemed by some modern historian to be a major encounter. Engagements which, in this author's judgment, appear to have been nothing more than skirmishes – relatively small, brief, unintended clashes of no significant strategic value for either hostile party involved – have not, with rare exceptions, been selected for inclusion.

Also omitted are those battles discussed or alluded to by one or more ancient writers for which there is simply no identifiable name, location or landmark, a circumstance especially applicable to the Late Empire. Likewise I have generally avoided sieges, a particular form of hostile encounter that is commonly reported in sources pertaining to the Near Eastern wars of the Late Empire, but which occurred throughout the history of Rome. Some of these more celebrated events are included nonetheless, so readers will find descriptions of sieges ranging from Amida to Volandum.

Finally, I have chosen to end my study with the reign of Justinian I for two fundamental reasons: first, because he was the last emperor who aspired to reunite much of the former Roman Empire; and second, because he was the last imperial ruler to speak Latin, and as such symbolizes for me, in a very poignant way, the passing of a great age in Mediterranean history.

Part One

Introduction to Roman Imperial Warfare

The Roman Imperial Army

The Roman Legion,
First Century BC–early Fourth Century AD

'The Roman army, clashing their shields and spears together, as was their custom and uttering their battlecry, advanced against the foe.'

Polybius I.34.23

Throughout the long history of Imperial Rome, the army served as a touchstone of power for the state. The growth of Roman political influence was oftentimes synonymous with the expansion of military strength, and the power of the army became a measure of the state's vitality. In similar fashion, the evolution of the army reflected the social, political and cultural changes which shaped and reshaped the empire over the course of five-and-a-half centuries.

Unlike its Early Republican predecessor, the Roman army of the Late Republic and Principate consisted entirely of professional troops divided into legions and *auxilia*. By the time the Emperor Tiberius assumed the purple in AD 14 the army's total manpower strength was approximately 300,000, divided in roughly equal measure between the two component forces. This division was the continuation of a practice originating in the Republic.

Soldiers (*milites*) in legionary service were Roman citizens, and largely *voluntarii*, though conscription was still an option during the Empire, especially in times of crisis or preceding a major campaign.[1] As early as the emperorship of Augustus (30 BC–AD 14) most recruitment, particularly in Italy, was voluntary, while the *delectus* (levy) was increasingly reserved for the raising of legionaries in the provinces.

Provincial recruitment became more important for the Roman army throughout the first century as the enlistment of soldiers from Italy declined precipitously during the Early Empire. By the time of the Emperor Hadrian (AD 117–138) most recruits serving in the western legions were from Gaul, Spain and northern Italy, while those in the East consisted largely of soldiers drawn from the eastern regions of the Empire.[2]

Soldiers were typically recruited from the poorer citizen classes, and were expected to be in sound health and meet certain minimum height requirements. These qualifications of the candidate were determined through an interview, called a *probatio* or *inquisitio*, conducted by Roman authorities in Italy, while it was carried out by the local governor in each province.[3] This screening also involved a medical examination at which time the applicant's physical qualifications were assessed. According to Vegetius, recruits who entered service with the first cohort of a legion or a cavalry *ala* were required to be of strong carriage, and at least 5ft 10in tall.[4] In reality, the necessities of active service in the ancient world most probably resulted in many recruits not meeting this ideal height standard.[5] If accepted for army service, the *sacramentum* was administered, by which the *tiro* (recruit) swore personal allegiance to the emperor. He was then sent to his assigned unit to complete basic training before assuming the duties of a legionary.

Service was thereafter for a period of sixteen to twenty-five years, with most recruits entering active service in their late teens or early twenties.[6] Once posted to a unit, the soldier's time was divided between wartime and peacetime responsibilities. When not engaged in combat operations, units were routinely employed to provide physical labour for the completion of engineering projects ranging from road building to fort construction, but peacetime duties ordinarily involved mundane daily tasks such as patrols, drill, field training and camp fatigues.[7]

Soldiers received regular wages, which were supplemented by a portion of booty from campaigns and special bonuses called *donativa* paid on occasion by the emperors in recognition of their supreme authority, and to further secure the loyalty of the legions to their imperial person.[8] Each soldier (*miles*) was routinely paid three times a year, and from these payments stoppages were typically made for clothing and equipment, while a further portion was garnered by the *miles'* cohort in the form of savings. An additional annual payment was also made to a burial account (*ad signa*).[9] On the successful completion of his military service, the legionary was discharged with a gratuity equal to about thirteen years' pay.[10]

Upon leaving service, veterans were recognized by the Roman army as *missus honesta missione* (honourably discharged), *missio causaria* (discharged due to ill-health or injury)[11] or *missio ignominiosa* (dishonorably discharged).[12] During the emperorship of Augustus, veterans were often settled together in military colonies, though it became increasingly common from the late Julio-Claudian period onward for veterans to reside in a village (*canabae* or *vicus*) near their former legion's base, or even to return to their native province.

One determining factor was often whether the discharged soldier had acquired a family during his tenure of service. Until the emperorship of Septimius Severus (AD 193–211), soldiers of the Empire were prohibited from marrying. In many cases this restriction did not hinder their effort to establish a long-term relationship with local women and raise families.[13] Ultimately, this circumstance not only impacted the local economies where veteran settlements were established, but in a very real sense the future of the Roman army, as the male offspring of ex-soldiers commonly provided a rich pool of new provincial recruits for those legions posted semi-permanently on the Empire's frontiers.

Cohortal Legion, *c.*105 BC–313 AD

Between the era of Scipio Africanus (d. 183 BC) and the time of Julius Caesar (d. 44 BC), the manipular construction of the legion was superseded by a tactical organization based on the *cohors*. The exact evolution of this change is unknown. The historians Livy and Polybius allude to the cohort in their accounts of the fighting in Spain during the Second Punic War, but the *manipulus*, or maniple, was still the basic unit around which the 4,200-man legion was constructed, and appears to have remained so until the eve of the first century BC.[14] The cohort was essentially an amalgamation of three maniples, and early uses of a *cohors*, like that described by Polybius in his account of Scipio's battle against Indibilis, suggest this modification was valuable under certain situations as a more robust tactical response to an enemy threat.

By the first century BC a new 'cohortal' legion, consisting of 5,000–6,000 men arrayed in ten cohorts, replaced the earlier manipular formation. In composition, the cohort consisted of 480 soldiers, divided into six centuries of eighty men. The size of the first cohort was subsequently reorganized during the second half of the first century AD in order to accommodate five double centuries of approximately 800 legionaries in total. With the change from *manipulus* to *cohors*, the tactical distinctions between the older unit's heavy infantrymen called *hastati*, *principes* or *triarii* disappeared. In addition, the accompanying lightly-armed skirmishers known as *velites* were completely eliminated as a distinct fighting force. All troops were now armed alike with a spear called a *pilum*. These changes are typically ascribed by many modern scholars to the body of reforms introduced by the *consul* Caius Marius, in part because the last textual references regarding the maniple and *velites* in battle are found in Sallust's account of Caecilius Metellus' campaign against Jugurtha, in 109–108 BC.[15]

Attached to each legion was a small force of 120 cavalry, the *equites legionis*, and various support personnel. The contingent of cavalry was recruited from within the ranks of the legionaries, so consisted of Roman citizens. The primary role of the cavalry force was as scouts and couriers. Because of its ability to perform a variety of tasks, this type unit remained critical to the legion, and its size did not alter from the time of its inception until it was increased by the addition of some 600 riders during the emperorship of Gallienus.[16]

The Cohortal Legion: the officers, and career structure below the centuriate during the Principate

By the reign of Caesar Augustus, a *legatus* was recognized as holding permanent command of a legion by special appointment of the emperor. Whereas under the Republic a *legatus* was selected by a regional governor from among personal friends, family or political supporters; during the Empire the choice fell within the purview of the emperor to make the selection based on similar criteria. In no case were such posts ever determined by election. Legates were typically of senatorial rank, selected from among ex-*praetors* and ex-*quaestors*. This practice continued until the second half of the third century AD when the Emperor Gallienus issued an edict prohibiting senators from assuming army commands.[17]

In the Principate a provincial army was commanded by a governor (*legatus Augusti pro praetore*) whose title and rank were determined by the location of their posting: *propraetors* of senatorial rank governed provinces where legions were deployed, while those provinces without a permanent legionary presence were typically under the authority of a *procurator* of equestrian status. In both cases the appointed magistrate exercised the authority of an imperial *legatus*, while each legion in the provincial army was under the direct command of a *legatus legionis*.[18]

The *legatus legionis* was the senior officer in the legion. Because of past military and political service, this officer was commonly in his thirties, and might expect a two- or three-year posting. His authority extended over both the legion and supporting auxiliary units.[19]

Assisting the legate in his responsibilities was the *tribunus laticlavius*, recognized as the senior tribune and second-in-command of the legion. Such officers typically sought a political rather than military career, and as a result served only a one-year term of military service in the legion prior to age 25, before entering the Senate as a *quaestor*. Because of their unique station, each such officer wore a broad, or laticlavian, purple stripe on the toga, denoting their senatorial aspirations.[20]

Next in line of authority was the *praefectus castrorum*, who was the senior professional officer in the legion and commonly possessed years of field experience, having previously served as the senior centurion, or *primus pilus*, of a legion. His responsibilities included oversight of camp construction and maintenance, transport supervision of the legion's equipment during deployment, maintenance of supplies and munitions, and command of the legion's artillery during military operations. In the absence of the two senior officers, the *praefectus castrorum* commanded the legion. Over time, the authority invested in this position increased. After the reign of Septimius Severus (AD 193–211), the title was altered to *praefectus legionis*, and under Emperor Gallienus (AD 260–268) this officer supplanted the *legatus legionis* as the senior officer of the legion.[21]

Assigned to each legion were the *tribuni legionis augusticlavii*, five tribunes of equestrian rank who typically aspired to either civil or military careers. The expectation of military service was much higher for these officers than for their laticlavian counterparts, and each officer could anticipate additional military service in the *auxilia*. Young equestrians entering the army normally advanced through the following sequence of posts: *praefectus cohortis* (commanding officer of an auxiliary cohort – *peditatae* or *equitatae*); *tribunis angusticlavius*; and *praefectus alae* (officer commanding a cavalry detachment – an *ala*). Each such officer wore a narrow, or angusticlavian, purple stripe on their toga. The angusticlavian tribunes of a legion were usually about five to ten years older than the unit's laticlavian officer, and routinely possessed more service experience.[22]

Following the *tribuni angusticlavii* were the sixty centurions of the legion. Each centurion (*centurio*; plural *centuriones*) commanded one of the legion's centuries. The senior centurions were recognized as *prior centuriones* and the junior centurions as *posterior centuriones*. Because the distribution of the centurions continued to reflect the older three-part division of heavy infantrymen (*hastati*, *principes* and *triarii*) found in the manipular model, each centurion was still identified specifically as *hastatus prior*, *hastatus posterior*, *princeps prior*, *princeps posterior*, *pilus prior* or *pilus posterior*. The single exception to this arrangement was the centurions of the first cohort, known as the *primi ordines*. Accompanying the reorganization and enlargement of the *cohors I* in the first century AD was a reordering of its centurions in the following descending order of seniority: *primus pilus*, *princeps*, *hastatus*, *princeps posterior* and *hastatus posterior*.[23]

Below the rank of centurion, the command structure of a legion was relatively simple and straightforward, though it was characterized by a very wide array of specific posts and duty stations, all of which are not fully understood today.[24] These junior officers were denoted as either *principales* or *immunes*, and were as a rule exempt from the ordinary fatigues of the common legionary; *principales* because of privilege of rank and *immunes* because they performed special duties. *Principales* typically received double pay (a *duplicarius*) or pay-and-a-half (a *sesquiplicarius*) for their jobs, while *immunes* received the same base pay as all other soldiers.[25]

These officers were denoted also by their service responsibilities. Some posts were specifically associated with the operational activities of the centuries and cohorts, while others were defined by their administrative duties within the various *officia* of the provincial governor, legionary commander (*legatus legionis*), camp prefect (*praefectus castrorum*) and the tribune of the legion (*tribunus laticlavius*).[26]

Within the century there were three ranks below that of centurion: *signifer*,[27] *optio*[28] and *tesserarius*.[29] Of this trio, the *signifer* was the officer primarily responsible for the century's bookkeeping, pay, savings and operational paperwork. During field operations, command of the century in the absence of the centurion was the duty of the *optio*.[30] Promotion of the *optiones* was from cohort to cohort, advancement beginning in the *Cohors X* and progressing upward to the *Cohors I*.[31] Both he and the centurion were assisted by the *tesserarius*, who received the daily watchword and oversaw the posting of the century's pickets.

Below the *tesserarius* was the *custus armorum*.[32] The role of this subordinate officer is not clearly understood by modern scholars. It is known that he was associated with the legions' *armamentaria* (weapons stores), though the exact manner in which these officers performed their duties is largely uncertain. However, it is quite possible that they were responsible for the daily storage, maintenance, requisition and distribution of arms and equipment to active and on-duty personnel.[33]

A second body of junior officers in the legion was the various clerks, secretaries and assistants which collectively formed the administrative staff, the *tabularium legionis*. This office contained *librarii* (clerks), including the *librarii horreorum* responsible for granary records, and the *librarii depositorum* who collected soldiers' savings. Also included in this office were *exacti* (accounting clerks) and *frumentarii*, officers responsible for the collection and distribution of grain. The highest staff posts in the *tabularium legionis* were those of *commentariensis* (senior clerk) and *cornicularius* (office manager). The *cornicularii*, because they were adjutants to the legion's ranking officers, were in charge of the various *officia*, and thus helped to ensure administrative cooperation within the legion. All of this activity was centred around the *principia* (legionary headquarters) and *praetorium* (the legionary commander's residence).[34]

A proliferation of ranks and posts appeared during the second and third centuries AD below that of the centurion. Some of these positions were not characteristic of the first century imperial legion, but quite possibly represent a later and more refined organizational system for the maintenance and supply of the legionary unit.[35] Within the legion itself was a wide variety of specialists classified as *immunes*. Unlike the previous personnel mentioned, many of these individuals were responsible for providing a variety of support services including the actual manufacture or repair of weapons and armour. Numerous such craftsmen worked in the various *fabricenses* of the legion and were overseen in their production activities by the *praefectus fabrum*. Ancient sources confirm that these *officia* were clearly capable of providing a wide array of materials for consumption by a legion. A partial list of these posts is preserved in Justinian's *Digesta seu Pandectae*, which is itself copied from an earlier second century AD work provided by the praetorian prefect and military jurist Tarruntenus Paternus in his *de rei militari*. Among the posts recorded are: *specularii* (glass fitters); *fabri* (craftsmen and smiths); *sagittarii* (arrowsmiths); *aerarii* (coppersmiths); *buccularum structores* (helmet makers who specialized in the fashioning of cheek pieces); *carpentarii* (wagon makers); *scandulaarii* (roofers); *gladiatores* (swordsmiths); *aguilices* (water engineers);

acuarii (bowmakers); *plumbarii* (leadsmiths); *ferrarii* (ironsmiths); *lapidarii* (stoneworkers); *gui calcem cocunt* (lime burners); *gui silvan infindunt* (wood-cutters); *gui carbonem caedunt ac torrent* (charcoal burners); *in eodem numero haaberi solent lani* (butchers); *venatores* (hunters); *optio fabricae* (in charge of a workshop); *polliones* (millers of flour); and *custodes armorum* (armourers).[36]

The *Auxilia* of the Principate, 27 BC–AD 284

The legions of the Empire relied heavily on highly trained support units called *auxilia*. *Auxilia* were commonly of two types during the Principate: cavalry (*ala*, pl. *alae*) and infantry (*cohors peditata*, pl. *cohortes peditatae*). A first century derivative of the infantry cohort was the *cohors equitata* (pl. *cohortes equitatae*), a mixed unit of infantry and cavalry. Such units as these, regardless of their individual tactical composition, consisted entirely of non-citizens (*peregrini*) enrolled for twenty-five years' service.

The division of *auxilia* into infantry, cavalry and irregular troops provided the Roman army with an important element of tactical flexibility and thereby greatly augmented the strategic mission of the legions. As expansion declined and the Empire's borders began to solidify in the late first century, *auxilia* were increasingly used in conjunction with legionary forces to secure the frontiers.[37]

During the Republic and early Empire, auxiliary units were recruited in the provinces before deployment abroad, and each was given an identification number and *cognomen* (name). Unit names therefore commonly reflected the tribe, country, city or region of origin from which the auxiliary force was initially raised, or the emperorship under which the unit was first created. These descriptive names continued to be used to identify the unit even after subsequent local recruitment in the province of their posting had completely erased the unit's original cultural characteristics. Such dilution of regional character was furthered when the equipment and organizational structure of the various auxiliary units in the Empire was standardized in the late first century. Once all of the auxiliary forces in the Empire were similarly equipped, much of the units' individual identities were lost with the elimination of their native weapons and clothing.[38]

Because of the vast expanse of territory and the general nature of terrain in certain parts of the Empire, especially in regions like Syria and North Africa, mounted auxiliary troops were especially ideal for patrol and reconnaissance duties. Further, cavalry could respond much more quickly to sudden crisis situations along the fringes of Roman territory and were ideal for the tracking and pursuit of infiltrators, particularly if the breach was perpetrated by mounted riders.[39]

Roman auxiliary cavalry were of two types: the *cohors equitata* and *ala*.[40] Because of their skilled horsemanship, Gauls provided the largest percentage of mounted troops by the late first century, with significant contributions made by other European peoples including the Thracians, Celtiberians and Germans. At this time cavalry accounted for approximately one-sixth of the army's total manpower.[41]

Of the two basic types of units which contained cavalry, the *cohors equitata* was far more flexible for tactical purposes than the *ala* because it was a mixed formation consisting of cavalry and infantry. According to Pseudo-Hyginus in his *De Munitionibus Castrorum*, a *cohors miliaria equitata* contained 1,000 men, of which 240 were mounted troops. The *cohors quingenaria equitata* included 120 *equites*. These mounted elements were then primarily divided into eight and four *turmae* (troops or squadrons), respectively.[42]

Duty rosters which have survived on papyrus from Dura-Europos in Mesopotamia list cavalry from *cohortes equitatae* as commonly employed on scouting patrols, as dispatch riders, mounted escorts for infantry formations, supply convoys, foraging parties, camp harvesters, payroll shipments and travelling dignitaries.[43] In essence, these mounted detachments were used in an extensive variety of tasks where infantry was either ineffective or impractical.[44]

Like their mounted counterparts, infantry cohorts were organized as units of either 500 or 1,000 men. These were then subdivided into centuries. According to Pseudo-Hyginus, those units organized as *quingenaria* consisted of six centuries commanded by an equal number of centurions. The larger *cohors miliaria* was comprised of ten centuries of eighty men.[45]

The command structure within an auxiliary cohort below the rank of centurion was similar to that of the legionary cohort. However, the centurions of an auxiliary unit were promoted exclusively from the ranks and, unlike their legionary counterparts, remained for the duration of their service life within the same cohort. Below the rank of centurion every century contained an *optio*, *signifer*, and *terrerarius*, with each possessing duties similar to those already mentioned above for legionary officers.[46]

The size difference of the cohorts was also reflected in the ranks and title of their respective commanding officers. The senior officers of a *cohors quingenaria peditatae* was an equestrian who bore the title *praefectus cohortes* and was appointed to his post by a provincial governor. This contrasted sharply with the commanding officer of a military cohort, who was a tribune appointed by the emperor personally from a pool of infantry *praefect*. The most immediate notable difference between these two officers was in military experience. The latter typically possessed some military background, whereas an individual appointed to a prefecture in command of a *cohors quingenaria* might only possess experience as a civil magistrate, with no formal military training or field experience.

In contrast to the *cohors equitata* and *cohors peditata*, cavalry *alae* (wings) represented the most prestigious body of troops in the *auxilia*. Like its cohortal counterparts, the *ala* was organized as a unit of either 500 or 1,000 soldiers. According to Pseudo-Hyginus, the *ala quingenaria* contained sixteen *turmae* (troops or squadrons) of cavalry, and the *ala miliaria* twenty-four squadrons. Each *turma* consisted of thirty-two horsemen.[47] The troops of an *ala* were better paid and equipped than their counterparts in a *cohors equitata*, and seem to have been generally exempt from such tasks as escort or reconnaissance duties, responsibilities which typically befell cavalry in the mixed cohorts.

The command structure of the *ala* was, again as it was for the other auxiliary units discussed, a more simplified version of the legion's chain of command. The senior officer of an *ala* was the *praefectus alae*,[48] who was typically of equestrian social rank and in his late twenties or early thirties at the time of his posting.[49] The rank of *praefectus alae* clearly demonstrates the level of integration which existed among the legionary and auxiliary officer corps. For equestrians, the promotional ladder during military service was normally: *praefectus cohortis* (senior officer of a *cohors peditata*), *tribunus legionis* (an augusticlavian tribune in a legion) and *praefectus alae* (commander of an auxiliary cavalry wing). This alternation from auxiliary infantry unit, to front-line legion, to *ala* provided the equestrian officer with invaluable practical experience as an active service officer in both legionary and auxiliary formations.[50]

Below the *praefectus alae* in authority were the decurions of the *ala*. Each *turma* in the unit was commanded by a decurion (*decurio*). Officers below the rank of decurion were the *duplicarius* ('double-pay man'), roughly equivalent to an *optio* in a century, the *sesquiplicarius* ('pay-and-a-half man'), corresponding to the *tesserarius*, and the *curator*.[51] The exact order of precedence in the decurionate of an *ala* is unclear. It may have followed a system of rank and promotion similar to that of a legion's centurionate.

A portion of Hadrian's address of AD 128 to troops at Lambaesis in North Africa was directed toward the mounted troops of *Cohors VI Commagenorum equitata*. From the preserved fragments of this speech, there is a strong indication that the level of training and quality of equipment and material was of a higher standard for the *alae* than the *cohorts equitatae*. This and other evidence suggests that the *alae* were a more skillfully trained force of cavalry used only when hostilities erupted.[52] Under such circumstances, the *cohortes equitatae* assumed primary responsibility for the execution of day-to-day missions that required the presence of mounted troops.[53]

This is not to suggest, however, that the *alae* were completely inactive in peacetime. This is borne out by an inscription from Tingitana. A statue base from the community of Sala dated 28 October 144 records the gratitude of the decurions of the *municipium* to M. Sulpicius Felix, praefect of the *ala II Syrorum*, for constructing wall defences around the city and for providing patrols to protect workers in the countryside.[54]

In a discussion of this sort, pertaining to the ancillary troops which helped to reinforce the mission responsibilities of the legions, brief mention should also be made of the units known as *numeri*. A *numerus* was, through the strictest definition of the word, any unit of irregular troops which still retained its native weapons, costume and language. However, this term was also used in a more general context to describe any detached unit of troops which was not specifically attached to or representative of a particular legion or auxiliary unit. A number of third-century inscriptions record the term *numerus collatus*. What type of unit or body of soldiers the term specifically describes is uncertain, but they were perhaps detachments consisting of soldiers taken from several camps or units for the purpose of performing a specific task.[55]

From an array of sources including *diplomata* and tombstone inscriptions, evidence indicates that the *patria* of individual soldiers was very often not the same as the country of origin for those auxiliary regiments in which they served. By about AD 40, it appears to have been increasingly common for the units to accept recruits from the province in which they were posted rather than the unit's homeland.[56]

The value of relying on local recruitment increasingly outweighed the disadvantages initially associated with such practices in the first and early second centuries. During this period, imperial authorities faced a number of revolts in the Empire, including the North African uprising of Tacfarinas in AD 17–24, which were directly associated with locally raised auxiliary contingents.[57] In each case, the rebellions were either initiated or fueled by *auxilia* stationed in or near their homelands. Under such conditions, the Roman military establishment sought to post native units far from their *patria*.[58]

This practice clearly diffused the threat of similar rebellions, yet the army lost the critical tactical advantage inherent in posting native regiments to their own homelands where geographical familiarity was a distinct advantage in the maintenance of frontier security. Increasingly during the late first century, the potential for rebellion was overshadowed by the positive aspects offered by a system of local recruitment and posting. Aside from the tactical benefits, the logistical problems associated with massive troop relocation were also avoided, and the Roman army increased its gains even more by taking advantage of regional tribal rivalries to diffuse any nationalistic sentiments on the part of its auxiliary forces.[59]

Any concerns Roman commanders might have had regarding recruitment competition between the legions and auxiliary units were alleviated by the restrictions attached to the granting of citizenship after AD 140. From that date, the *auxilia* and legion drew upon two separate pools of local manpower: the auxiliary units included among the ranks of its recruits the sons of ex-auxiliaries, the *ex-castris*; and the legions maintained their combat strength through recruitment in the veteran settlements.[60]

Evidence also suggests that a select emphasis was placed on the recruitment and deployment of the various auxiliary forces, especially in the units' abilities to respond to highly mobile, mounted adversaries. As a result, a number of *auxilia* in areas like Numidia and Proconsular Africa consisted, all or in part, of mounted archers, especially for those units recruited in Syria and the East. Many of these bowmen were assigned to regiments consisting of both mixed cavalry and infantry, or squadrons made up exclusively of horse troops. The incorporation of archers and cavalry thus provided an important element of swift tactical mobility and striking power which was otherwise unavailable from the more traditional Roman infantry formations.[61]

During the early second century, Emperor Hadrian formed the first unit of *cataphractarii*, the *ala Gallorum et Pannoniorum*.[62] These heavily-armoured troops, unique in the early Empire, became increasingly important by the late Imperial period. As a result, the number of these units in the Roman arsenal grew as the value of mounted forces became more critical to the defence of the Empire.

The Roman Army, mid-Third–Fifth Century AD

'*The Romans in unison sounded their warcry, as usual rising from a low to a louder tone, of which the national name is barritus.*'

Ammianus Marcellinus, 31.7.11

At the end of the Principate, the Roman army was still composed of legions, auxiliary cohorts and *alae*, but certain innovations were clearly present which denoted the changing military conditions in the Empire during the period modern scholars identify as the Third Century Crisis. The period from AD 235 to 284 was an unstable episode in the history of the Roman Empire, characterized by a precipitous decline in centralized authority amplified by civil war, assassination and usurpation. Over twenty emperors ruled during this era, and numerous other legionary and provincial commanders were put forward by regional armies as claimants to the purple. The disorder manifesting itself inside the borders of the Empire was complemented by significant external threats to the integrity of the Roman state. By mid-century, the danger posed by powerful peoples like the Goths and Sassanid Persians was acute. In June of 251, the Emperor Decius was killed in a disastrous defeat attempting to check a Gothic invasion of Moesia, Dacia and Thracia. Nine years later, a Persian army inflicted a major defeat on an Imperial army at

Edessa that resulted in the capture and imprisonment of the Emperor Valerian. Such battlefield disasters only underscored the disintegration of government order in the Empire, which contributed to the loss of several provinces including Gaul, Britannia, Hispania, Egypt, Palestine and Syria by 260. Such haemorrhaging continued largely unabated until the last quarter of the third century, when several emperors including Aurelianus (270–275) successfully slowed the downward spiral of the Empire.

These same adverse forces also stimulated important changes in the Roman army.[63] Until the end of the Severan period, battles continued to be fought by Roman commanders employing traditional legionary formations. Full legions were routinely deployed under Marcus Aurelius (161–180), and complete legions were still used in battle as late as the emperorship of Caracalla (211–217), but changing conditions in the Empire during the remainder of the third century gradually dictated a fundamental alteration in the deployment of legionary troops for major campaigns.[64] Whereas Roman field armies were previously composed of several legions, such campaign forces increasingly came to consist of multiple units called *vexillationes*, each of which typically consisted of a pair of cohorts detached from a parent legion, to form composite armies for foreign service. The use of *vexillationes* accelerated in the years following the death of Severus Alexander (222–235), and this pattern of deployment became more pervasive by the mid-third century. In contrast, the once formidable legions were gradually relegated to static provincial service along the frontiers of the Empire. By the reign of the Emperor Diocletian, the composition of field armies was fundamentally altered, and it was no longer common for entire legions to be deployed for campaign.

Following his assumption of power in AD 284, Diocletian created a Tetrarchic system of government to aid in the ordered restoration of stable authority throughout imperial territories. He also introduced certain innovations to the structure of the military, along with modifications to the administration of the frontier regions. During his tenure of power, Diocletian increased the number of legions, though the exact number is unknown, perhaps from thirty-nine to sixty-nine.[65] Simultaneously, he decreased the size of these new legionary units included in the field armies to approximately 1,000–1,200 men each.[66] But such changes to the legion do not appear to have been universal, and the basic infrastructure of the older legions on the frontier may have remained essentially that which had evolved during the Principate: units of 5,000-plus men each divided into ten cohorts.[67] Of note, however, was the continued reliance by Roman army commanders on *vexillationes* drawn from these larger combat units, ensuring that the traditional legions rarely, if ever, possessed their full manpower complement. At the immediate disposal of Diocletian was a small mobile field army, the *sacer comitatus*. Its tactical structure and unit composition are not completely certain, but its size ensured that infantry and cavalry *vexillationes* were routinely and necessarily detached from the frontier armies in order to reinforce the *comitatus* during significant military operations.[68] The flexibility of the *comitatus* also meant that Diocletian's fellow tetrarchs each maintained a similar force for their own personal use.

The increasing use of *vexillationes*, particularly contingents of cavalry, to supplement the distribution of legionary and auxiliary forces on the frontier was a notable change in the tactical deployment of the army during the final stages of the Principate; a practice that reflected the continued overall shift toward the use of detached units of infantry and cavalry, assembled into large composite forces, instead of traditional legions for major military actions. Though the Diocletianic modifications reflect an ongoing evolutionary trend in the basic structure of the army, pronounced strategic change did not occur until the reign of Constantine (312–337), under whose leadership the composition of the Roman army was fundamentally altered.[69] Constantine realigned the army to establish two primary branches of regular troops: static frontier forces consisting of infantry *legiones*, *cohortes* and *numeri*, and cavalry *alae*, *cunei* and *vexillationes*; and mobile field armies likewise comprised of light and heavy cavalry and infantry units.[70] The frontier troops, called *limitanei*, garrisoned the *limes*, or borders of the Empire, while the mobile field armies, or *comitatenses* (sing. *comitatus*), were maintained in reserve to be deployed wherever significant hostile incursions of the imperial frontier occurred. Constantine also added new elite units of infantry and cavalry called *palatini* to the field armies. Unlike the *limitanei* and *comitatenses*, these latter forces were closely associated with the emperor's person. This would remain the basic distribution of regular troops until the end of the Western Roman Empire. According to the *Notitia Dignitatum*, twelve field armies existed at the turn of the fifth century, with numerous divisions of *limitanei* arrayed along the Empire's frontiers.

Despite such changes, any consideration of a perceived resuscitation in the vitality of the late Roman army must necessarily take into account the role played in imperial defence by foreign mercenaries. In its basic construction, the Roman army of the later fourth and fifth centuries was comprised of two components: regular troops and mercenary forces raised from among those federate barbarian peoples living inside the Empire, as well as residing beyond the imperial frontiers. In the late Roman army, regular troops were broadly subdivided into three categories: *limitanei*, *comitatenses* and elite mounted divisions attached to the praesental army called *palatini*. A part of these palatine forces were units of the Imperial Guard called *Scholae Palatinae*, which served as a personal guard for the emperor.[71]

In conjunction with the deployment of these regular army units in the late Empire was the mustering of sizable contingents of barbarians identified as either *foederati* or *buccellarii*. The Roman reliance on such mercenary troops accelerated during the reign of the Emperor Theodosius I (379–395), and was indicative of a decline in overall imperial defence, particularly in the Western Empire during the fifth century.[72]

Limitanei

A typical border province may consist of an army of two legions and several auxiliary units, under the command of a local *dux* (pl. *duces*) who might in turn be subordinate to a regional army commander called a *comes rei militaris*.[73] Regardless of speculation among modern scholars regarding the smaller Diocletianic legions, units of *limitanei* appear to be bodies of trained regular troops organized into complete ten-cohort legions. Even with the realignment of the army under Constantine, perhaps sixty per cent of Rome's total manpower force remained on the frontiers of the Empire.[74]

By AD 400, individual cohorts declined in both strength and quality, together with a corresponding and steady drop in recruitment since the Early Empire. By the fifth century, the decline in recruitment was further complicated by the manpower losses to the *comitatenses* who routinely drew away from the *limitanei* the most promising recruits and experienced soldiers.[75]

The *limitanei* consisted of both cavalry and infantry units. Cavalry units in the *limitanei* were designated as *vexillationes, alae* or *cunei*.[76] The terms *vexillatio* and *ala* indicate the unit's origin rather than a particular fighting style, and the normal strength of all mounted units, regardless of designation, numbered 500.[77] Within the ranks of the *limitanei*, the term *ripenses* denoted higher tier units of legions, *auxilia, cunei equitum* and *equites*.[78] Rather than serving in line-of-battle, *limitanei* cavalry were typically used to patrol the *limes*, act as internal security and pursue raiders and bandits which penetrated into the frontier zones. In essence, the *limitanei* policed the border and dealt with low intensity threats to Roman territory. Within the *limitanei*, both cavalry and infantry were capable of challenging small-scale incursions; however, should a frontier zone be breached by large-scale invasion or penetration, the *limitanei* were used to garrison and otherwise stiffen the defences of threatened towns. Given this role, the *limitanei* infantry probably retained most or all of their artillery.[79] Shattered and understrength *limitanei* were sometimes incorporated into the mobile field armies as *pseudocomitatenses*. This designation was applied strictly to infantry. After the disaster at Adrianople in AD 378, many units were transferred from the *limitanei* to the field armies as *pseudocomitatenses*.[80]

Mobile Field Armies

The particular defensive posture of the *limitanei* along the frontiers was made relevant by the inclusion of mobile field armies to the empire's strategic defence. The overall effectiveness of these mobile forces was maximized by the creation of regional field armies deployed in outlying locations like Illyricum, Britannia, Mauritania Tingitana, and Africa, together with larger concentrations of praesental forces based in Thracia, Gaul, and Italy. While the regional armies served to reinforce the *limitanei* in its ongoing mission of static defence along the frontiers, the praesental army (*praesentalis*) responded to particularly acute threats which proved beyond the capability of *limitanei* and regional field armies to check alone.

As its name implies, the praesental army was commanded personally by the emperor. He was assisted in his command by a group of officers collectively called the *magistri praesentales*. These officers were the *magister militum* (Master of Soldiers), *magister equitum praesentalis* (Master of Cavalry) and *magister peditum* (Master of Infantry).

All units originating in the praesental army, whether cavalry or infantry, were designated *palatini*. By the early fifth century, numerous palatine units had been transferred to regional field armies to reinforce units designated *comitatenses*, but retained their higher palatine rank.[81] Likewise, some units of *comitatenses* were posted to the praesental armies. Incomplete evidence suggests that the cavalry was likely organized into 500-man units known as *vexillationes palatinae* or *vexillationes comitatenses*. Fragmentary evidence implies, however, that under normal field conditions actual unit size was somewhat less than the ideal manpower figure.[82] Infantry in the praesental army were organized into 1,000–1,200-man units known as *legiones palatinae*. Because of field conditions these units were also likely deficient in manpower, and probably typically numbered less than their ideal strength.

In like manner to the application of the palatine designation in the praesental army, all regional field army units (infantry or cavalry), were denoted as *comitatenses*. By the early fifth century numerous units of *comitatenses* were transferred to praesental armies to reinforce the *palatini*, but retained their lower status.[83] Cavalry in the regional field armies were organized into 500-man units known as *vexillationes comitatenses*. Because of the harsh field conditions commonly experienced, these units likely numbered no more than 400 men under routine circumstances. Infantry in the regional field armies were organized into 1,000–1,200-man *legiones comitatenses*. Like their mounted counterparts, it is likely that these units were also typically understrength.[84]

Battlefield Elements: Late Roman Cavalry

During the fourth century, Roman cavalry fell into one of three broad categories: conventional heavy cavalry, heavily-armoured cavalry called *cataphractarii*, or light cavalry. These units were typically organized into 500-man *vexillationes*.

The unit composition and armament of conventional heavy cavalry was likely similar to auxiliary cavalry of the early Empire. Incomplete physical and textual evidence suggests such soldiers were suited in traditional forms of light armour, such as chain mail, scale or lamellar, and commonly armed with a shield, lance and javelins.

Within the ranks of the Late Roman army, heavily-armoured cavalry included units identified as *cataphractarii* and *clibanarii*; terms that imply the origin of the units rather than different fighting styles. In contrast to conventional heavy horse squadrons, cavalry identified in ancient sources as cataphracts and *clibanarii* were often mounted on heavily-armoured horses, and the riders fitted with a generous array of body armour.[85] Each cataphract wore a knee-length, long sleeved (and sometimes hooded) coat of scaled armour. This was worn over a cloth tunic, cloth ankle-length pants and soft leather, ankle-high boots. The horse was also covered in similar armour which protected the head, neck and torso of the animal. Though typically associated with the wars of the Late Roman Empire, the first regular unit of cataphracts was, in fact, formed by Emperor Hadrian (117–138) in the early second century. Squadrons of cataphracts consisted of lance-wielding troopers and, less commonly, armour-clad mounted archers. In like fashion, a combination of plate and scale armour completely enclosed the body of those cavalrymen designated *clibanarii*. The head of the rider was fully encased in a metal helmet, his limbs contained in circlets of iron plates, the torso protected by a coat of scale or rectangular plates and the hands and joints covered with fine chain mail. The head, neck and body of the horse was also fully fitted in scale armour.[86] Squadrons of *clibanarii* were first used in AD 312 in Italy against the forces of Constantine during his war with Maxentius. Such horsemen may have been equipped with lance and bow.

Whereas heavy cavalry were intended primarily for purposes of shock action in battle, light cavalry provided a critical element of flexibility to the army, both in their tactical capability on the battlefield and in their ability to respond swiftly to hostile incursions on the frontier. Formations of light cavalry typically consisted of either javelin-armed riders or horse archers (*equites sagittarii*), each organized into 500-man units identified as either *vexillationes*, *cunei* or *alae*.[87]

Battlefield Elements: Late Roman Infantry

Late Roman infantry consisted of two broad categories: light and heavy. As discussed above, the new field armies included Diocletianic legions that were smaller than the classic imperial legion of the Early Empire, consisting perhaps of only 1,000–1,200 men. Joining these new-style legions within the ranks of the field armies were units of a new type called *auxilia*. Organized into 500–600-man heavy infantry units, the *auxilia* of the Late Roman

Empire bore no relation to the earlier *auxilia* of the Principate, and all were identified as *palatini*. These units appear to have been wholly new creations formed sometime during the early fourth century from among the tribal peoples of Gaul and the Rhineland region.[88] Their impact on the battlefield was almost immediate. By mid-century, ancient writers list units of *auxilia* among those bodies of troops vital to Roman victories in both the eastern and western portions of the empire. These forces, identified by such names as *Bracchiati, Cornuti, Victores, Batavi* and *Iovii*, proved indispensable to Roman generals seeking decisive victories against both German and Persian adversaries.[89]

In addition to the heavy infantry divisions, both legions and *auxilia*, there were specialist units of light troops, including *sagittarii* (archers), *funditores* (slingers) and *exculcatores* (javelineers). Like their republican and early imperial counterparts, *velites* and *auxilia*, light infantry of the Late Empire offered Roman generals greater tactical flexibility when confronting the enemy.

From the Decline of the Roman West to the Death of Justinian in the East

The strategic circumstances that once gave rise to many of Rome's great battles during the Republic and Early Empire altered as time passed. For Roman troops posted on the borders, challenges of local defence and security varied from one frontier to another during the last centuries of imperial authority, but the geopolitical forces which in the earlier ages led to war with one or more major centralized Mediterranean state like Carthage or Macedon were gone. By the third century, only one notable exception existed, and this enemy lay to the east, across the Euphrates River.

Persia remained the Roman Empire's principal antagonist, first under the rule of the Parthians and later the Sassanid dynasty. In the age-old contest between these established powers, the opposing armies were typically well-matched, resulting in very few lasting territorial gains being achieved by either side in the later fourth and fifth centuries; and the same was true during the era of Eastern Roman history ending with the death of Justinian I in 565.

Throughout these centuries, fighting in the East was routinely concentrated along the shared borders between Persia and Rome. As a result, area strongholds like Dara or Amida naturally came to assume preeminent importance within the greater scope of strategic operations in and around Armenia and the Mesopotamian Basin. Because of their inherent value, such prominent locations were commonly a focal point for attacking armies during a number of notable campaigns or armed expeditions initiated by both sides. Tensions between the two ancient superpowers went largely unabated throughout this long period, even after the implementation of various truces between Justinian and King Chosroes I (531–579) in the three decades prior to the emperor's death.

During these same centuries, Roman armies faced challenges of a different nature in regions like North Africa, Gaul, Germania and the Balkans, where persistent tribal threats worked to constantly challenge the integrity of imperial authority. The difficulties presented by the tribal peoples in and around these provinces of the Empire commonly demanded strategic and tactical solutions markedly different from those implemented against the current Sassanid threat or even employed to combat the earlier enemies of the Republic and Principate.

Roman forces in the north periodically faced acute threats from different Germanic tribes along the Rhine, including the Franks and Alamanni; while further east in the vicinity of the Danube, the Sarmatian and Gothic peoples, and later the Huns and Avars, habitually placed a tremendous amount of pressure on imperial defences.

On the southern frontier, the threat from tribal peoples in North Africa was never comparable to the danger presented by the Germanic, Hunnish and Slavic powers in Europe and Asia, but was nonetheless a challenge which demanded the full attention of the Roman army. The dry and often harsh environmental conditions which extended from Egypt to Mauretania Tingitana presented the army with unique strategic, tactical and logistical problems. Because the military danger was far more severe in both barbarian Europe and the Sassanid East, the number of Roman units stationed along the southern frontiers of the Empire was also more modest, only adding to the difficulty of securing a frontier that extended from the upper Nile River to south of the western Atlas Mountains.

In each of these regions, the character of the Roman army gradually altered; almost always as a result of declining central authority, social and economic changes within the Empire, changes introduced over time in the relationship between an indigenous population and Roman units resident in the particular location, and the evolving tactical comportment of any hostile forces present.

Beginning in the third century, set-piece battles involving large formations of infantry and cavalry became increasingly rare on all imperial fronts. Instead, Roman frontier defence, including massed military responses to hostile raids and border incursions, became steadily reliant on smaller units whose speed and tactical dexterity were more capable of dealing with the type of small-scale mobile warfare which occurred with increasing frequency throughout most of the late Empire.

Some two centuries later, it was quite common for Roman authorities to incorporate into the army ethnic units from the native population found on both sides of the frontier. These 'barbarian' recruits were commonly identified in Roman records as *laeti*, *gentiles*, *tributarii* or *dediticii*, meaning they were associated with groups of federate peoples who were permitted to settle within imperial territory. Once established inside the boundaries of the Empire, these bodies of indigenous troops were thereafter obligated by treaty to guard and defend the immediate border. Such units proved increasingly invaluable as the exigencies of imperial defence resulted in a steady withdrawal of *limitanei* from many areas of the western frontier by the early fifth century. But such alterations in strategic policy were the by-product of greater changes – social, economic and material – within the Empire that were irrevocably altering the nature of the Roman state and driving toward an irreversible decline.

In time, divergent forces great and small contributed to a steady contraction of the Empire, commensurate with a continual diminution of Roman power throughout Europe, the Near East and the Mediterranean region. The gradual loss of territorial control in these geographical locations eventually ended with the complete eclipse of all power emanating from Rome. By the beginning of the sixth century, leadership of the Roman world devolved to the eastern imperial capital of Constantinople, the only surviving source of state authority which still possessed the means to actively project an emperor's power.

In the following decades, Germanic groups gradually assumed control of the western portions of the Empire. Accompanying this change was the slow dissolution of the remnants of the once mighty Western Roman army, its disappearance seemingly in step with the decline of Roman influence in these lands.

The loss of Roman authority in Western Europe closed an important chapter in ancient history, and brought to an end perhaps the single most formidable war machine in antiquity. In the Balkans, Anatolia and the Levant, 'Roman' armies retained their tactical prowess for several more generations, and proved central to the longevity of the Eastern Roman, or Byzantine, Empire. Their abilities on the battlefield, especially while under the leadership of sixth-century generals like Flavius Belisarius or Narses, served as a fine testament to the legacy of their legionary predecessors, but eventually even Byzantine armies of a later age succumbed to the Arab conquests which consumed Eastern Europe and the southern and eastern shores of the Mediterranean Sea. That the Roman state, in both its western and Byzantine forms, survived for so many centuries is, in itself, indisputable evidence of the singular greatness of its army.

The Roman Navy from the early Principate to the Death of Justinian

The cessation of the civil wars in the late Republic that climaxed with the accession of the emperor Caesar Augustus also brought to an end the need for large Roman warfleets. With the close of hostilities, large numbers of ships were demobilized and destroyed, and the preponderance of the remaining fleet divided between two major naval installations at Misenum and Ravenna in western and eastern Italy respectively.

Since the Roman state no longer faced a major foreign or domestic naval threat, the strategic mission of the fleet gradually altered to one of supporting the Empire's military operations. To this end, the task of maritime security and transport became the mainstay of the *Classis Misenatium* and the *Classis Ravennatium*, while the responsibility of providing close support for major army campaigns and lesser combat operations devolved to the various provincial fleets stationed in the outlying regions of the Empire.[90]

In this new support role, the navy eventually relinquished use of the three-banked battleships of the Republic and early Principate, the *trireme* and *quinquereme*, for the faster and more nimble one- and two-banked *liburna*, which was itself in turn supplemented by the *navis lusoria*, a transport of the Late Empire. Both vessels were known for their speed and exceedingly shallow draft, and so were ideally suited for use in bays, estuaries and rivers.[91]

In time, the changed nature of the navy's role in imperial defence led to an inability to properly respond to major strategic threats to the security of the Empire. In the third century, when the eastern provinces experienced significant invasions by several powerful tribes including the Goths, Gepids and Heruli, Roman naval capabilities had so diminished that imperial fleets could no longer effectively check large-scale seaborne incursions into the Black, Aegean or eastern Mediterranean Seas.

Despite such threats, and even after a brief resurgence of internecine naval encounters during the wars of the early fourth century, the absence of any major standing Roman battle fleet comparable to those of the early Empire remained unaltered. This was still the state of affairs a century later when imperial authorities faced a serious naval threat from the Vandal Kingdom of North Africa. Even a demonstration by an eastern imperial fleet in Sicilian waters in 441 under Areobindus was not enough to stop Vandalic ships plundering at will throughout the central and western Mediterranean, and so the depredations continued.

In reality, the ability to achieve any semblance of naval superiority in the western Mediterranean Sea was already beyond the capability of Western emperors by the mid-fifth century. Any hope for such restoration now rested solely with Byzantine Romans.

In the sixth century, a resurgence of naval power occurred under the Emperor Justinian I (527–565), initially inspired in large measure by the growing Ostrogothic challenge emanating from Italy. Roman armies permanently extinguished the Vandal threat in 535, and then proceeded to prosecute a Gothic War for the next two decades. This latter contest played out on land and sea.

In the protracted struggle, the centrepiece of Byzantine warfleets was the *dromon*, the most significant ship design since the advent of the classical *trireme*, and a direct evolutionary offshoot of the venerable *liburna*. Among the notable changes brought about by the introduction of the single-banked *dromon* were the application of lateen sails and the addition of a wooden spur above the waterline to replace the bow-mounted ram (ἔμβολος or *rostrum*) of the *trireme* and *liburna*.[92] Of equal consequence, the *dromon*[93] was faster than the standard *liburnae* of the Late Empire and, unlike some of the earlier vessels, was fully decked.[94]

The climactic naval battle in the ongoing war between the Ostrogoths and Romans happened off the Adriatic coast of Italy, near the town of Sena Gallica (modern Sinigaglia).[95] There, a Byzantine fleet achieved a final, decisive victory over a Gothic flotilla in 551. With this victory, Justinian began the restoration of Roman naval supremacy in the Mediterranean that would last until decisively challenged by the Muslims in the seventh century. Thereafter, a robust navy remained central to the security of the Byzantine state for centuries to come. Equally, the Battle of Sena Gallica was the final significant naval battle in antiquity.

The Ancient Sources

The Reliability of the Ancient Sources

The array of ancient sources available to the modern historian seeking to resurrect an accurate understanding of an ancient battle of the Late Roman era is diverse, but such works are not abundant and those that are obtainable are almost invariably prejudiced to some extent in critical interpretation. Late imperial sources are oftentimes heavily burdened by the bias of their creators, whether subconscious or deliberate, making the information available to a modern researcher problematic at best for an accurate interpretation of events.

The very nature of some sources calls into question the accuracy or even overall value of their content. The *Scriptores Historiae Augustae*, for instance, presents serious problems to any modern researcher. Long identified by scholars of various generations as a work of dubious content, seemingly as much fiction as fact, the ambiguous nature of the *SHA* allows no meaningful path for scholars seeking to extrapolate genuine historical information from the 'evidence' presented; but its uniqueness as a source document has continually provided the collection a certain intrinsic value despite its general reputation of unreliability. This has not, however, deterred its continued use; and a vigorous debate among each new generation of scholars inevitably revolves around the merits of the work, or lack thereof.

In addition, some late Roman histories can clearly be seen to very closely draw upon certain commonly shared texts, resulting in a duplication of information in several sources. An example of this can be found in works by Eutropius, Aurelius Victor and Sextus Festus among others, in which portions of each demonstrate a certain commonality of information long theorized to have originated from a single source. In this case, the common text is the so-called *Enmannsche Kaisergeschichte*, the existence of which was first postulated by the late nineteenth-century German historian Alexander Enmann.[96] Though the *Kaisergeschichte*, if it ever truly existed, is no longer extant, its influence is presumed to be based on the intertextual similarities contained in numerous subsequent histories. Though each of the later works contains passages of unique origin, the larger body of replicated information only diminishes the overall value of the individual sources to the total corpus of available knowledge.

By contrast, other works, though they have their own detractors, simply prove less nettlesome to researchers, and the worth of their information far outreaches any impediments put forward by modern criticism. Counted among these are such works as Ammianus, Procopius and Agathias. Procopius has been long identified as the last great historian of western antiquity, and Agathias, whose *Histories* is a generally well-regarded continuation of Procopius, is perceived to be a competent source for events during the immediate years preceding 558. In like manner, the surviving books of the *Res Gestae* by Ammianus Marcellinus are seen to be a solid treatment of events from 353 to 378, particularly as it relates to Julian's campaign against the Sassanid Persians. Even these works are not, however, without a certain amount of author-infused bias, so like all ancient works, it goes without saying that a modern historian should employ each with due caution.

Beyond the above cited examples are also a host of lesser, more obscure or fragmentary sources which present their own unique challenges to historians. Perhaps most significant among these are the chronicles, popularly written works by individuals like Hydatius, Marcellinus Comes and Prosper of Aquitaine, as well as ones like the *Gallic Chronicle* which were produced by anonymous writers. As a general rule, the author of a *chronicon* rarely compiled his work with a discriminating eye, so such records do not typically prioritize events of great importance over those of lesser significance. The chronigraphical tradition represents a separate body of written evidence for scholars to consult, and a discriminating eye should likewise be applied to the use of these sources.

Note Regarding Battlefield Numbers

One of the most unrelenting problems facing the student of ancient warfare is the validity of numbers related to an army's size and to the casualties suffered as a result of a battlefield encounter. In truth, all numbers cited in ancient sources should be viewed with scepticism by a modern historian. There was very rarely any means by which ancient writers, often far removed in time and place from the actual event, might acquire an accurate count of the casualties suffered in a major engagement, let alone deliver a figure with the level of accuracy expected of today's military authorities. For these same reasons, information pertaining to the size of a field army at the moment of battle is also problematic, and so must likewise be approached with due caution.

Some ancient writers offer figures which are very evident exaggerations, while others provide numbers that are seen to be more plausible by modern researchers. The acceptance of the latter is typically based on a variety of factors, including the type and volume of evidence present, the availability of supporting or corroborating information and the overall reliability of the particular writer or source from which the numbers are drawn. For instance, it is reasonable to conclude that historians like Ammianus or Procopius of Caesarea, because they were not only contemporary with the events they were describing but even participants of one sort or another, were in a better position than most to relate battlefield statistics with a certain expectation of accuracy. Even so, such sources are still viewed with strong qualification by the prudent scholar.

Also, it should be understood that ancient writers were susceptible to the expectations of their audience, and the temptation to skew the numbers in order to satisfy the bias of their readers, or to reflect the author's own political or social prejudice, was certainly great. In like fashion, the transmission of numbers through subsequent editions and translations of a work only enhanced the likelihood of human error, and it is reasonable to conclude that over time such changes might occur either by accident or design while in the hands of a scribe.

Ancient Authors and Their Works Relevant to this Study

When studying an ancient battle, it is important to have an understanding of the original sources from which the accounts are drawn. Though no historian should slavishly adhere to the descriptions provided by ancient and medieval writers, their works do serve as the fundamental starting point for any further critical investigation. To this end, basic insight into the background of the early author provides the modern researcher with an appreciation of the inherent value of the extant source.

AGATHIAS SCHOLASTICOS (*c.*532–580). A sixth-century Greek historian from Myrina in Asia Minor, Agathias wrote his *Histories* in five books. The work covers the period from 552 to 557 and was intended by the author to resume where Procopius' historical narrative ended. The *Histories* largely concentrates on foreign policy and the affairs of the Roman army under Narses. (Frendo, 1975)

AMBROSE. Born *c.*340 in the city of Augusta Treverorum (Trier, Germany) in the Roman province of Gallia Belgica, Ambrose was consecrated Bishop of Milan in 374. In this capacity he became one of the most important Roman Christian church leaders of the fourth century. A prolific writer, his complete corpus includes some ninety-one *epistulae*. (McLynn, 2014)

AMMIANUS MARCELLINUS. A fourth-century Latin historian born to a Greek family in Antiocheia, Ammianus accompanied Emperor Julian on his Persian campaign of 362–363. His *Res Gestae* originally consisted of thirty-one books, but only books 14–31 survive. The extant books cover the period from 353–378. (Loeb)

APPIAN. Born *c.*95 in Alexandria, Egypt, to an upper-class family of equestrian rank, Appian served in high offices in his native province before moving to Rome, where he worked first as *advocatus fisci* before being appointed *procurator* during the reign of Antoninus Pius. Appian died about 165. He composed his *Roman History* in twenty-four books, though only portions of the total work are extant. Most significant are books 13–17 of the *Roman History*, which focus on the civil wars of the later Republic. (Loeb)

AUGUSTINE OF HIPPO. Aurelius Augustinus was born in the Numidian city of Tagaste in North Africa in 354. For the first decade of his adulthood Augustine taught rhetoric in Carthage, Rome and Milan. While in Milan he came under the influence of Ambrose, Bishop of Milan, and it was during this time that he abandoned Manichaeism and converted to Christianity. He was baptized in 387 and ordained a priest in 391. Four years later he was appointed Bishop of Hippo Regius. It was here that he died in 430 during the Vandal siege of the city. A prolific writer, among his best known works are *Confessions* (*Confessiones*) in thirteen books and the *City of God* (*De civitate Dei*) in twenty-two books. (Loeb; Brown, 2000)

CASSIUS DIO. Born sometime around 160 in Bithynia in Asia Minor, Cassius Dio Cocceianus (though commonly rendered in Greek, *Δίων ο Κάσσιος*) came from a prominent Roman family. A member of the Senate by the emperorship of Commodus (180–192), Dio subsequently had a distinguished career as praetor, *suffect* consul, proconsul of Africa and governor of Dalmatia and Upper Pannonia. During these years he wrote his seminal work, *Roman History*, which recounts in eighty books some 1,400 years of Roman history from the age of Aeneas to the year 229. Books 36–54 and 56–60 are almost complete. All other volumes of the history survive only in part or in fragments. (Loeb)

CLAUDIAN. Claudius Claudianus was a Latin poet born in Alexandria, Egypt, around 370. In 395, he came to Italy and eventually settled in Milan. While there, his poetic talents garnered for him intimate access to the court of the Western Roman emperor, Honorius, and the patronage of the general, Flavius Stilicho. Once established in court circles, he produced a series of historical epics over the next decade, including *On the Consulate of Stilicho* (*De Consulatu Stilichonis*), *On the Gildonic War* (*De Bello Gildonico*) and *On the Gothic War* (*De Bello Gothico*). Modern scholars conclude his death occurred *c.*404. (Bowen, 1954; Cameron, 1970)

CORIPPUS. Flavius Cresconius Corippus was a sixth-century poet from North Africa. He served in various official capacities, including imperial treasurer and chamberlain of the Emperor Justinian. Two epic poems are ascribed to him: *In praise of the younger Justin* (*In laudem Iustini minoris*), in four books; and an earlier work, composed about 550, entitled *Tale of John* (*Iohannis*). This latter poem recounts the Byzantine campaign led by the *magister militum* John Troglita against the Mauritanians. The *Tale of John*, also called *On the Libyan war* (*De bellis Libycis*), is composed in eight books and is the leading source for the events of the war. (Shea, 1998)

EUSEBIUS OF CAESAREA. Eusebius was a Roman historian and early fourth-century Bishop of Caesarea Maritima. The author of numerous works related to aspects of early Christian church history, one of his most recognized is the *Ecclesiastical History* (*Historia Ecclesiastica*), completed sometime around 324. The work, in ten books, broadly recounts early Christian history from the first century until the early fourth century. Largely because the work embodies the bias of its author, the historical community since Edward Gibbon has given the work a mixed reception, ranging from open disdain to a carefully considered acceptance of its value to Late Roman history. (Loeb; Cameron and Hall, 1999; Drake 2002)

EUTROPIUS. Supporting evidence indicates that Flavius Eutropius, the latter fourth-century Latin author of the *Abridgement of Roman History* (*Breviarum ab urbe condita*), was a *magister memoriae* in the city of Constantinople, and that his public career may have spanned a rising echelon of offices most notably under the emperors Julian and Valens. Compiled in ten books, the *Breviarum* broadly records Roman history from Romulus through to the Emperor Jovian, and the narrative generally focuses on the military events of each age. (Burgess, January, 2001; Rohrbacher, 2002)

FESTUS. The late fourth-century historian Festus of Tridentum, author of the *Breviarium rerum gestarum populi Romani*, was a career bureaucrat whose service included *magister memoriae* and Proconsul of Asia. The *Breviarum* was completed *c.*370, and is a largely superficial compilation of Roman history from its foundation until the year 369. The author dedicated the work to Emperor Valens, and chose to concentrate primarily on the political and military exploits of the Roman state during both the Republican and Imperial eras. Of particular note is the second half of the *Breviarum*, which offers a chronological survey of Rome's wars with Persia. (Kelly, 2010)

FLORUS. Born in North Africa during the emperorship of Vespasian, Lucius Annaeus Florus was the author of *Epitome* (*Epitome de T. Livio Bellorum omnium annorum DCC Libri duo*), a work which broadly describes the history of Rome from Romulus to Caesar Augustus. The information in the *Epitome* is drawn primarily from the work of Livy, though Florus' text suffers from certain deficiencies such as chronological and geographical inaccuracies. Annaeus Florus died *c.*130, during the final years of the reign of Hadrian. (Den Boer,1972)

GALLIC CHRONICLE OF 452 AND 511. The *Chronica Gallia a CCCCLII* and the *Chronica Gallia a DXI* are chronicles compiled in the form of annals by anonymous authors who were most likely resident in southern Gaul in the latter fifth and early sixth centuries. The first records a number of significant events between the accession of Theodosius I as co-emperor in 379 and the Hunnic invasion of Italy in 452. The second work likewise begins in 379 but continues to the year 511. Each chronicle focuses on events in the western part of the Empire, particularly in Gaul. The reliability of dates in the two documents has been a point of intense disagreement for generations of classical scholars, but most modern historians tend to favour the chronicles as important contemporary sources for events in the fifth century. The author of the *Chronicle of 511* used both the earlier work as well as the chronicle of Hydatius as important sources of information. (Mathisen and Shanzer, 2001)

GREGORY OF TOURS. Georgius Florentius was born in France in the early sixth century and appointed Bishop of Tours in 573 by the Frankish king, Sigebert I. He completed his *Decem Libri Historiarum*, more commonly known as the *History of the Franks* (*Historia Francorum*), in 594 shortly before his own death. The work is in ten books and is the principal source for the history of the Merovingian kings. (Dalton, 1927)

HERODIAN. Intertextual evidence suggests that Herodian lived from approximately 170 until sometime after the publication of his *History of the Empire from the Death of Marcus* in the years following 240. The common assumption among modern historians is that he lived in Syria, perhaps in the city of Antioch. Herodian's history covers the period from 180 to 238. Modern historians have long recognized that the work suffers from errors in dating and the inclusion of historical and geographical inaccuracies. In general, the work has received a mixed reception from historians over the centuries. John of Antioch made liberal use of Herodian's work, while others like John Zonaras used the *History* simply as a supplement to Cassius Dio's *Roman History*. (Loeb; Bowersock, 1975)

HYDATIUS. The fifth-century Gallaecian bishop Hydatius composed his *Chronicle* in 468–469. The work is valuable to modern historians as a unique source of information on pre-Islamic Spain and the history of the fifth century. (Burgess, 1993)

ISADORE OF SEVILLE. Isadore of Seville was Archbishop of Seville from 601 to 636, during the era of Gothic rule in Spain. An author of several works, including the *Etymologiae*, he composed his *History of the Gothic, Vandal, and Suevic Kings* (*Historia de regibus Gothorum, Vandalorum, et Suevorum*) in the early seventh century. The work traces the history of the West Goths from 256 to 624. The primary sources from which he draws his *Historia* include

Jerome's continuation of the *Chronica* by Eusebius, the *Historiae* of Orosius and Hydatius' *Chronica*. Modern scholars consider Isadore to be the most reliable extant source for the history of the West Goths from 590 to 624. Two versions of the *Historia* survive, one in shorter form which dates to 619 and a longer completed in 624. (Donini and Ford, 1966)

JOHN OF ANTIOCH. A seventh-century Christian monk, John of Antioch was the author of the *Historia chronike* (Χρονικὴ), a record of historical events from Creation to the death of the Byzantine emperor Phokas (602–610). Only fragments of the chronicle remain extant. (Cross and Livingstone, 2005; Van Nuffelen, 'Antioch', 2012)

JORDANES. The sixth-century historian Jordanes completed *The Origin and Deeds of the Goths* (*De origine actibusque Getarum*), or *Getica*, in Constantinople in early 551. The work is an abridgement of the now lost multi-volume *History of the Goths* by the sixth-century Roman statesman, Cassiodorus. The *Getica* is particularly valuable to modern scholars because it serves as the primary contemporary source on both the Gothic and Hunnic peoples. Jordanes' treatment of the Huns is largely based on the lost work of the fifth-century Byzantine historian, Priscus. (Croke, 1987; Kazhdan, ed., 1991)

JOSEPHUS. The first-century Jewish historian Yosef Ben Matityahu (Flavius Josephus) was born in Jerusalem to a wealthy family connected to the former Hasmonean rulers of Judea. In the First Jewish War (66–73) he commanded Galilean forces during the Roman army's siege of Jotapata. Following the capture and destruction of the city, Josephus gained the patronage of the Roman general and emperor, Vespasian, as well as the friendship of his son, Titus. Through his association with the imperial family he received Roman citizenship and elected to adopt the name *Flavius*. After the war, Josephus completed *The Jewish War* (*Bellum Judaicum*) which covers Jewish history from the reign of Antiochos IV Epiphanes to the Roman destruction of Jerusalem in AD 70. Less than two decades later he wrote *Jewish Antiquities* (Ἰουδαϊκὴ ἀρχαιολογία), which together with his earlier work provides modern historians valuable insight into the social and religious events of first century Judea. (Loeb)

LACTANTIUS. Lucius Caecilius Firmianus Lactantius was a rhetorician who served as tutor in Latin to Crispus, son of Emperor Constantine I. Born a pagan, his conversion to Christianity while an adult influenced the nature of his writings. The particular moral perspective found in Lactantius' only historical work, *On the Deaths of the Persecutors* (*De Mortibus persecutorum*), reveals the author's particular religious bias toward those Romans from Nero to Maximus who are identified as the leading persecutors of Christians between the early first and fourth centuries. (Bardenhewer, 1908)

LIBANIUS. Born in Antioch, Syria, in 314, the life of the pagan Sophist and rhetorician Libanius spanned most of the fourth century, making his writings valuable sources for modern historians seeking insight into aspects of Eastern Roman politics, culture and society. Among his most notable works are some sixty orations, a number of which were composed in memory of the Emperor Julian, with whom Libenius once shared a friendship. His *Funeral Oration for Julian* was one of several composed between 362 and 365. (Loeb)

MARCELLINUS COMES. An Illyrian by birth, Marcellinus Comes spent much of his life in Constantinople in the service of the Eastern Roman emperors, Justin I (518–527) and Justinian I (527–565). Incomplete evidence suggests he died shortly after completing his *Chronicle* in 534. Marcellinus intended his work to be a continuation of the *Ecclesiastical History* by Eusebius of Caesarea. As such, the *Chronicle* records events in the Eastern Empire from 379 to 534. An anonymous author covered the work's final period to 566. The evident bias of Marcellinus toward heretics and the presence of numerous factual inaccuracies challenge the credibility of the work. (Croke, 1995)

MEROBAUDES. Flavius Merobaudes was a fifth-century poet and orator. Included among the few surviving fragments of his work is a portion of a panegyric on the third consulship of Aetius Patricius, which occurred in 446. Merobaudes is also presumed by some researchers to be the Spanish author of the short poem *De Christo*, but cannot be definitively proven. (Clover, 1971)

MIDRASH. The *midrash* (pl. *midrashim*) is a form of rabbinic literature derived from biblical text. There are two types: *midrash aggada* and *midrash halakha*. *Aggada*, which means literally 'story' or 'telling' in Hebrew, explores the ethics and values of a word or verse in biblical texts in order to derive the sermonic implications. In like fashion, *midrash halakha* derives laws and legal practice from the scriptures. Among the oldest works of midrashic literature is the *Lamentations Rabbah* (*Midrash Eichah*), which is included among the *aggadic midrashim* on the books of the *Tanach*, the canon of the Hebrew Bible. (*Encyclopaedia Judaica*)

OLYMPIODORUS OF THEBES. Olympiodorus was a fifth-century poet and historian born in the city of Thebes, Egypt, in the late fourth century. His public career unfolded during the reigns of emperors Honorius and Theodosius II, and he is most remembered for a diplomatic embassy to the Huns in 412. Olympiodorus was the author of the *History*, a work which recorded the history of the Western Roman Empire from 407 to 425. The *History* is largely lost; only fragments remain extant. The *Bibliotheca* by Photius, the ninth-century Byzantine Patriarch of Constantinople, offers a valuable summarization of Olympiodorus' work. Evidence from Photius and the surviving fragments suggest the *History* was a source for the later historians Zosimus,

Sozoman, Philostorgius and perhaps even Procopius of Caesarea. (Blockley, 1983; Matthews, 1970; Treadgold, 2004)

OROSIUS. Born in the later fourth century, the historian and Christian writer Paulus Orosius began the composition of his most widely recognized work, *Seven Books of History against the Pagans* (*Historiarum adversus paganos libri septem*), while in the North African city of Hippo Regius. The work is a superficial treatment of world history from the Creation until 417, though the author did draw upon earlier historians like Livy, Caesar and Suetonius among others. Modern historians place most value on the record of events from 378 to 417. (Rohrbacher, 2002)

PANEGYRICI LATINI. Panegyrici Latini is a collection of twelve panegyrics, most of which were composed by unknown authors. With the exception of the first oration, composed by Pliny the Younger *c.*100, the remaining speeches appear to date from the latter third century to the late fourth century. Eight of the panegyrics were presented in Gaul, and each of the twelve is given to honour a particular man of power. Among these are the emperors Trajan, Julian and Constantine I. (Nixon and Rodgers, 1994)

PLINY THE ELDER. The natural philosopher Caius Plinius Secundus, more popularly called Pliny the Elder, was born in Como in Transalpine Gaul in AD 23 to a family of equestrian rank. A prolific writer, his only extant work is *Natural History* (*Naturalis Historia*), an encyclopedia published *c.*78. The work, composed in thirty-seven books, covers a wide array of subjects including astronomy, geography, anthropology, zoology, botany, mineralogy and pharmacology. (Loeb)

PLUTARCH. Born about the mid-first century in the small Greek town of Chaeronea in Boeotia, the philosopher Plutarch died after 120. The author of numerous works, among his most significant is the *Parallel Lives*, a collection of over two dozen extant biographies, mostly arranged in pairs that include one distinguished Greek and Roman political or military figure. (Loeb)

POSSIDIUS. Friend of St Augustine for almost forty years, Possidius was born *c.*365 and became associated with Augustine's monastery in Hippo soon after its foundation in the early 390s. In 397 Possidius succeeded to the Bishopric of Calama, a North African city in the Roman province of Numidia. Sometime between 432 and 439 he completed the *Life of St. Augustine* (*Vita S. Augustini*), considered by modern scholars to be a reliable source on the life of Augustine of Hippo. (Weiskotten, 1919)

PRISCUS. Born in Thracia in the early fifth century, the Greek historian Priskos (Priscus) of Panium was the author of the later-titled *History of Byzantium* (Βυζαντινή Ιστορία) in eight volumes. (Blockley, 1983)

PROCOPIUS OF CAESAREA. Procopius was a sixth-century Byzantine historian from the Roman province of Palaestina Prima. In 527 he was appointed the *adsessor* for the great Byzantine general, Flavius Belisarius. The relationship lasted until after the Roman seizure of Ravenna from the Ostrogoths in 540, when Procopius appears to have left Belisarius' staff. One of his most significant works, the *History of the Wars*, chronicles the Persian, Vandalic and Gothic wars of Emperor Justinian I (527–565). The first two books treat the Byzantine conflict with the Sassanid Persians, the next two volumes recount the struggle against the Vandals of North Africa and books V–VIII focus on the Gothic war in Italy. Procopius' works remain the central source for the history of Justinian's reign. (Cameron, 1996; Kaldellis, 2004; Loeb)

PROSPER OF AQUITAINE. Prosper of Aquitaine was a fifth-century Christian writer from the region of Aquitaine in south-western Gaul. His most significant work is the *Chronicle* (*Epitoma chronicon*), composed over a period of two decades and updated for a final time by the author in 455. Of particular value to modern historians is Prosper's treatment of the Hunnic invasions of Gaul and Italy in 451 and 452, due in large measure to the dearth of sources for this period. (Muhlberger, 1990)

SCRIPTORES HISTORIAE AUGUSTAE. The *Scriptores Historiae Augustae or Historia Augusta* is an extant collection of some thirty biographies about the Roman emperors from Hadrian to Carinus. Most of the biographies recount the lives of a single emperor, though some consist of more than one emperor when the individuals under study possess a notable association of some sort. The work was purportedly composed by six separate authors – Aelius Spartianus, Julius Capitolinus, Vulcacius Gallicanus, Aelius Lampridius, Trebellius Pollio and Flavius Vopiscus – though this claim is rejected by most modern scholars, who assign the entire collection to a single writer. The nature of the texts, a rich compilation of fact and fiction, has excited much controversy among historians for several generations. Nonetheless, *Historia Augusta* continues to elicit the attention of modern scholars because the biographies recount the exploits of Roman emperors, their heirs and the various imperial claimants of the second and third centuries, a period for which there is otherwise a shortage of evidence. (Loeb)

SEXTUS AURELIUS VICTOR. Very little is known about the Roman historian and politician Sextus Aurelius Victor. Extant evidence suggests he was born in the early fourth century in North Africa near the city of Cirta (Constantine, Algeria), perhaps on a small prosperous farm in the vicinity of the capital. Though apparently of humble birth, Victor achieved an illustrious career as a politician and bureaucrat. Emperor Julian appointed Victor consular governor of Pannonia Secunda in the summer of 361, and almost three decades later he attained the prestigious office of urban prefect of Rome, suggesting that he had obtained important posts during the intervening years, perhaps including a proconsulship. It appears Victor completed his most important historical work, *De Caesaribus*, sometime immediately before the assumption of his governorship in Pannonia. The work is a brief survey of the Roman emperors from Caesar Augustus to Constantius II, but unlike contemporaries such as Eutropius and Festus, Victor is a moralist. The text is thus punctuated with passages which express the views of the author, and his style is clearly influenced by the work of the late Republican writer, Gaius Sallustius Crispus. (Bird, 1994)

SIDONIUS APOLLINARIS. The poet Caius Sollius Apollinaris Sidonius (Modestus), commonly styled by modern scholars as simply Sidonius or Sidonius Apollinaris, was born in the early fifth century to a distinguished Roman family in the city of Lugdunum (Lyons) in Gaul. Both his grandfather and father served as Praetorian Prefect of the province during Sidonius' youth. He received a sound education befitting one of his social status in Gaul. The Western Roman Emperor Anthemius (467–472) created Sidonius *praefectus urbanus* and senator in *c.*468 and made him a patrician the following year. Soon afterwards, he became Bishop of Auvergne. His work is in two groups, the *Epistulae* and the *Carmina*. Counted within this latter collection are his three panegyrics. Sidonius' work is considered an important source in the life of the fifth-century Gallo-Roman nobility during a time when the region was transitioning from Roman to Frankish rule. (Loeb; Waarden and Kelly, 2013)

SOCRATES OF CONSTANTINOPLE. The Christian writer Socrates of Constantinople, also called Socrates Scholasticus, was born in the city of Constantinople in the latter fourth century. His work, the *Ecclesiastical History* (Εκκλησιαστικης Ιστορία or *Historia Ecclesiastica*), covers the reigns of eight Eastern Roman emperors from the accession of Constantine I in 406 to the year 439 in the reign of Theodosius II. The author intended the work to be a continuation of the fourth-century *Ecclesiastical History* by Eusebius of Caesarea. (Rohrbacher, 2002)

SOZOMEN. Salminius Hermius Sozomen was a fifth-century Christian historian born in the region of Palestine. The recipient of a monastic education in his homeland and legal training in Beirut, he later practised law in Constantinople. His *Ecclesiastical History* (*Historia Ecclesiastica*) is in nine books. Only the last is incomplete. (Rohrbacher, 2002)

STRABO. The Greek philosopher and historian Strabo was born to a prominent family in the Pontic city of Amasia in 64 or 63 BC. He completed his most significant work, *Geography* (*Geographica*), sometime in the early first century AD, likely immediately prior to his death. For modern scholars, the *Geography* is a valuable source for insight into different regions of the Near Eastern and Mediterranean world. (Loeb)

SUETONIUS. The life of the Roman writer Caius Suetonius Tranquillus appears to have spanned the latter third of the first century and perhaps the first three decades of the second century. He came from an equestrian family, his father Suetonius Laetus having served as a *tribunus angusticlavius* in the Thirteenth Legion during the Battle of Betriacum. Among his numerous extant writings, the only complete work is the *Lives of the Caesars* (*De Vita Caesarum*), a biography of Roman leaders from Julius Caesar to Emperor Domitian. The *Lives* is notable for its invaluable insight into the histories of the first emperors, but the text is commonly anecdotal. (Loeb)

SYNCELLUS. Georgios the Synkellos (Syncellus) was an advisor and assistant to Tarasios (784–806), the Byzantine Patriarch of Constantinople. Sometime after the death of Tarasios, Synkellos retired permanently to a monastery. It was in this capacity that he composed the *Selection of Chronography* (Ἐκλογὴ Χρονογραφίας). The work is a chronological listing of historical events from the biblical Creation to the emperorship of Diocletian (284–305) and reflects the author's preoccupation with matters of Christian church orthodoxy, biblical history and the life of Christ. Modern scholars consider the *Chronography* an insightful source because it draws upon numerous histories and chronicles from Egypt and the Near East, including the lost chronicle of Eusebius of Caesarea. (Adler and Tuffin, 2002)

TACITUS. Born in the mid-first century to a wealthy Roman family, the political career of the historian Publius (or Caius) Cornelius Tacitus included a consulship in 97 or 98 and the governorship of Asia province a decade and a half later. The author of the *Agricola* and *Germania*, Tacitus completed two larger histories pertaining to the events of the early Principate. The first, called the *Histories*, was originally compiled in fourteen books and covered the events of the Flavian period, beginning with the civil wars that brought Vespasian to power. Tacitus' final work was the *Annals*, for which intertextual evidence suggests he was still writing as late as 117. Of this multi-volume work, to which modern scholars have assigned a total of sixteen books, numbers 1–6 survive in a single manuscript, though portions of books 5 and 6 are missing, books 7–10 are no longer extant and books 11 and 16 of the collection are incomplete. The *Annals* covers the reigns of the Julio-Claudian emperors, though an account of Augustus does not exist. Both the *Histories* and the *Annals* are highly valued by modern historians of Roman Imperial history, though a certain sharp bias can be detected in the author's discussion of the emperors. (Loeb)

ZONARAS. John Zonaras was a twelfth-century Greek historian and author of the *Epitome of Histories* (*Epitome historiarum*), which chronicled events to the death of the Byzantine emperor Alexios I Komnenos in 1118. Zonaras draws upon both the works of Flavius Josephus and Cassius Dio Cocceianus, though his Late Roman sources are much disputed by modern scholars. (Banchich and Lane, 2009)

ZOSIMUS. Zosimos (Zosimus) was a *comes* and *ex advocatus fisci* (Photius, *Bibliotheca*, Code 98), and intertextual evidence suggests that he was a Greek of the late fifth to early sixth century. His *New History* (*Nea Historia* or *Historia Nova*) is in six books, and focuses on the first four centuries of Roman Imperial history to 409, just before the Gothic siege of Rome. His primary sources are Eunapios for the period from 270–404, thereby incorporating the influence of Dexippos, and Olympiodoros for 407–409 (Zosimos, 5.27.1). Zosimos recounts the decline of the Empire, focusing on its increasing barbarization and the decline of paganism. An acknowledged pagan, the author is essentially anti-Christian in tone. (Ridley, 1982)

Part Two

Battles of the Roman Empire

Alphabetical and Chronological
List of Battles

Alphabetical List of Battles

Chronological List of Battles

First Century BC (100–1 BC)

First Century (AD 1–99)

28 Baduhennawood
43 Medway River
43 Camulodunum
50 Severn River
53 Milvian Bridge
58 Volandum
61 Isle of Mona
61 Camulodunum
61 Watling Street
62 Rhandeia
66 Bethoron
67 Gamala
67 Jotopata (June–July)
69 Baden
69 Cremona (April)
69 Forum Julii
69 Locus Castorum
69 Bedriacum (October)
69 Trapezus
69 Rhenus River
69 Rhenus River
69 Insula Batavorum
69 Bonna
69 Gelduda
69 Gelduba (December)
69–70   Castra Vetera (Autumn–
   Spring)
69 Via Salaria (December)
69 Rome
69 Placentia
70 Jerusalem (March–September)
70 Rigodulum (Summer)
70 Augusta Treverorum (Summer)
70 Castra Vetera (Autumn)
70 Castra Vetera (Autumn)
70 Arenacum
70 Batavodurum
70 Helinium (Autumn)
70 Bingium
70 Vada
73 Masada
84 Mons Graupius

87 Tapae
88 Tapae
89 Antunnacum

Second Century (AD 100–199)
101 Tapae
134–135   Bethar
162 Elegia
166 Ister River
172 Ister River
174 Battle of Thundering Legion
193 Cyzicus
194 Nicaea
194 Issus
197 Lugdunum

Third Century (AD 200–299)
217 Nisibis
218 Immae
231 Euphrates River
238 Carthage
243 Rhesaena
244 Misiche
249 Verona
250 Nicopolis ad Istrum
250 Augusta Traiana
251 Philippopolis
251 Abrittus
253 Barbalissus
253 Interamna Nahars (August)
259 Edessa
259 Mediolanum
259 Mursa
260 Corycus
267 Nessos River
268 Naissus
268 Mediolanum
268 Benacus Lake (November)
270 Haemus Mons
270 Ister River
270 Ister River
271 Placentia

271	Metaurus River (Winter)
271	Ticinum
272	Immae
272	Daphne
272	Emesa
272	Palmyra
274	Catalunian Plains
276	Tarsus
278	Licus River
285	Verona
285	Margus River (May)
296	Calleva Atrebatum
296	Callinicum
297	Satala
298	Lingonae
298	Vindonissa

Fourth Century (AD 300–399)

312	Augusta Taurinorum
312	Brixia
312	Verona
312	Milvian Bridge (28 October)
313	Campus Serenus
316	Cibalae (8 October)
316	Plain of Mardia
322	Ister River
323	Adrianople
324	Callipolis
324	Chrysopolis (18 September)
344	Singara
350	Nisibis
351	Mursa
353	Mons Seleucus
355	Lake Briantia
356	Durocortorum
356	Brotomagus
356	Senonae
357	Argentoratum (August)
357	Hercynian Forest
358	Batavia
358	Ister River
359	Tigris River

359	Amida
359	Acimincum
360	Singara
363	Euphrates River (Spring)
363	Euphrates River (Spring)
363	Sumere
363	Maranga (22 June)
363	Samarra (26 June)
363	Samarra (27 June)
363	Maiozamalcha
363	Tigris River
366	Thyatira
366	Nacolia (26 May)
366	Catalunian Plains (July)
367	Solicinium
368	Piri Mons
371	Vagabanta
374	Valeria
376	Marcianopolis
376	Ad Salices
376	Salices
377	Dibaltum
378	Rhenus River
378	Argentaria
378	Adrianople (9 August)
381	Ister River
386	Ister River
388	Siscia
388	Poetovio (Summer)
394	Frigidus River (5–6 September)
394	Aquileia (5–6 September)
398	Tabraca

Fifth Century (AD 400–499)

401	Timavus (November)
403	Verona
403	Pollentia (6 April)
406	Faesulae
410	Rome
411	Arelate
413	Ocriculum

425   Arelate
428   Vicus Helenae
430   Arelate
430   Hippo Regius
432   Ariminum
435   Arelate
436–439   Narbo Martius
438   Singilis River
439   Tolosa
447   Utus
451   Catalunian Plains
452   Aquileia
456   Agrigentium
456   Corsica
456   Urbicus River (5 October)
456   Placentia (16 October)
468   Hermaeum Promontorium
469   Vicus Dolensis
471   Rhodanus River
472   Rome
486   Noviodunum

Sixth Century (AD 500–599)
527   Melabasa
528   Mindouos
530   Daras
530   Satala (Summer)
531   Callinicum (19 April)
533   Ad Decimum (14 September)
533   Tricamaron (December)

534   Mammes
535   Mount Bourgaon
535   Panormus
535   Salonae
535   Salonae
536   Membresa
536   Perusia
536   Scardona
536   Narnia
537   Scalae Veteres
537   Ponte Salario (22 February)
537   Porta Salaria
537   Rome
537   Porta Pinciana
540   Auximus
540   Tarbesium
542   Faventia (Spring)
542   Mucellium (Spring)
543   Leptis Magna
543   Anglon
544   Tebesta
544   Cillium
545   Siccaveneria
546   Tiber River
546   Rome
547   Rome (May)
547   Sufetula
547   Plain of Gallica
548   Fields of Cato (Spring)

Battles of the Roman Empire
31 BC–AD 565

Abrittus, AD 251, July – Unable to stop Germanic tribes from crossing the Danubian frontier and ravaging throughout Moesia and portions of Thracia during the previous year, Emperor Trajanus Decius again led an army into the region in a concerted effort to drive the invaders out of Roman territory. Near the town of Abrittus (Razgrad) the Romans confronted the forces of the Gothic king Kniva during the barbarians' homeward march. The raiding band, consisting of a coalition of various German tribes, divided into three divisions and prepared to face the legions of Decius. Once the battle began the Romans defeated two of the enemy formations, but then made the fatal mistake of allowing themselves to be trapped on unfavourable ground. Mired by marshy terrain and unable to manoeuvre for tactical advantage, the imperial army was almost completely destroyed. Thousands of Romans perished in the disaster, including the emperor and his oldest son, the co-*Augustus* Herennius Etruscus. The loss of Decius also marked the first death of a Roman emperor in battle against a foreign enemy.

Sextus Aurelius Victor, *Liber De Caesaribus*, 29; Anonymous (Sextus Aurelius Victor), *Epitome of the Emperors*, 29.3 (T. Banchich, trans.); John Zonaras, *Epitome of Histories*, 12.20; Zosimus, *New History* 1.23.1–3; Lucius Caecilius Firmianus Lactantius, *On the Deaths of the Persecutors*, 4; Jordanes, *The Origins and Deeds of the Goths*, 103.

Acimincum, AD 359 – While preparing to offer an address during peace negotiations with the Limigantes of Sarmatia, Emperor Constantius II was unexpectedly rushed by an angry mob. As the attackers charged the tribunal they were briefly slowed by imperial attendants who were all wounded or killed in the encounter, but the delay permitted armed soldiers to reach the emperor in time to ensure his safety. A general struggle quickly erupted as arriving Roman troops moved against the Limigantes. In the battle which followed near the community of Aciminum in Pannonia, the Sarmatian forces suffered severe casualties, all being either killed or driven to flight. Roman losses were minimal.

Ammianus Marcellinus, *Res Gestae* 19.11.10–15.

Actium, 31 BC, September 2 (Roman Civil Wars, Wars of the Second Triumvirate) – This naval battle marks the end of a series of inconclusive

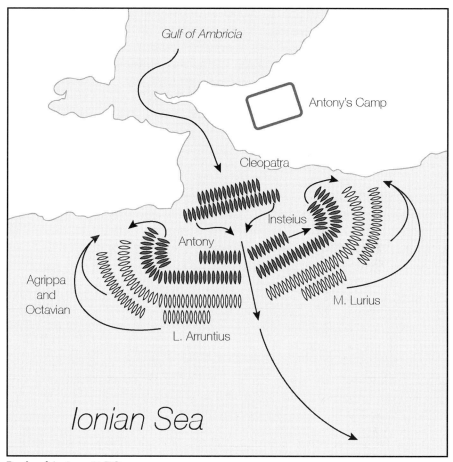

Battle of Actium, 31 BC

engagements between the forces of Marcus Antonius and Caius Octavius, and the decisive turning point in the Roman domination of Ptolemaic Egypt. At dawn the two fleets engaged one another west of the Actium Promontory at the mouth of the *Sinus Ambracius* (Ambracian Gulf) in western Greece. Although Antony's fleet possessed a numerical and size advantage in ships over that of Octavian's squadrons, the latter ultimately benefited from lighter, faster and more manoeuvrable Liburnian vessels (though the exact figures offered by ancient sources vary widely for both fleets). The centre squadron of Octavian's fleet was commanded by Lucius Arruntius; the left wing by Marcus Vipsanius Agrippa; and the right by Octavian himself. Arrayed against this formation on the right was Antony, with Lucius Gellius Publicola, Marcus Octavius and Marcus Insteius in the centre and Caius Sosius commanding the left wing of the fleet. The Egyptian squadron of Cleopatra VII remained behind this line, held in reserve. The battle was initiated by the Antonian left. Octavian immediately responded to this attack by ordering the ships of his right to backwater so as to draw Sosius' squadrons out of the gulf's narrows and into deeper waters of the Ionian Sea, where his lighter Liburnian craft would be at most advantage. Cohesion finally eroded in the Antonian formation when Agrippa sought to extend his left and envelope Antony's right, forcing Publicola to advance against him and thereby separate from the centre. The combination of these moves weakened the left and centre of the Antonian formation. It was at this decisive moment that the sixty ships of Cleopatra's squadron took flight through Antony's line, further disrupting the hard-pressed fleet. At sight of the Ptolemaic queen's withdrawal, Marcus Antonius abandoned his forces and followed the retiring Egyptian vessels. The battle continued despite the absence of Antony. After ten hours of combat, the beaten remnant of the now leaderless fleet finally surrendered to Octavian, having suffered some 5,000 dead.

Plutarch, *Antonius*, 60.50–62.4; Appianus (Appian), *Civil Wars*, 1.5, 6; Lucius Annaeus Florus, *Epitomy* 2.21.4–9; Dio Cassius, *Roman History*, 50.12–35.

Ad Decimum, AD 533, 14 September (Vandal War, Wars of Justinian I) – Three months after its departure from Constantinople, a Roman fleet carrying an invasion force bound for Vandal North Africa landed some 150 miles (241km) south-east of Carthage at Cape Vada (Capoudia). The army, commanded by the general Flavius Belisarius, moved toward its destination following the Mediterranean coast through Leptis Minor and Hadrumetum. Near the town of Ad Decimum, located approximately 8 miles (13km) southwest of Carthage, the leading elements of Belisarius' army unexpectedly encountered Vandal forces. A Roman vanguard of 300 cavalry led by John the Armenian clashed with enemy troops under Ammatas, brother of the Vandal king Gelimer. A second Roman detachment further inland on the left, consisting of 600 Hunnic horsemen, engaged some 2,000 Vandal riders led by Gibamund on a nearby salt plain. In both instances the Romans routed the enemy with heavy losses, but an additional force of Roman federate cavalry, arriving too late to contribute to the fighting, was suddenly driven off by the appearance of Gelimer's vanguard. Unaware that the main Vandal army was in the vicinity, Belisarius and the primary formation of Roman troops finally reached the site of the skirmishes. While there, the general and army were shortly alerted to the rapid approach of the enemy van from the south, led by Gelimer himself. Yet any advantage afforded by this swift advance was lost when the king, upon encountering the lifeless body of his brother, who was killed in the day's earlier action, delayed his attack, permitting the Roman general ample time to rally his scattered forces in preparation for battle. In the general struggle which followed, the flower of the Vandal army was largely

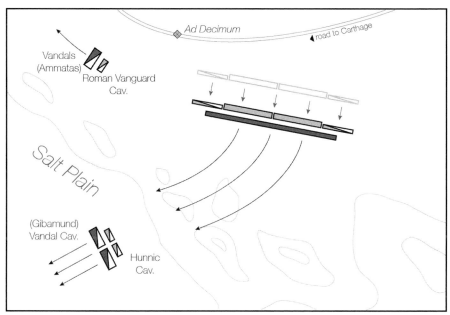

Battle of Ad Decimum, AD 533

destroyed. Gelimer and the remnants of his force fled toward Bulla Regia near the northern Numidian coast, while the victorious Belisarius claimed possession of Carthage.

> Procopius of Caesarea, *History of the Wars* (*The Vandalic War*), 3.18–19; *Chronicle of Pseudo-Zachariah Rhetor*, 9.17c.

Ad Salices, AD 376 (Gothic Wars) – Approximately 12 miles (19km) from Marcianopolis (Devnya, Bulgaria), near the town of Ad Salices, an army led by the Eastern Roman generals Profuturus and Trajanus prepared to engage a much larger force of Goths raiding in the region of Thracia. They were soon joined by reinforcements under the Western Roman *comes domesticorum* Flavius Richomeres, who immediately assumed overall command of the campaign. The Roman troops encamped some distance from the Gothic wagon *laager* in anticipation of attacking the barbarians should they attempt to relocate their camp. The Goths were content to remain within the protection of encircled wagons until the return of their cavalry from pillaging raids. With the arrival of these errant horsemen, both armies prepared for battle. On the morning of the great contest, the Goths immediately occupied some nearby high ground from which they intended to charge the enemy line. The Romans assembled into formation and then declared their readiness for action by sounding their war-cry, the *barritus*. The battle opened with an exchange of missile fire between light skirmishing troops, before the main divisions of heavy infantry collided in the centre. The fighting proved intense, and the Goths were briefly able to penetrate the Roman left wing, forcing Richomeres to commit some of his reserves to redress the broken line. Thereafter, the contest degenerated into a stubborn trial of arms between opposing armies. On the periphery of the struggle, Roman and Gothic cavalry engaged in a violent contest, while contending bowmen subjected their enemies to an unrelenting shower of arrows. With the onset of nightfall, the fighting finally ended with neither side able to claim a victory.

Ammianus Marcellinus, *Res Gestae*, 31.7.5–16.

Adrana River, AD 15 – In retaliation for the Chatti's participation in the destruction of three Roman legions in the Teutoburg Forest in AD 9, Germanicus Caesar, the nephew and adopted son of the Emperor Tiberius, initiated a campaign into the territories of the German tribe. The Roman army, consisting of four legions and 10,000 auxiliaries, cut a wide swath of destruction through the countryside before reaching the Adrana (Eder) River, a small tributary of the Fulda River. Here, Chatti warriors attempted to stop the Romans from constructing a bridge, but were driven off by the legions' *ballistae*. Once Germanicus crossed the river, his forces attacked and burned Mattium, the capital of the tribe. After the destruction of the city, the army proceeded to devastate the surrounding land before withdrawing toward the Rhenus (Rhine) River.

Publius Cornelius Tacitus, *Annals*, 1.56.

Adrianople, AD 323, 3 July (Wars of Constantine I) – The seven years of fragile peace shared between the eastern Emperor Licinius and his western counterpart, Constantine I, deteriorated into a resumption of war in the spring of 323. Following the renewal of hostilities, Licinius established his army near the city of Adrianople (Edirne) in Thracia. His imperial rival soon marched against him from Thessalonica and encamped a short distance away on the opposite bank of the Hebrus (Maritsa) River. The following day, Licinius arrayed his army of 150,000 infantry and 15,000 cavalry on open ground to the north-west of the city near the confluence of the Tonoseius (Tunca) and Hebrus rivers, but Constantine was not willing to hazard a water crossing while his opponent waited in full battle formation. Over the course of the next days, the proximity of Licinius' army prevented Constantine from traversing the river, as any attempt to cross the watercourse would place his army at the mercy of the awaiting eastern troops. He eventually settled upon a deception to move his army safely across the Hebrus. Upon learning of a location sufficiently narrow to permit men and horses to ford the river, the emperor ordered bridge materials collected at a location far removed from the chosen crossing point. With the enemy misled by the construction of the decoy, Constantine secretly gathered 5,000 infantry and archers and 800 cavalry on a wooded hill in preparation for an assault. He then led a select force of horsemen across the river at the predetermined place and charged Licinius' formation. The unexpected attack threw the eastern legions into disorder, allowing time for the remainder of the western army to cross the Hebrus and reassemble for battle. There followed a difficult struggle that ended around sunset when Constantine's men overran the enemy camp. By that time the main divisions of Licinius' army were put to flight. Eastern losses amounted to almost 34,000 dead. The following morning, Constantine accepted the surrender of those defeated forces now scattered about in the countryside and throughout the immediate vicinity of the previous day's fighting. His imperial rival fled to Byzantium.

Zosimus, *New History*, 2.22.3–7.

Adrianople, AD 378, 9 August (Gothic Invasion of the Eastern Empire) – Seeking to stop a Gothic invasion of the Eastern Roman Empire, an army under the command of Emperor Flavius Julius Valens engaged a sizable force of Goths, Alans and Huns, led by the Visigothic chieftain Fritigern 12 miles (19km) from the community of Adrianople in the province of Thracia. Around midday, the Roman army, while still in marching order, encountered

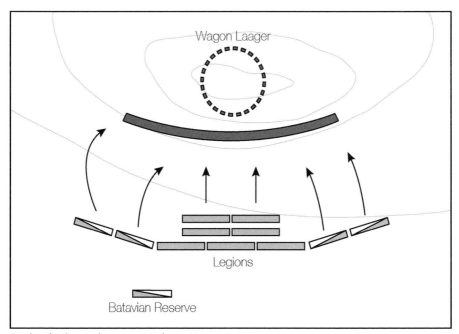

Battle of Adrianople, AD 378 (Phase 1)

the barbarian *laager*. Valens hastily deployed the army into battle formation, with the legions arrayed in the centre and supported by strong formations of cavalry on both wings. A force of Frankish Batavi cavalry was held in reserve. Fritigern declined battle immediately to await the return of some 5,000 Gothic cavalry under the chieftains Alatheus and Saphax, away on a foraging expedition. In order to hamper the Roman deployment, the Goths ignited grassfires to further exhaust the legionaries, who were already suffering the effects of fatigue, thirst and the summer heat. After failed negotiations, Valens ordered a general advance against the enemy camp. Almost immediately, the Roman line became dangerously attenuated as cavalry on the left charged the Gothic position. As the main Roman force approached the *laager*, large numbers of returning Goth, Hun and Alan horse suddenly launched a furious attack which shattered both wings of Roman cavalry. The right formation of Roman horse was completely broken; and the left, now isolated, was crushed by the massive Gothic assault. The remnants of the two Roman wings were either driven from the field or back on the flanks of the Roman infantry. Faced with this calamity, the Batavi deserted. Now devoid of all mounted support, the legions were quickly enveloped by Gothic cavalry, as Fritigern's infantry abandoned its defensive position in the *laager* and initiated an intense charge against the exposed ranks of the Roman infantry. In the ensuing battle, Valens' army was destroyed piecemeal. Perhaps two-thirds of the Roman

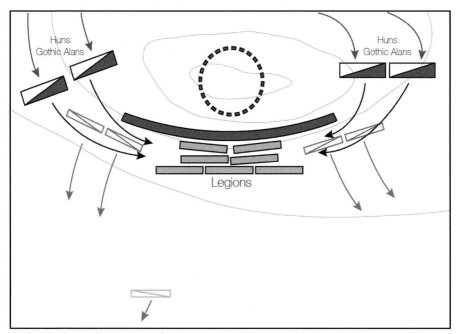

Battle of Adrianople, AD 378 (Phase 2)

army at Adrianople died – 20,000 soldiers, including the emperor, his senior command officers and thirty-five tribunes – in one of the greatest military disasters in late Roman imperial history.

Ammianus Marcellinus, *Res Gestae*, 31.13.1–16; Zosimus, *New History*, 4.24.1–2; Socrates Scholasticus, *Ecclesiastical History*, 4.38; Sozomen, *Ecclesiastical History*, 6.40; Consularia Constantinopolitana, 378 (CM 1.243); Libanius, Oration 24.3–5; Jerome, Chronicon, 2395.

Agrigentum, AD 456 – A Roman fleet and army under the command of Flavius Ricimer, the *comes* of the Western Empire, defeated the Vandals of King Geiseric near the port city of Agrigentum (Agrigento) on the southern coast of Sicily. Ricimer subsequently defeated Geiseric a second time off Corsica.

Hydatius, *Chronicle*, 170 [Mom. 177]; Sidonius Apollinaris, *Carmen*, 2.367.

Amasias River, 12 BC – In a naval action on the Amasias (Ems) River, the Roman general Nero Claudius Drusus defeated the Bructeri, a German tribe occupying lands between the Amasias and Luppia (Lippe) rivers.

Strabo, *Geography*, 7.1.3.

Amida, AD 359 (Persian Wars, Wars against the Sassanids) – Following the defeat of a Roman force near the Tigris River, a large Persian army under Sassanid king Shapur II then approached the strategic fortress of Amida (Diyarbakir). The outpost, situated in northern Mesopotamia on the west bank of the Tigris River, possessed a considerable civilian population as well as a sizeable complement of Roman troops. Along with the community's regular garrison of the *Legio V Parthica*, the defenders included six additional legions, among which was the Thirtieth Ulpia, Tenth Fretenses and two veteran Gallic legions, the *Magnentius* and *Decentius*. Also gathered inside the walls of the community were two units of light cavalry, the *Superventores* and *Praeventores*, as well as an elite squadron of mounted archers. Upon arrival, the Persians immediately invested the city. Early efforts by the king to persuade the occupants to surrender failed, and the Romans responded to the succession of assaults which followed with a liberal discharge of missiles, including those fired by *ballistae* and *scorpions*. Overcrowding, and a brief outbreak of pestilence, exacerbated the difficult conditions inside Amida, but the army continued to offer stiff resistance to all Persian attempts to reduce the city's defences. At one point the Gallic legions launched a devastating night attack on the unsuspecting enemy, resulting in 400 Roman dead, but inflicting significant casualties on the Persians. Thereafter, Shapur brought up towers and other siege-works in an endeavour to overcome the defenders. At last, having constructed earthen ramps, the Persians successfully overtopped the walls. With its defences ruptured, the fortress was soon subjected to a thorough sacking and its inhabitants killed. The Roman army was generally destroyed by the losses accrued during the seventy-three day siege and subsequent capture of the city. Persian casualties included 30,000 dead.

Ammianus Marcellinus, *Res Gestae*, 18.8–19.9.9.

Andematunum, AD 298, see Lingonae, AD 298.

Andernach, AD 89, see Antunnacum, AD 89.

Andomatunum, AD 298, see Lingonae, AD 298.

Anglon, AD 543 – Having learned that Persian armies were weakened from plague, Roman Emperor Justinian ordered an invasion of Persarmenia, which was at that time under the governorship of Nabedes. As the Romans approached the village of Anglon, they discovered that the Persians had fortified the location with a sizable trench, and awaiting their arrival behind the earthworks was Nabedes and his entire force of 4,000 men. Taken aback by the unexpected presence of the Persians, the Roman army nevertheless arrayed for battle, though it was presently poorly assembled in marching order and was in no way prepared to challenge the enemy. The Romans deployed in three divisions. The Roman general Valerianus commanded the left wing and Peter the right. Arrayed in the centre were the troops under Martinus. As the Romans approached the Persians, the rugged terrain disrupted their formation, weakening the entire battle line as it neared Nabedes' position. The battle opened with a Roman charge led by Narses. This assault was led by a contingent of German Heruli. After intense hand-to-hand fighting, the enemy line eventually broke under the force of Narses' attack, but the momentum of the pursuit carried the Romans into an ambuscade. When the Roman attack was sufficiently expended by the ambush, Nabedes responded with a countercharge of the entire Persian host. The attack proved irresistible, and large numbers of Romans died in the resulting rout, brought down by the intense fire of numerous mounted bowmen.

Procopius of Caesarea, *History of the Wars* (*The Persian War*), 2.25.5–34; *Chronicle of Pseudo-Zachariah Rhetor*, 10.0, 10.10a.

Angrivarian Wall, AD 16 (German War) – Near a large earthwork constructed to divide their tribal lands from those of the neighbouring Cherusci, the Angrivarii, led by their chieftain Arminius, determined to engage the legions of the Roman provincial governor, Germanicus Caesar. Arminius deployed his infantry on a narrow portion of marshy ground located between a river and forests, and stationed his cavalry inside a nearby grove of trees. Fully apprised of the Germans' tactical disposition, Germanicus responded by dividing his forces. He ordered one part of his infantry to advance across open ground toward the tree line and the remainder to scale the Angrivarian wall, which was presently defended by elements of German troops. The cavalry, under the command of Lucius Seius Tubero, was instructed to secure the plain. As the legions moved to close with Arminius' warriors, those cohorts pressing toward the wood reached the forest's edge with little difficulty; but the units given the task of climbing the earthen barrier were stopped by heavy resistance. Unable to make significant progress against the German defenders on the wall without accruing a considerable loss in men, Germanicus withdrew his legions a short distance and then swept the top of the works with fire from slingers and *scorpions*. The missiles from the machines, together with volleys of shot, inflicted heavy casualties among the enemy, permitting the legionaries to move in and secure control of the rampart. Germanicus and the Praetorian cohorts then charged into the forest, followed by those legions atop the wall. Thereafter, the two armies settled into an intense struggle made more terrible by the constraints of the difficult terrain; the Romans confined by river or hills, and the Germans by marshland. The large size of Arminius' force further restricted his army's ability to manoeuvre to best advantage in the limited space, and hampered the warriors' means to freely wield their weapons. By contrast, the compact formation employed by the legions permitted them to more capably drive home their attack. While fighting continued, Germanicus soon recognized the desperate plight of the enemy and ordered the legions to offer no quarter, determined to completely destroy the opposing army and thereby end the war. By nightfall the victory was complete.

Publius Cornelius Tacitus, *Annals*, 2.19-21.

Antioch, AD 218, see Immae, AD 218.

Antioch, AD 272, see Immae, AD 272.

Antunnacum, AD 89 – During the early months of 89, the governor of *Germania Superior* (Upper Germany), Lucius Antoninus Saturninus, led a revolt against Domitianus after the emperor made defamatory public comments against him. By means of extortion, Saturninus acquired legionary support from the *Legio XXI Rapax* and *Legio XIV Gemina* at Moguntiacum (Mainz) after seizing the units' savings. He then secured additional military assistance from German tribes across the Rhenus (Rhine) River. Meanwhile, Roman forces from the provinces of *Germania Inferior* (Lower Germany) and Spain moved to end the uprising. The *legatus* Aulus Bucius Lappius Maximus marched south-east from Lower Germany with two legions, the *Legio I Minervia* and *Legio VI Victrix*, while Marcus Ulpius Trajanus led a single legion, the *Legio VII Gemina*, toward the Rhineland from Hispania Terraconensis. Before these latter troops could reach Germany, the armies of Saturninus and Lappius converged near the town of Antunnacum (Andernach) on the west bank of the Rhenus. There, Lappius decisively defeated his opponent when a premature thaw prevented the German reinforcements from crossing the ice-covered river to join in the battle. Saturninus died in the fighting.

> Caius Suetonius Tranquillus, *Domitian*, 6–7; Dio Cassius, *Roman History*, 67.11.1–2; Anonymous (Sextus Aurelius Victor), *Epitome of the Emperors*, 11 (T. Banchich, trans.); Pliny the Younger, *Panegyricus*, 14.2–4.

Aquileia, AD 394, 5–6 September, see Frigidus River, AD 394.

Aquileia, AD 452 – Though decisive, the Roman defeat of the main Hunnish army of King Attila on the Catalunian Plains of Gaul left the Western *magister militum*, Flavius Aetius, too weak to deliver a second and perhaps fatal blow to the barbarian army. The victory did, however, force the king to abandon his Gallic campaign and retreat eastward. After the loss, the Huns crossed the Alps and descended into northern Italy, where Attila proceeded to devastate the region and besiege the Roman city of Aquileia. The community withstood the assault for three months, but eventually succumbed to the investment when the attackers breached the defensive walls. Attila then sacked and utterly destroyed the city. Afterwards he advanced southward, but his army was hindered in its progress by disease and a shortage of food supplies. While his forces slowly moved toward the Padus (Po) River, a second Roman army, sent by Emperor Marcianus and commanded by the Eastern Roman general Aetius, crossed the Ister (Danube) River and attacked Hunnish territory. These auxiliaries devastated Attila's settlements north of the river, further influencing the king's eventual decision to abandon Italy and return home.

> Marcellinus Comes, *Chronicle*, 5th indiction, Sporacii et Herculanii, in year 452 (Croke); Hydatius, *Chronicle*, 146 [Mom. 154].

Arbalo, 11 BC – In the early spring, a Roman army under the command of Nero Claudius Drusus crossed the Rhenus (Rhine) River, and advanced into the territory of the Usipetes. After subjugating the German tribe, the legions of Drusus constructed a bridge over the Lupia (Lippe) River and entered into the lands of the Sugambri (Sicambri). Because these peoples were presently at war with a neighbouring tribe, the Chatti, and had invaded their homeland, the Romans were able to cross through the country unhindered. Following a brief sojourn into the region, the onset of winter and a shortage of provisions caused Drusus to withdraw toward the Rhenus. During the return march, the Sugambri constantly harassed the legions. In a narrow pass, the Romans were caught in an ambuscade that threatened to destroy the army, but the enemy grew overconfident and attacked the cohorts in a disorderly manner. In the resulting contest the legions defeated the tribesmen. Once Drusus resumed his march, the Sugambri also renewed their harassment of the Roman column, but refused to risk a second major confrontation.

Dio Cassius, *Roman History*, 54.33; Pliny the Elder, *Natural History*, 11.18.

Archaeopolis, AD 551, Spring (Lazic War, Wars of Justinian I) – The Roman capture of Petra in the early spring was followed by a Persian campaign against the Lazic capital of Archaeopolis, located north of the Phasis (Rioni) River. The assault on Archaeopolis was led by the Persian general Mermeroes and a sizable army consisting largely of cavalry. Eight war elephants and an auxiliary contingent of 4,000 Sabirian Huns completed the expedition's complement. Defending the city was a garrison of 3,000 Roman soldiers under the officers Babas and Odonachus. The rugged nature of the elevated ground around Archaeopolis served to hinder the Persian investment, and Mermeroes finally elected to concentrate both his elephants and siege engines against a particular gate on a lower part of the city's walls. At about the same time, a Lazic traitor set fire to the capital's grain magazines in an effort to further burden the already beleaguered defenders. While the Persians continued to confidently press their attack against the city's defences, the besieged garrison suddenly burst through the gates and launched an assault against the startled attackers. The unexpected sally threw Mermeroes' forces into confusion, permitting the Romans to completely rout the disorganized opposition. Persian losses from the battle amounted to 4,000 dead. Roman fatalities are not stated by Procopius.

Procopius of Caesarea, *History of the Wars* (*The Persian War*), 8.13.1–34, 41–44.

Campus Ardiensis, AD 316, see Mardia, AD 316.

Arelate, AD 411 – The inability of the Western Roman Emperor Honorius to effectively deal with a German invasion of Gaul in 406 inspired the rise of the usurper Flavius Claudius Constantine in Britannia during the early months of the following year. In summer 407, Constantine crossed the English Channel and landed on the mainland at the head of the Britannic legions, intent on aiding the beleaguered province. Once there, the Gallic legions offered their support to the pretender. This event was soon followed by the defeat of the Suevians, Asding Vandals and Alans, who had crossed the Rhenus (Rhine) River unchecked on the last day of December in the previous year. Constantine afterwards advanced into eastern Gaul, while the barbarian invaders, quickly recovering from their loss, resumed their pillaging of the western and central portions of the province. After Constantine occupied the city of Arelate (Arles) in southern Gaul, Honorius attempted to dislodge him by force of arms, but these efforts failed until the arrival of Roman forces from Italy in the summer of 411, led by the capable general Flavius Constantius. While the siege wore on, Constantine sent his *magister militum*, Edobichus, across the Rhenus in a bid to garner the aid of the Franks and Alamanni. He returned to Arelate with a large army of reinforcements, but was soundly defeated by the legions of Constantius and his fellow general, Ulphilas. With all hope of escape now gone, Constantine surrendered to the awaiting forces and was sent to Italy. He was executed on the orders of Honorius while some 30 miles (48km) from Ravenna.

Salminius Hermius Sozomen, *Ecclesiastical History*, 9.13; Olympiodorus, *fragment* 17 (Blockley); Zosimus, *New History*, 6.2–6, 13; Paulus Orosius, *Seven Books of History against the Pagans*, 7.42; Gregory of Tours, *History of the Franks*, 2.9 (Dalton).

Arelate, AD 425 – While the Romans were preoccupied with the imperial usurper Joannes (423–425), Visigothic ruler Theodoric, King of Toulouse, invaded Roman territory with the intention of seizing the city of Arelate (Arles). This effort failed when Roman forces under the command of the general Flavius Aetius forced the Goths to retire.

Prosper of Aquitaine, *Chronicle*, 1290 (i. 471); *Gallic Chronicle*, 102 (i.658); Mommsen, *Ges. Schr.* iv, 535.

Arelate, AD 430 – Not far from the city of Arelate (Arles), a Roman force under the command of the *comes*, Flavius Aetius, destroyed a band of Visigoths. The defeat followed the capture of the Gothic chieftain Anaulfus.

Hydatius, *Chronicle*, 82 [Mom. 92]. This battle is perhaps the contest noted by the fifth-century poet Flavius Merobaudes as Mons Colubrarius. See, Flavius Merobaudes, *Panegyric* I.10 (Friedrich Vollmer, ed., *Fl. Merobaudis reliquiae, Monumenta Germaniae historica: Auctores antiquissimi*, vol. xiv, 1905).

Arelate, AD 471, see Rhodanus River, AD 471.

Arenacum, AD 70 (Revolt of Civilis, Batavian Revolt) – The defeat of Civilis at Vetera (Xanten) did not deter the German leader from recruiting a new army in preparation for another offensive against the Romans. Outside the town of Arenacum, a German force attacked an indeterminate number of Roman soldiers from the *Legio X Gemina* while they were cutting trees near their fortifications. The extent of the fighting is unknown, but resulted in the deaths of several legionaries, five centurions and the *praefectus castrorum*. The remainder of the troops defended themselves from inside the camp.

Publius Cornelius Tacitus, *The Histories*, 5.20.

Argentaria, AD 378 – When an army of 40,000 Lentiensian Alamanni entered the northern frontiers of the Empire, Emperor Gratian dispatched a legionary force under the veteran general Nannienus. He was joined by Mallobaudes, who was commander of the household guard and king of the Franks. The two armies met in battle near the community of Argentaria (Colmar) south of Argentoratum (Strasbourg) on the plain of Alsace. Both sides suffered significant casualties in the fighting, but the Romans ultimately succeeded in routing the Germans with heavy losses. Of the total force of Alamanni, only one-quarter were able to escape the disaster. Among the dead was the Lentiensian king Priarius.

Ammianus Marcellinus, *Res Gestae*, 31.10.6–10; Anonymous (Sextus Aurelius Victor), *Epitome of the Emperors*, 47.2 (T. Banchich, trans.).

Argentoratum, AD 357, August – After the Alamanni resumed their raids into Roman Gaul, a legionary army marched eastward from Durocortorum (Reims, Rheims) under the leadership of the 25-year old *Caesar*, Julian, cousin of Emperor Constantius II. Near the city of Argentoratum (Strasbourg), the Romans encountered a larger Alamannic force led by seven kings, including the high-king Chonodomar. When Julian reached the outskirts of Argentoratum, he assembled the army for battle. It consisted of 13,000 men arrayed in two lines, each consisting of legions and *auxilia palatini*, with squadrons of *catafractarii* and mounted archers deployed on the right wing. To the left, the *magister militum*, Severus, commanded a detachment of infantry. Opposing the Roman centre was the main German formation of 35,000 warriors, and across from Julian's mounted squadrons was the Alamannic cavalry under Chonodomar, which was joined by elements of light infantry. The battle opened with an exchange of missiles as the contending lines closed in a violent struggle. On the left, the legions locked shields in close formation and

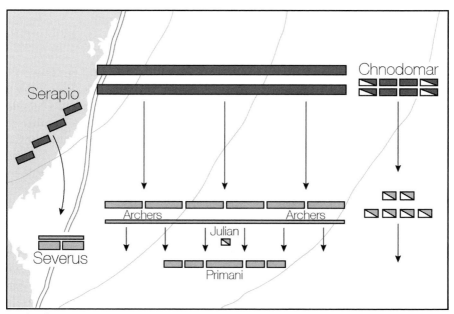

Battle of Argentoratum, AD 357 (Phase 1)

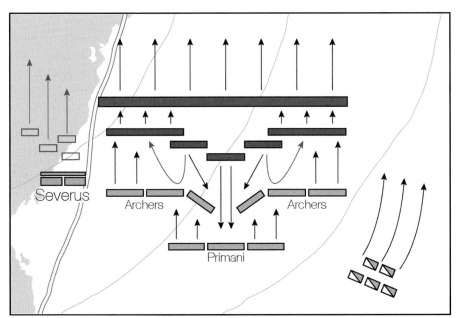

Battle of Argentoratum, AD 357 (Phase 2)

eventually drove back the mass of Germans, but the same was not repeated on the right wing where the *catafractarii* were put to flight by the combined work of the Alamannic horse and light infantry. Julian quickly managed to rally the cavalry, though the success of Chonodomar's horsemen inspired the German foot soldiers to launch a powerful assault against the Roman front-line. The legions and *auxilia*, together with two veteran units of *auxilia palatina*, the *Cornuti* and *Brachiati*, resisted the attack for some time before a concerted effort by a select band of German warriors completely penetrated the Roman centre. As the enemy charged through the breach and attacked the second line of Roman infantry, one legion, the *Primani*, successfully contained the assault. The effect of this failed action not only exposed the Alamannic foot to the danger of a double envelopment but turned the momentum of the battle in favour of the Romans. Julian's army counter-attacked with renewed vigour. Now exhausted and suffering from heavy losses, the German formation collapsed. In the flight which followed, many Alamanni sought safety by crossing the Rhenus (Rhine) River. Roman losses amounted to 243 soldiers and four *tribuni*, while battlefield deaths among Chonodomar's army totalled 6,000.

Ammianus Marcellinus, *Res Gestae*, 16.12.1–56, 63; Zosimus, *New History*, 3.3.1–3; Libanius, *Funeral Oration for Julian*, 138,140–141; Anonymous (Sextus Aurelius Victor), *Epitome of the Emperors*, 42.13 (T. Banchich, trans.).

Argentovaria, AD 378, see Argentaria, AD 378.

Ariminum, AD 432 (Roman Civil Wars) – An ongoing power struggle between the rival Roman generals, *magister equitum* Flavius Aetius and Bonifacius, the *comes Africae*, climaxed in a major battle near the town of Ariminum (Rimini), 30 miles (48km) south-east of Ravenna. The contest ended six years of growing tension between the two great commanders, which began in 426 when Aetius intrigued against his counterpart, resulting in Bonifacius briefly losing favour in the imperial court at Ravenna. When the plot was eventually exposed, the African governor quickly regained the support of the palace, and the empress regent, Galla Placidia, recalled him to Italy to serve as *magister militum praesentalis*. With the acquisition of this powerful military office she hoped Bonifacius might provide a counterbalance against the growing strength of Aetius. These circumstances inevitably led to civil war in Italy and a major battlefield clash between the armies of the opposing generals. At Ariminum, near the Adriatic coast, the two sides fought a protracted engagement. Despite Aetius' superior generalship, his enemy won the battle. But the victory was short-lived. Having been badly wounded during the fighting, Bonifacius succumbed to his injuries several months later. As a result, the defeat at Ariminum proved only a temporary setback for Aetius, who shortly recovered his standing in Italy.

> Procopius of Caesarea, *History of the Wars* (*The Vandalic War*), 3.3.14–36; Priscus, *frag.* 30; John of Antioch, *frag.* 201 (Blockley); Hydatius, *Chronicle, c.*89 [Mom. *c.*99]; *Gallic Chronicler of 452, c.*109–116; Prosper of Aquitaine, *Chronicle, c.*1310.

Ariminum, AD 553 (Gothic War, Wars of Justinian I) – In the autumn of 553, while visiting the town of Ariminum on a military matter, the Roman general Narses clashed with a force of 2,000 Frankish cavalry and infantry plundering the Italian countryside. As the Roman detachment of some 300 cavalry approached, the Germans abandoned their pillaging and assembled into a defensive posture consisting of a central formation of infantry flanked by cavalry on both wings. A stand of nearby forest insulated the Frankish rear from assault. Unwilling to risk a frontal confrontation with such a formidable array of mounted troops and heavy infantry, the Romans elected to soften their opponents' ranks with volleys of arrows and javelins before closing with the enemy in hand-to-hand combat. When these efforts failed to significantly penetrate the Frankish shield wall, Narses resorted to the use of a ruse to draw the enemy troops away from the tree line and onto the surrounding plain. Following a final demonstration, the Roman horsemen suddenly broke and fled. The feigned retreat compelled the opposing cavalry to give chase, joined by a portion of the infantry. The resulting pursuit badly disrupted the Frankish formation. Once the enemy was scattered about the plain and sufficiently removed from the safety of the forest, a predetermined signal from Narses caused the Roman cavalry to suddenly wheel about and charge the unsuspecting Germans. Taken completely off guard, the Franks were unprepared to confront their attackers and were thrown into a panic. The Romans quickly pressed their advantage and sliced into their confused enemy. Caught at a disadvantage, the Frankish cavalry quickly turned their mounts and galloped for the safety of the woods; but more than 900 foot soldiers, unable to outrun Narses' charging horsemen, died in their attempt to escape.

Agathias Scholasticos, *The Histories*, 1.21–22.6.

Arsanias River, AD 62, see Rhandeia, AD 62.

Augusta Taurinorum, AD 312 (Wars of Constantine I) – In the spring, Emperor Constantine I departed from Gaul with an army of some 40,000 men and crossed the Alps through the Mont Cenis pass (Cul du Mont Cenis). Near Augusta Taurinorum (Turin), his forces clashed with those of his imperial rival, Maxentius. As Constantine's divisions approached the town, they encountered the enemy already fully arrayed in a wedge-shaped battle formation. Observing large numbers of *clibanarii* in the centre of the opposing line, Constantine assumed personal command of his own mailed horsemen and assembled them across from Maxentius' awaiting armoured squadrons. When the engagement began, the *clibanarii* immediately concentrated their attack against Constantine's *cataphracti*, who quickly gave ground ahead of their more heavily-armoured counterparts. This deliberate retreat served to draw the charging enemy cavalry beyond the rest of Maxentius' line, even as Constantine's wings swept forward to threaten a double envelopment. As the *clibanarii* persisted in their pursuit, Constantine's line slowly began to bow inward, constraining the movement of the attackers, who were soon isolated within the ranks of the opposing formation and completely destroyed. The loss of these armoured cavalry squadrons preceded the rout of Maxentius' entire army, which suffered massive casualties in the flight.

Anonymous, *Panegyrici Latini* [AD 313] 12.6.2–5; Nazarius, *Panegyrici Latini* [AD 321] 4. 21–24.

Augusta Traiana, AD 250 – While pursuing a coalition army of Germanic tribes led by the Gothic king Kniva, a Roman army under Emperor Trajanus Decius was surprised and badly defeated near the Thracian town of Augusta Traiana (Boroa; Stara Zagora). The loss proved a temporary strategic setback for the Romans and forced the emperor to withdraw northward to the town of Oescus in Moesia. There the emperor was able to join with Roman forces under the local governor, Trebonianus Gallus, in preparation for a second contest with the Goths.

Sextus Aurelius Victor, *Liber De Caesaribus*, 29; John Zonaras, *Epitome of Histories*, 12.20; Jordanes, *The Origins and Deeds of the Goths*, 102.

Augusta Treverorum, AD 70, Summer (Revolt of Civilis, Batavian Revolt) – Soon after Cerialis' victory at Rigodulum (Riol), the Germans and Gauls initiated a second battle near Augusta Treverorum (Trier). The contest began with a night attack against the Roman encampment, situated on the banks of the Mosella (Mosel) River opposite the town. The Ubii and

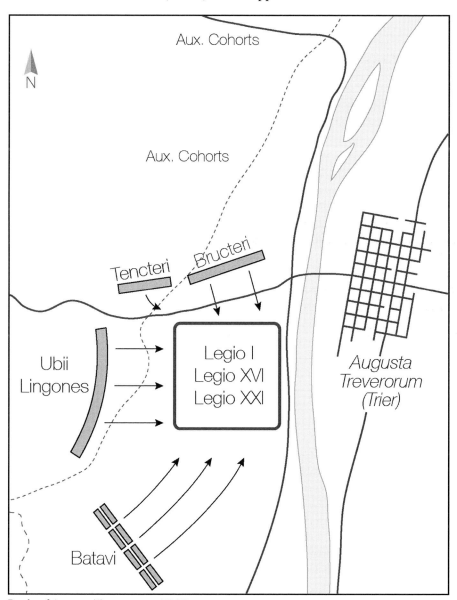

Battle of Augusta Treverorum, AD 70

Lingones were stationed in the centre of the approaching battle line. The Bructeri and Tencteri anchored the left flank, and Batavian cohorts were positioned on the right. Descending undetected from a line of tree-covered low hills to the west, the intensity of the massed assault successfully breached the Roman defences on the first charge and threw the legionary defenders into confusion. At the same time, the attackers routed the auxiliary cavalry and seized the middle of the bridge spanning the Mosella River. The Roman general Quintus Petilius Cerialis, who was not in the *castrum* at the time, arrived shortly after the battle began and quickly gathered a select force to recover the structure. While the struggle for the bridge moved toward its conclusion, the situation remained chaotic inside the camp. The veteran troops of *Legio XXI Rapax* worked desperately to form into cohorts, but were hampered by the confines of the *castrum* and the army's baggage and tents. Nearby, the *Legio I Germanica* and *Legio XVI Gallica*, both still demoralized by their past surrender at Bonna (Bonn), were badly disorganized and close to defeat. Once the Romans secured control of the bridge, Cerialis entered the camp and quickly moved to organize a defence. He reproached the First and Sixteenth legions for their indiscipline and then worked to rally the men, even as the reconstituted cohorts of the nearby Twenty-first Legion finally launched a decisive counter-attack that drove the tribesmen back. The force of this charge broke the courage of the entire German and Gallic host, who began to flee the fortifications in complete disorder. Following this victory, Cerialis captured and destroyed the enemy encampment later that same day.

Publius Cornelius Tacitus, *Histories*, 4.76–78.

Augustodunum, AD 21 (Revolt of Sacrovir) – In the provinces of Gallia Lugdunensis and Gallia Belgica, a rebellion occurred among a number of communities burdened by heavy debt to Roman authorities. The insurrection involved a number of Celtic peoples, including the Treviri, Aedui, Andecavi and Turoni. Within a short time Roman forces ended all of these uprisings except the one involving the Aedui. After devastating the villages of the Sequani on the frontiers of *Germania Superior* (Upper Germany), the *legatus* Caius Silius marched against Augustodunum (Autun), the capital of the Aedui, with two legions. About 10 miles (17km) from the town, the Romans clashed with a 40,000-man army of Aeduian warriors led by Julius Sacrovir, an Aeduian and former Roman auxiliary soldier. The tribal army consisted of some 8,000 heavy infantry, armed like legionaries and deployed in the centre of the battle line, with other well-armed divisions placed on each wing. In the rear, Sacrovir stationed a reserve of poorly armed men. Once Silius completed the arrangement of his legions, with cavalry posted on the wings, he launched a frontal assault against the enemy. The attack was momentarily delayed by the Aeduian infantry, before all were either cut down or routed from the field.

At the same time, the squadrons of Roman horse enveloped the opposing formation, helping to further collapse the Celtic ranks. When disaster became apparent, Sacrovir and his closest supporters fled the scene of fighting. The Aeduian leader committed suicide in a local villa near Augustodunum.

Publius Cornelius Tacitus, *Annals*, 3.45–46.

Auximus, AD 540 (Gothic War, Wars of Justinian I) – In an effort to further extend Roman authority over portions of central Italy, the general Flavius Belisarius and an 11,000-man army marched against a sizable concentration of Gothic troops in the Picentine hill town of Auximus, located near the Adriatic coast approximately 80 miles (129km) south-east of Ravenna. The garrison was under the leadership of the Ostrogothic king, Vittigis. When the Romans arrived in the vicinity of the town, Belisarius ordered his men to encamp around the base of the hill preparatory to initiating a siege. As the army began to bivouac by units, it became apparent to the Goths that the various enemy camps were spaced relatively far apart and would not be able to easily reinforce each other during an attack. Determined to exploit the situation to best effect, Vittigis launched an assault in late afternoon against those Roman contingents situated to the east of Auximus, some of whom were still preoccupied with the construction of their camps. Sufficiently warned of the approaching enemy force, the Romans successfully blunted the attack before resolute fighting finally routed the enemy. The victors quickly followed in the train of retreating warriors, attempting to overtake them as they climbed the hill toward the safety of Auximus, but midway up the slopes the Goths suddenly turned to face their pursuers. Emboldened because of the advantage afforded by their elevated position, the enemy prepared to make a stand even as the Romans attempted to press home their attack. In the course of the struggle, many of Belisarius' men were killed by arrows from above. Fighting continued until nightfall, when both armies elected to retire from the field.

Procopius of Caesarea, *History of the Wars* (*The Gothic War*), 6.23.9–12.

Baden, AD 69 – The Helvetii, angered that the *Legio XXI Rapax* had stolen money intended to reimburse the Gallic tribe for the cost of its services to garrison a local Roman fort, detained some soldiers carrying letters between the legions in Germania and Pannonia. As punishment for the tribe's audacity, the Roman general Aulus Caecina devastated the lands of the Helvetii and then assaulted the town of Baden, located on the west bank of the Limmat River, 14 miles (22.5km) north-west of Zurich. All resistance by a local force of poorly trained Helvetians collapsed when Caecina trapped them between the Twenty-first Legion and a strong detachment of Rhaetian infantry and cavalry. The tribesmen, now mostly wounded as a result of the exchange, fled the field and sought refuge on Mount Vocetius (The Botzberg), but were pursued by a cohort of Thracian infantry and driven from the high ground. The fugitives were then brutally hunted down by German and Rhaetian *auxilia* when they sought shelter in the surrounding forests. Thousands of Helvetian men, women and children were subsequently massacred or sold into slavery in retaliation for the tribe's resistance.

Publius Cornelius Tacitus, *Histories*, 1.68.

Baduhennaweld, AD 28, see Baduhennawood, AD 28.

Baduhennawood, AD 28 – The Frisians of *Germania Inferior* (Lower Germany), oppressed by Roman demands for payment of an annual tribute deemed excessive by the tribesmen, revolted after twelve years of peaceful relations with imperial authorities. When word reached the province's *pro-praetor*, Lucius Apronius, he summoned detachments (*vexillationes*) from the legions in *Germania Superior* (Upper Germany), together with picked units of auxiliary cavalry and infantry, and advanced down the Rhenus (Rhine) River into the lands of the Frisians, located along the North Sea coast. Near the Rhenus, close to a location known as Baduhennawood, the Romans encountered the Frisii in full battle array. After sending an *ala* of Canninefate cavalry and an entire contingent of German auxiliary infantry on a march around the enemy rear, Apronius promptly lost all tactical advantage by failing to initiate a coordinated attack using both his *auxilia* and legionary *vexillationes*. As a result, the Canninefates were driven off first along with the accompanying infantry, followed by four *termae* of Roman cavalry subsequently deployed in support. The *propraetor* then dispatched three cohorts of auxiliary infantry, shortly joined by two more, and finally, after some delay, all of his remaining mounted *auxilia*. Having deployed them at intervals, all were in turn repulsed. Recognizing the seriousness of the situation, Cethegus Labeo, the *legatus* of the *Legio V Alaudae* who was presently charged by Apronius with command of the last auxiliaries, requested the legions move forward in relief. His own Fifth Legion was the first to engage the enemy, and drove off the Frisii after a sharp clash. Its swift action saved the battle for the *propraetor* and permitted the exhausted and badly mauled *auxilia* to withdraw. Pockets of fighting lingered until the following day. Deserters later reported that 900 Roman captives were subsequently slaughtered at a sacred site called the Grove of Buduhenna, while an additional 400 others committed suicide at a second location after fearing their capture by the Frisians.

Publius Cornelius Tacitus, *Annals*, 4.72–73.

Barbalissos, AD 253, see Barbalissus, AD 253

Barbalissus, AD 253 – A breakdown in relations between Rome and Persia inevitably led to the resumption of war between the two empires. With the renewal of hostilities, a Persian army under the Sassanid king Shapur I departed southern Mesopotamia and crossed into Syria at the city of Anath, where it defeated a local Roman garrison. The Persians then continued their march to the north-west, following the Euphrates River, and overran the Roman strongholds of Birtha and Sura before crushing a 60,000-man Roman army in battle outside the walls of Barbalissus (Qal'at Balis). The defeat proved a critical strategic loss for Rome, permitting Shapur the immediate opportunity to sweep into Syria unhindered and creating the conditions necessary for the eventual capture of Antioch and Dura Europos by the Persians.

Res Gestae Divi Saporis, 4 (inscription at Naqsh-i Rustam); Michael I. Rostovtzeff, 'Res Gestae Diviv Saporis and Dura', *Berytus* 8:1 (1943), pp. 24–25.

Batavia, AD 358 – At the behest of their Saxon kinsmen, the Chamavi raided into Roman territory and expelled the Frankish Salii from Batavia (Betuwe), a large island situated between the Vacalis (Waal) and Rhenus (Rhine) rivers in *Germania Inferior* (Lower Germany). In response, the Roman *Caesar*, Julian, led his forces against the invaders and defeated them.

Ammianus Marcellinus, *Res Gestae*, 17.8.5; Zosimus, *New History*, 3.6.1–3.

Batavia, AD 69, see Insula Batavorum, AD 69.

Batavodurum, AD 70 (Revolt of Civilis, Batavian Revolt) – At the town of Batavodurum in *Germania Inferior* (Lower Germany), a German force attempted to disrupt the construction of a Roman bridge over the Vacalis (Waal) River, but was stopped by legionaries of the *Legio II Adiutrix*. The assault failed to destroy the bridge, and all fighting ended at nightfall.

Publius Cornelius Tacitus, *The Histories*, 5.20.

Bedriacum, AD 69, 24 October (Year of the Four Emperors, Roman Civil Wars) – The Roman civil war that followed the Emperor Nero's death in early summer of AD 68 resulted in the rapid manifestation of four claimants to the imperial purple by the spring of the following year. The power struggle eventually led to the assassination of Emperor Galba in January AD 69 after only seven months in power; the suicide of his successor Otho following his army's defeat at Cremona in April; and the emergence of a violent contest between Aulus Vitellius, governor of *Germania Inferior* (Lower Germany), and Titus Flavius Vespasianus, the general appointed by Nero to crush an ongoing revolt in Judaea. Near the town of Bedriacum (Calvatone) in northern Italy, legions loyal to Vitellius and Vespasian joined in a violent battle to determine the future of the Empire. Following a sharp but largely inconclusive engagement on the first day, both armies prepared for a major battle that night. Shortly after dusk, the Flavian commander Marcus Antonius Primus drew up his army across the Via Postumia, an elevated roadway which extended between the towns of Cremona and Bedriacum, and generally followed the left bank of the Padus (Po) River. He positioned the *Legio XIII Gemina* on the causeway, and on the left flank in an open plain he deployed the *Legio VII Galbiana* and the *Legio VII Claudia*. To the right, Antonius stationed the *Legio VIII Augusta* on a secondary road. It was joined by the *Legio III Gallica*, which found itself hampered on the far right by its placement among dense thickets. A detachment of praetorians was then drawn up next to the Third Legion and auxiliary cohorts were posted on each wing. The Flavian cavalry, numbering some 4,000, secured the flanks and rear of the entire formation. Lastly, ahead of the legions ranged a select force of Suebian tribesmen.

Opposite Antonius' front line, the darkness heavily obscured a formidable Vitellian battle formation. The approaching army was presently leaderless, as its general, Aulus Caecina Alienus, was in irons after plotting to defect to the Flavians. The absence of their senior commander, combined with the dark of night, served to create some initial confusion within the ranks of the Vitellians. On the extreme right, the *Legio IIII Macedonica* advanced in the company of the Fifth and Fifteenth legions, which were stationed in the centre along with vexillations of the *Legio IX Hispana*, *Legio II Augusta* and the *Legio XX*

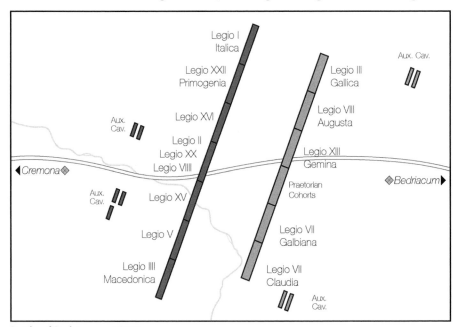

Battle of Bedriacum, AD 69

Valeria Victrix. On the left, the Sixteenth and First legions were joined by the *Legio XXII Primigenia*. Within the ranks of each was included a liberal distribution of soldiers from the depleted cohorts of the *Legio XXI Rapax* and *Legio I Italica*. Completing the arrangement was the army's cavalry and *auxilia*, which were arrayed around the main body of heavy infantry. Some distance from Bedriacum, the contending armies met in a decisive confrontation. The battle lasted throughout the night, and proved to be a savage, confusing struggle whose outcome remained uncertain until dawn when the men of the *Legio III Gallica*, imbued with a certain Syrian custom after many years of service in the orient, turned and saluted the rising sun. The Vitellians misunderstood the gesture, and concluded that the Third Legion was acknowledging the arrival of reinforcements. Using the dissemination of this misinformation to best advantage, the Flavian cohorts vigorously advanced as if supported by fresh divisions. The ruse worked to further demoralize an enemy already weakened by a lack of leadership, and Antonius seized the opportunity to launch an assault against the opposing line. The forceful attack broke the Vitellian formation, and a subsequent attempt to reform proved futile because the oppressed cohorts were driven back among their own supply wagons and artillery. Unable to recover, Vitellius' forces dissolved into headlong retreat toward Cremona, pursued by the victorious troops of Vespasian.

  Publius Cornelius Tacitus, *The Histories*, 3.17–26.

Bedriacum, AD 69, 14 April, see Cremona, AD 69, 14 April.

Benacus, AD 268, see Lake Benacus, AD 268.

Beroe, AD 250, see Augusta Traiana, AD 250.

Beroia, AD 250, see Augusta Traiana, AD 250.

Bethar, AD 134–135 (Bar Kokhba Revolt, Jewish Wars) – In the autumn of AD 132, the Jews again rebelled against Roman authority and initiated a protracted guerrilla war against legionary forces in the province of Judaea. The Roman Emperor Hadrian responded to the crisis with a massive military build-up in the region and summoned the celebrated general Julius Severus from Britain to assume command of the campaign. Over the next several months, the Roman army gradually regained control by the systematic reduction of rebel strongholds such as Herodium and Tekoa. After the capture of Jerusalem, the rebel leader Simon bar Kokhba and his followers withdrew to Bethar, located approximately 8 miles (13km) south-west of the city. There, Roman forces, which included elements of the *Legio V Macedonica* and a *vexillatio* from the *Legio XI Claudia*, established two camps and then constructed a line of siege works around the community. After a months-long investment of the fortress, the Romans managed to breach Bethar's walls and massacre the entire complement of Jewish defenders.

Eusebius of Caesarea, *Ecclesiastical History*, 4.6.1–4; *Mishnah, Ta'anit*, 4.6; *Corpus Inscriptionum Latinarum*, iii 14155.2 (Clermont-Ganneau, *Comptes-rendus de l'Academie des Inscription et Belles-Lettres*, 1894, 13.f); Midrash, *Lamentations Rabbah*, 2 (Solomon Buber, ed., p. 51a–52a. See also Jacob Neusner, *Lamentations Rabbah*, 1989).

Beth Horon, AD 66, see Bethoron, AD 66.

Bethoron, AD 66 (First Jewish Revolt, Jewish Wars) – The news of an uprising in Judaea convinced Cestius Gallus, the Roman military commander in Syria, to send troops to suppress the rebellion, particularly in the city of Jerusalem where growing dissent had led to the deaths of several soldiers. Gallus moved to check the disorder with one legion, the *Legio XII Fulminata*, and accompanying *auxilia*. Within a short time, Roman forces controlled Bezetha in the Jezreel Valley, but encountered sufficient resistance to thwart their efforts to seize the Temple Mount to the south. Unable to make any further progress against the insurgents, Gallus elected to withdraw from the city. The Jews closely pursued the departing Roman column as it moved north-west toward the town of Lydda. By the time the army neared the Bethoron Pass some 11 miles (18km) from Jerusalem, the enemy's attacks had resulted in numerous casualties and the loss of the legion's baggage. With the onset of nightfall the harassment temporarily ended, but Gallus was fully aware that the chase would resume at first light, and chose to undertake a night march to avoid his pursuers. Abandoning his siege artillery, the Roman commander left a 400-man rearguard to delay the enemy long enough to permit the rest of his army to escape. The next morning, the Jews discovered the remaining contingent and destroyed it in a brief, sharp clash. The victors then returned to Jerusalem. Within a matter of days, Gallus and the remnants of the Twelfth Legion reached the safety of Caesarea Maritima, having lost a total of 5,300 heavy and light infantry and 380 cavalry.

Flavius Josephus, *The Jewish War*, 2.19.7 – 9; Publius Cornelius Tacitus, *Histories*, 5.10; Caius Suetonius Tranquillus, *Vespasianus*, 4.

Bezetha, AD 66, see Bethoron, AD 66.

Bingium, AD 70 (Revolt of Civilis, Batavian Revolt) – With the arrival of the Roman general Quintus Petilius Cerialis and three fresh legions, Gallic and German support for the Batavian Revolt began to collapse. While the uprising otherwise floundered, one Treviran rebel leader named Julius Tutor, a former Roman officer of *auxilia*, briefly rallied a tribal force that included levies from the Treviri, Vangiones, Triboci and Caeracates, as well as a veteran band of legionary deserters. In a preliminary encounter, these troops massacred a cohort of Roman *auxilia* scouting ahead of a larger contingent of auxiliary infantry moving northward from Raetia under the command of Sextilius Felix. Despite this minor victory, the growing awareness among the tribes of Cerialis' massive show of military power soon persuaded all but Tutor's fellow Treviran tribesmen to seek reconciliation with Rome. With his support waning, Tutor withdrew to Bingium (Bingen), after destroying the bridge across the Nava (Nahe) River. While thinking himself secure in this new location he was surprised by Sextilius, whose cohorts successfully forded the river and fell upon the unsuspecting Treviri. In the encounter the Romans defeated the tribesmen and put them to flight.

Publius Cornelius Tacitus, *The Histories*, 4.70.

Bonn, AD 69, see Bonna, A.D. 69.

Bonna, AD 69, Autumn (Revolt of Civilis, Batavian Revolt) – Outside the Roman *castrum* at Bonna (Bonn), a single 3,000-man Roman legion, the *Legio I Germanica*, supported by cohorts of Belgian *auxilia*, attempted to block the passage of eight veteran Batavian auxiliary cohorts returning home from Moguntiacum (Mainz) after being recalled from Roman service by their tribal chieftain Julius Civilis. The Batavian leader, a former Roman auxiliary officer, was responsible for leading an ongoing rebellion against Roman authority in *Germania Inferior* (Lower Germany). The legion's commander, Herennius Gallus, sought to capture the unsuspecting Batavian *auxilia* by a sudden sally of his forces from the camp at Bonna, but the Germans recognized the trap and quickly closed ranks and prepared to offer battle. Once the fighting started, the veteran soldiers put the less experienced Belgian auxiliaries to flight, precipitating a general rout of the legion. As the legionaries and their Gallic allies fled to the safety of their camp, the Batavians charged in pursuit. In the chaos which followed, large numbers of Gallus' men died in the crush to enter the *castrum* or were cut down by the Batavians while seeking protection within the ramparts. After the fighting ended, the German units continued on to their homeland.

Publius Cornelius Tacitus, *The Histories*, 4.20.

Bourgaon, AD 535, see Mount Bourgaon, AD 535.

Briantia, AD 355, see Lake Briantia, AD 355.

Brescia, AD 312, see Brixia, AD 312.

Brixia, AD 312 (Wars of Constantine I) – Outside the northern Italian community of Brixia (Brescia), the forces of Emperor Constantine I defeated a contingent of cavalry loyal to his co-emperor and rival, Maxentius. The victory was won with only a single assault. The beaten squadrons afterward fled to the city of Verona, the location of a major army under the command of

Maxentius' praetorian prefect, Ruricius Pompeianus. After his victory at Brixia, Constantine resumed his army's march into the Veronese heartland for a showdown with the legions of his rival.

Nazarius, *Panegyrici Latini* [AD 321] 4.25.1–2.

Brotomagus, AD 356 – As the *Caesar* Julian and a Roman army approached the community of Brocomagus (Brumath), located west of the Rhenus (Rhine) River, they encountered a sizeable band of Alamanni. The emperor arrayed his forces in a concave, or crescent, formation. When the battle opened and the struggle became hand-to-hand, the two wings of the Roman line closed in on the enemy ranks, overwhelming the German host.

Ammianus Marcellinus, *Res Gestae*, 16.2.12–13.

Brumath, AD 356, see Brocomagus, AD 356.

Brotomagus, AD 356, see Brocomagus, AD 356.

Busta Gallorum, AD 552, see Tadinae, AD 552.

Caer Caradoc, AD 50, see Severn River, AD 50.

Caesian Forest, AD 14 – In Germany, word of Emperor Augustus' death in Nola, Italy, was almost immediately followed by a revolt among the legions stationed along the Rhenus (Rhine) River. Subsequent to the restoration of order, the situation remained dangerously unstable and the army's commander, Germanicus Caesar, initiated a campaign against the German Marsi, partly to distract the legions from the recent round of disorder. After constructing a bridge, Germanicus crossed over the Rhenus with an army of 12,000 legionaries, twenty-six auxiliary cohorts and eight *alae* of cavalry. The columns cut a path through the Caesian Forest as far as the *limes* of Tiberius. Establishing their *castrum* near this line of demarcation, the legions prepared to invade the lands of the Marsi. Once the army reached the tribe's territory, Germanicus divided the legions into four columns. They then proceeded to devastate the countryside and slaughter the unsuspecting population for some 50 miles (80km) around. In response to the carnage, the neighboring Bructeri, Usipetes and Tubantes took up arms against the invaders. When Germanicus was satisfied with the results of the expedition, he prepared to withdraw to the Rhenus, fully cognizant that the Germans lay in wait for the returning army. Accordingly, he arrayed the marching column in anticipation of an attack. Deploying a squadron of cavalry and ten auxiliary cohorts as a vanguard, he then sent the *Legio I Germanica* after them and ordered the baggage train to follow. On the left flank, he positioned the *Legio XXI Rapax*, and to the right the *Legio V Alaudae*. Lastly, the *Legio XX Valeria Victrix* followed with the remainder of the *auxilia* trailing as a rearguard. The German assault did not occur until the entire length of the Roman column was completely within the confines of the forest. As the army moved forward, the enemy launched a sudden attack against the front and flanks in an effort to stop the column's advance, while a powerful charge against the rear completely crumpled the light-armed cohorts. In response, Germanicus ordered the Twenty-first Legion to wheel against the mass of Germans wreaking carnage on the rear-guard. The counter-attack struck the serried ranks of the tribesmen with enough force to completely penetrate the German formation and drive the shattered remnants out of the tree line and into the clearing. Thrown into disorder, the warriors were badly defeated. At the same time, the cohorts in the van repelled their attackers and emerged from the woods in good order. After passing the night in a well-fortified camp, the army finished the remainder of its march uninterrupted.

Publius Cornelius Tacitus, *Annals*, 1.49–51.

Calleva Atrebatum, AD 296 (Carausian Insurrection) – Seven years after declaring himself *Augustus* of an independent Britannia, the usurper Marcus Carausius was assassinated by one of his lieutenants, Allectus, who then assumed supreme authority of the island in 293. The break-away province then remained separated from the Western Empire for an additional three years before a Roman invasion fleet led by the Western *Caesar*, Constantius Chlorus, crossed the English Channel in an attempt to restore Britain to imperial rule. While Constantius led half of the flotilla from Bononia (Boulogne), a second naval force sailed from the mouth of the Seine River under the command of the praetorian prefect, Julius Asclepiodotus. A heavy fog obscured this latter fleet from an enemy squadron operating near the Isle of Vectis (Isle of Wight), allowing the ships to reach the British mainland undetected. Once ashore, Asclepiodotus' army burned their vessels and advanced north-east in the general direction of Londinium (London), forcing Allectus to move west-north-west from the East Sussex coast in order to engage the invaders. His departure preceded the arrival of Constantius' fleet along the same shoreline. Near Calleva Atrebatum (Silchester), Allectus' troops clashed with those of Asclepiodotus and were defeated, the renegade ruler being among those killed in the fighting. The Frankish survivors of the rebel army then fled to London and began plundering the city, but were massacred when they encountered a stray contingent of Constantius' soldiers that had become separated from the main invasion force. With the death of Allectus, Britannia once again became an imperial province under the ruler-ship of the Western *Augustus*, and Constantius Chlorus was hailed as a liberator by the native population.

Eutropius, *Abridgement of Roman History*, 9.22; Paulus Orosius, *Seven Books of History against the Pagans*, 7.25; Anonymous, *Panegyrici Latini* 8 [AD 297?], 8.12–17; Sextus

Aurelius Victor, *Liber De Caesaribus*, 39. For additional discussion see also N.Shiel, *The Episode of Carausius and Allectus*, British Archaeological Reports (BAR) 40, Oxford, 1977; D. Eirchholz, 'Constantius Chlorus' Invasion of Britain', *Journal of Roman Studies* 43 (1953), 41–46; S. Frere, *Britannia*, 3rd ed., London, 1987.

Callinicum, AD 296 – While the Roman Emperor Diocletian was in Egypt attempting to suppress a rebellion, a Persian army under the Sassanid ruler Narses invaded the province of Syria. In response, the Eastern *Caesar* Galerius crossed the Euphrates River with an army in an attempt to intercept the king's forces. North of the river, between the city of Callinicum (Raqqa) and the town of Carrhae, the two armies joined in battle. Narses' forces were far more numerous than those of Galerius, and the Romans were badly defeated in the struggle. The loss temporarily undermined Rome's strategic control of the region. The next year, Galerius assembled a second army from legionary forces collected in Illyricum and Moesia, and initiated a campaign into Armenia. There, the Romans badly defeated a Persian army. The victory allowed Galerius to recover those lands lost to Narses during the previous year.

Eutropius, *Abridgement of Roman History*, 9.24–25.

Callinicum, AD 531, April 19 (Persian Wars, Wars of Justinian I) – On the southern bank of the Euphrates River, opposite the community of Callinicum (Raqqa), a Persian army under the general Azarethes engaged a Roman

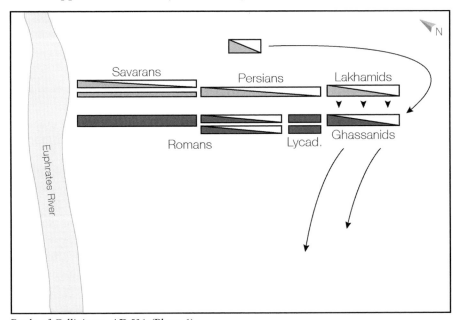

Battle of Callinicum, AD 531 (Phase 1)

force led by Belisarius. The Romans drew up for battle with the infantry placed on the left wing against the river, squadrons of cavalry deployed in the centre, and on the right flank, where the ground rose sharply, Belisarius stationed the Saracen king, Arethas, and a detachment of Arab Ghassanid auxiliary cavalry. Azarethes elected to array his army in similar fashion opposite the Romans, placing elements of Arab Lakhmid cavalry on the left wing and Persians to the right, including squadrons of Savaran cataphracts. When the battle opened, archers on both sides immediately discharged flights of arrows, resulting in significant casualties among the two armies. The Persians proved to be better bowmen, but the heavier shields and body armour of the Romans resulted in fewer fatalities. Desperate fighting continued for several hours without resolution until select elements of Persian horse, perhaps *gyan-avspar peshmerga*, concentrated an attack against the Roman right wing, shattering the Arab formation and penetrating the line. The resistance offered by the nearby Lycaonian infantry also buckled under the shock. Once through, the Persians wheeled right against the now exposed centre and charged the rear of the Roman cavalry, which collapsed under the sudden pressure of the assault. As the Roman line disintegrated, Belisarius and a contingent of riders, together with a nearby band of Massagete horsemen, held their ground. After severe fighting, the Persians finally succeeded in destroying most of the Massagetae and inflicted significant losses among the remaining Roman cavalry. Belisarius and the survivors then retreated toward the

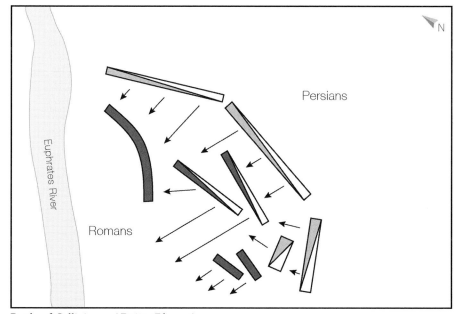

Battle of Callinicum, AD 531 (Phase 2)

river and joined with the beleaguered remnants of the infantry formation, still massed behind a wall of shields. The fighting again intensified as the enemy cavalry vainly sought to break up the Roman line. Following numerous failed attempts to overrun the Roman position, the Persians ended the assault at nightfall. The remaining Romans were ferried across the Euphrates to the safety of Callinicum the next day, while the Persians elected to discontinue the action and retire homeward.

Procopius of Caesarea, *History of the Wars* (*The Persian War*), 1.18.13–50; *Chronicle of Pseudo-Zachariah Rhetor*, 9.4a.

Callipolis, AD 324 (Wars of Constantine I) – A war fleet under the command of Crispus, the eldest son of Emperor Constantine I, sailed to Callipolis (Gallipoli) at the mouth of the Hellespont and engaged a rival fleet under Licinius' admiral, Abantus. Because of the narrowness of the channel near its mouth, Crispus elected to open the battle with only eighty *triaconters*, while Abantus committed 200 vessels to the battle in an effort to surround the opposing squadrons. When the battle commenced, the smaller fleet easily manoeuvred to best advantage in the restricted waters, allowing Constantine's admirals to engage the enemy in good order. The contest quickly turned against Abantus, whose warships were hampered by the narrowness of the location and fully exposed to the assaults of their less encumbered foes. Nightfall put an end to the fighting. The next day, around noon, a southerly wind caught Licinius' fleet near the Anatolian coast and inflicted additional losses.

Anonymous Valesianus, Pars Prior, *The Lineage of the Emperor Constantine*, 5.26; Zosimus, *New History*, 2.23–24.3.

Campi Catalaunii, see Catalunian Plains, AD 274, AD 366, AD 451.

Campus Ardiensis, AD 316, see Mardia, AD 316.

Campus Castorum, AD 69, see Locus Castorum, AD 69.

Campus Mardiensis, AD 316, see Mardia, AD 316.

Campus Mauriacus AD 366, see Catalunian Plains, AD 366.

Campus Mauriacus AD 451, see Catalunian Plains, AD 451.

Campus Paramus, AD 456, see Urbicus River, AD 456.

Campus Serenus, AD 313, 30 April – The power struggle between the rival Eastern Roman emperors Maximinus Daia and Licinius culminated in an epic clash near the city of Heraclea Perinthus (Marmaraereglisi). In preparation for hostilities with his counterpart, Maximinus crossed the Bosporus from Asia with an army of some 70,000 men. He quickly besieged the city of

Byzantium, forcing Licinius' garrison in the city to capitulate after only eleven days. The army then marched approximately 55 miles (88.5km) west, to the coastal city of Heraclea. The slow pace of Maximinus' legions contrasted with the rapid progress of Licinius, who approached from the northwest with an army of 30,000 troops. After securing control of Heraclea, Maximinus advanced along the Adrianople highway to confront Licinius. The two armies drew up on a barren plain called Campus Serenus, between the towns of Tzirallum (Corlu) and Drizipara. Despite the opposing army's larger size, Licinius ordered his troops to charge the enemy's ranks. The bold and unexpected attack threw Maximinus' forces into confusion. Without opportunity to reorganize or effectively check the momentum of the assault, the army suffered massive casualties, not only in the chaos of battle but in the subsequent rout. When the fighting ended, Licinius was master of the Eastern Empire. The defeated Maximinus abandoned his legions and fled into Anatolia, having lost 35,000 men during the encounter.

Lucius Caecilius Firmianus Lactantius, *On the Deaths of the Persecutors*, 45–47; Eusebius of Caesarea, *Ecclesiastical History*, 9.10; Zosimus, *New History*, 2.17.3.

Camulodunum, AD 43 (Invasion of Britannia) – After the Roman defeat of a substantial force of Catuvellauni at the River Medway, the army's commander, Aulus Plautius, went in pursuit of the tribesmen as they withdrew north-westward beyond the Thames River to the fortified city of Camulodunum (Colchester). Skirmishing ensued once the Romans were across the river, and the legions incurred a number of casualties among the marshland beyond the river. Around this time, the Catuvellaunian leader Togodumnus was slain, but resistance among the Celts remained substantial, compelling Plautius to temporarily halt the army's advance and await the arrival of reinforcements led by Emperor Claudius. When the imperial army arrived with additional equipment, including artillery and elephants, the legions resumed their campaign and defeated the Catuvellauni in battle. Camulodunum fell to the Romans soon afterward.

Dio Cassius, *Roman History*, 60.20.5–21.4.

Camulodunum, AD 61 (Revolt of Boudicca) – In Britannia, the callous injustice of a Roman *procurator* named Decianus Catus provoked the Iceni to rebellion. Led by their queen, Boudicca, the tribesmen were soon joined in the insurrection by the neighbouring Trinobantes. Incited to war, thousands of Celtic rebels soon overran and destroyed the Roman colony of Camulodunum (Colchester), killing some 20,000 settlers and their families. When word of the attack reached Quintus Pelitius Cerialis, commander of the *Legio IX Hispana*, he attempted to rescue Camulodunum, but en route to the colony his relief column clashed with Boudicca's army. In the resulting struggle, the

Celts destroyed the entire force of Roman infantry. Only Cerialis and his cavalry managed to escape the disaster.

Publius Cornelius Tacitus, *Annals*, 14.32.

Cape Bon, AD 468, see Hermaeum Promontorium, AD 468.

Cape Hermaeum, AD 468, see Hermaeum Promontorium, AD 468.

Cape Mercury, AD 468, see Hermaeum Promontorium, AD 468.

Capua, AD 554, see Casilinus River, AD 554.

Caranalis, AD 551, Autumn (Gothic War, Wars of Justinian I) – Aware that the Ostrogothic king Totila had sent a fleet to Corsica and Sardinia with sufficient troops to defeat the Roman garrisons stationed on the two Mediterranean islands, John, the *magister militum per Africam*, dispatched an army from North Africa to the larger island of Sardinia. Once ashore, Roman forces advanced against the city of Caranalis (Cagliari) on the island's southern coast. Because the Goths maintained a significant garrison in the community, the Romans considered it prudent to invest the city rather than attempt its capture by direct assault. In response, Ostrogoths attacked Roman forces encamped around Caranalis and inflicted heavy losses. Soon afterward, the entire Roman expeditionary fleet, together with the remnants of the defeated army, evacuated Sardinia and returned to Carthage.

Procopius of Caesarea, *History of the Wars* (*The Gothic War*), 8.24.33–37.

Carrhae, AD 217, see Nisibis, AD 217.

Carthage, AD 238 – In the spring of 238, a local revolt against Emperor Maximinus Thrax began in the North African community of Thysdrus. The uprising was led by the provincial *proconsul*, Marcus Antonius Gordianus, and his son, both of whom sought to usurp the imperial throne. The rebellion quickly collapsed, however, when Capellianus, the military governor of the neighbouring province of Numidia, moved against the insurrection with the *Legio III Augusta*. The two sides clashed near the city of Carthage. Unable to successfully resist the strength and discipline of the legionary troops, the larger force of untrained civilian militia led by the younger Gordianus soon fled in disorder. Among the casualties was Gordianus himself, killed in the fighting or trampled in the crush of fugitives seeking to escape the battlefield. His father committed suicide shortly after learning of the defeat.

Scriptores Historiae Augustae (*Gordianii*), 15; *Scriptores Historiae Augustae* (*Maximini duo*), 19.1–3; Herodian, *Roman History*, 7.9.1–10.

Casilinum, AD 554, see Casilinus River, AD 554.

Casilinus River, AD 554, October – During the spring of 553, an army of 75,000 Frank and Alamanni warriors, under the leadership of the Alamannic chieftains Butilinus and Leutharis, crossed the Alps and descended into Italy. The Germanic army then ravaged the northern half of the peninsula before dividing into two armies near Rome. Butilinus advanced south along the western coast of Italy, plundering the regions of Campania, Lucania and Brutium before reaching the Straits of Messina, while his brother and fellow chieftain, Leutharis, moved his forces toward the Adriatic coast and marched southward to the port of Hydruntum (Otranto). Upon learning that the Roman general Narses was amassing a large army in Rome, Butilinus and his band retraced their steps northward, intent on returning to their homelands with the rich store of spoils before their opponents could fully mobilize. Outside the Campanian city of Capua, not far from the banks of the Casilinus (Volturno) River, the two armies met. The Germans numbered 30,000 warriors, while the Roman force totalled only 18,000 men. Narses arranged his troops for battle by placing heavy infantry in the middle, with archers, slingers and light infantry positioned in the rear. An open space remained in the centre of the Roman line, awaiting the arrival of the allied Heruli, who were hesitant to join in the contest after a quarrel with the Roman general. Arrayed on both wings were squadrons of cavalry. Butilinus drew up his forces for battle across the field. The German host consisted almost exclusively of heavily armed Frankish and Alamannic infantry. Observing the gap in the

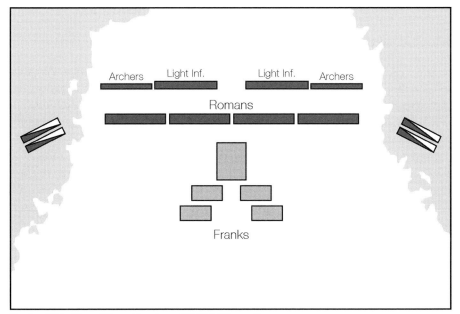

Battle of Casilinus River, October, AD 554 (Phase 1)

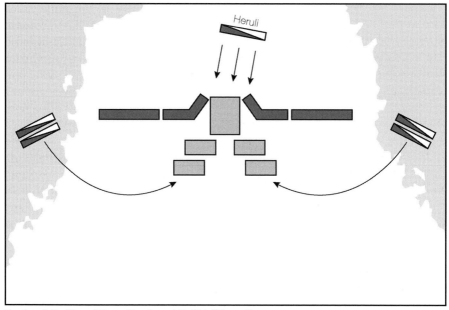

Battle of Casilinus River, October, AD 554 (Phase 2)

Roman line, the barbarian chieftain arranged his army in a large wedge-shaped formation, intent on penetrating the opposing ranks and dividing Narses' command. The Franks immediately drove through the Roman line when the battle began, but were simultaneously subjected to the amassed missile fire from Narses' mounted bowmen as the two wings wheeled inward against the enemy's unprotected rear. The German formation, already locked in a fierce hand-to-hand struggle with the Roman infantry, was unable to disengage in order to turn and face the cavalry assault, and suffered heavy casualties. In the midst of the carnage, some of Butilinus' troops managed to break through the attenuated ranks of the Roman centre, but were suddenly attacked by the Heruli, who had finally arrived at their place in the battle line. Trapped between a wall of Roman and allied infantry, and unable to escape the intense missile fire from Roman cavalry and light-armed troops, the Frankish army perished almost to a man.

Agathias Scholasticos *The Histories*, 2.4–9.

Castellum, AD 89, see Antunnacum, AD 89

Castra Vetera, AD 69, Autumn–AD 70, Spring (Revolt of Civilis, Batavian Revolt) – A series of late summer military victories over Roman forces around the Vacalis (Waal), Rhenus (Rhine) and Mosa (Meuse, Maas) rivers in *Germania Inferior* (Lower Germany) ultimately permitted thousands of

German tribesmen to concentrate against the region's main Roman legionary base at Vetera (Xanten). Julius Civilis, a chieftain of the Batavi and former Roman auxiliary officer who was responsible for the current revolt, led the attack. Stationed there behind formidable defences were the *Legio V Alaudae* and the *Legio XV Primigenia*, both recovering after their earlier defeat at Insula Batavorum. Civilis besieged the garrison with a sizable concentration of manpower, including tribesmen of the Batavi, Teneteri and Bructeri, together with eight cohorts of Batavian auxiliaries who were until recently in the service of Rome. Once the investment began, it quickly became apparent to the legions' commanders, Munius Lupercus and Numisius Rufus, that Civilis intended to assault the camp using Roman siege tactics. They accordingly began strengthening the palisade and ramparts of the *castrum*. Civilis was also aware that the complement of each legion was badly depleted, amounting to no more than 5,000 men in total. This situation ensured that the besiegers outnumbered the besieged. Compounding the hardship for the Romans was the fact that the camp was located on a shallow slope, and could be approached by an enemy from level ground. Early attempts by the Germans to breach the camp's defences using crude siege machinery failed, but Civilis continued to employ the Batavi in the construction of siege works, while keeping the Romans under perpetual attack by German tribesmen from across the Rhine. The legions offered unflagging resistance, and eventually the Batavi leader gave up hope of seizing the *castrum* by force alone. At this time, a Roman relief column, consisting of the *Legio XXII Primigenia*, *Legio I Germanica* and *Legio XVI Gallica*, reached the village of Gelduba (Krefeld) approximately 25 miles (40km) to the south. While the Roman general, Caius Dillius Vocula, temporarily delayed his advance at Gelduba, Civilis determined to destroy the approaching legions before they reached Vetera. His plan ended in defeat, and he was forced to retire after having lost all eight Batavian auxiliary units in the fighting. Thereafter, Vocula and his legions relieved the *Legio V Alaudae* and *Legio XV Primigenia*, but an unexpected attack on the Roman base at Moguntiacum (Mainz) by other German tribes to the south-east forced Vocula to retire from Vetera. The departure of the Twenty-second, Sixteenth and First legions was accompanied by the withdrawal of some troops from the Fifth and Fifteenth legions. Their loss proved fatal to the future defence of the *castrum*. Though re-equipped and provisioned, the undermanned legionary forces at Vetera were in no condition to withstand a protracted siege once Civilis resumed his investment. With Vocula gone and Marcus Hordeonius Flaccus, the Roman governor of *Germania Superior* (Upper Germany), now 40 miles (64km) to the south in Novaesium (Neuss) and too far away to aid Vetera, the Germans once again pressed their assault against the two isolated legions. In the end, trapped and without hope of succour, the legions' commander, Munius Lupercus, surrendered the fort to Civilis. Shortly afterwards, the German leader granted the Roman garrison permission to depart Vetera peacefully, but the legions were betrayed some 5 miles (8km) outside the camp and largely destroyed in an ambuscade.

Publius Cornelius Tacitus, *The Histories*, 4.21–60.

Castra Vetera, AD 70, Autumn (Revolt of Civilis, Batavian Revolt) – In the spring of AD 70, the arrival of a major Roman army under the command of the general Quintus Petilius Cerialis placed the Batavian revolt in grave jeopardy. Its leader, Julius Civilis, a chieftain of the Batavi and former Roman auxiliary officer, continued to lead his German and Gallic forces with great alacrity; but the Romans used the advantage afforded by the presence of four legions – the *Legio VI Victrix, Legio II Adiutrix, Legio XXI Rapax* and *Legio XIV Gemina* – to slowly turn the war to their favour. In the autumn, these divisions, together with the *Legio I Germanica* and *Legio XVI Gallica*, marched toward Castra Vetera (Xanten), where Civilis was encamped with a sizeable German army. Upon drawing near the enemy position, the Roman army stopped, its approach interrupted by a wide marshy plain which separated the legions from the tribal host. The already wet ground was further saturated at this time by flood water, after Civilis altered the course of the Rhenus (Rhine) River by the construction of a dam across the main channel. Once battle was joined, the Roman infantrymen found themselves hampered by the weight of their armour, which restricted mobility in the morass. The situation proved no better for the cavalry, whose effectiveness was largely neutralized by the deep marsh. This circumstance was fully exploited by the Germans, who were long acclimatized to the local conditions. They quickly took advantage of the Romans' plight to surround the cohorts on the flanks and rear. This tactic also served to block any attempt by the Romans to withdraw to higher ground. The battle then degenerated into a confused struggle, as isolated pockets of fighting erupted either in deep water or where small islands of dry earth permitted solid footing for the combatants. Ultimately, the adverse conditions proved insurmountable for both sides, and each eventually returned to their camps, having achieved nothing decisive from the day's action.

Publius Cornelius Tacitus, *The Histories*, 5.14–15.

Castra Vetera, AD 70, Autumn (Revolt of Civilis, Batavian Revolt) – The failure of both Germans and Romans to achieve a decisive victory over the other in a previous engagement again drew the two armies together for a second day of fighting. In this battle, fought near Castra Vetera (Xanten) on a plain beside the Rhenus (Rhine) River, the Roman general Quintus Petilius Cerialis deployed his army in two lines; the auxiliary cavalry and infantry arrayed in a *simplex acies*, with his six legions held in reserve. He then retained a special detachment of select troops under his personal command to address any emergencies that might arise once the struggle began. Standing opposite the Romans was a strong formation of German warriors, arranged in columns. On the right, the barbarian leader, Julius Civilis, placed the Batavi and Cugerni; and to the left, near the river, he positioned the tribes from across the Rhenus. The Germans opened the battle with a volley of missile fire, hoping to provoke the Romans into launching a reckless assault across a marshy plain to their front, but Cerialis refused to abandon his location on dry ground. The Germans then charged the Roman formation. The *auxilia* absorbed this initial shock, but were gradually driven back by the persistent pressure of the enemy attack. As the Germans continued to push forward, the legions entered the battle and capably stopped the advance. The battle thereafter became a contest of strength. While the two armies fought for advantage, a Batavian deserter led two troops of Roman cavalry around the marshland and in behind the German position. Upon a given signal, the horsemen charged the enemy rear, while the legions simultaneously initiated a strong frontal attack. The force of the combined assaults proved irresistible, and the Germans immediately broke ranks and fled in complete disorder toward the Rhenus. Because nightfall was approaching, and rain was starting to fall, Cerialis refused to pursue the defeated enemy. This Roman victory ultimately proved to be the decisive battle in the year-long Batavian Revolt.

Publius Cornelius Tacitus, *The Histories*, 5.16–18.

Catalunian Plains, AD 274, March – With the end of the Palmyrene campaign in the East, the Roman Emperor Aurelian determined to reconquer Gaul, which had remained beyond the control of his imperial predecessors since 259 when the pretender, Postumus, formed the province into a semi-independent kingdom within the Empire. After returning to Europe, Aurelian led his army into northern Gaul to challenge Caius Pius Esuvius Tetricus, an elder Roman senator who was the latest ruler of the *imperium Galliarum*. The two armies met near the town of Durocatalaunum (Chalons-en-Champagne; arch. Chalons-sur-Marne). Possessing only a tenuous hold over his mutinous troops, the Gallic 'emperor' abruptly betrayed his legions during the course of fighting and surrendered himself to Aurelian. Tetricus' army continued the battle for some time, even without its leader, but eventually lost. Both sides suffered heavy casualties in the engagement. Aurelian's victory resulted in the complete restoration of Gaul to the empire.

Eutropius, *Abridgement of Roman History*, 9.10,13; *Panegyrici Latini* [AD 311], 5.4.3; *Scriptores Historiae Augustae* (*Tyranni Triginta*) 'Tetricus Senior', 24.2; *Scriptores Historiae Augustae* 'Aurelian', 32.3; Sextus Aurelius Victor, *Liber De Caesaribus*, 33.

Catalunian Plains, AD 366, July – During the winter a strong force of Germanic Alamanni raided into Gaul, where it was eventually challenged by a

Roman army under the generals Charietto and Severianus. In the ensuing battle, the legions were soundly beaten and both generals slain. The following summer a second Roman army, led by the *magister equitum* Jovinus, moved against the various bands of Alammani still plundering the Gallic countryside. Near Scarponna (Charpeigne) and again on the banks of the Mosa (Moselle) River, the Romans intercepted bands of Alammani, badly defeating the interlopers each time. Soon after these victories, Roman scouts located a third division of Alamanni near the town of Durocatalaunum (Chalon-en-Champagne, archaic Chalons-sur-Marne). On reaching the vicinity of the enemy position, the Romans constructed a fortified encampment and rested in preparation for battle the following day. At first light, the legions arrayed on the Catalunian Plains. Jovinus immediately recognized that the superior numbers of the enemy placed the flanks of the Roman force at risk of envelopment and elected to attenuate his battle line by arranging the cohorts of infantry and cavalry squadrons in loose order. Shortly thereafter the fighting began and evolved into an intense struggle that continued throughout the day, only ending with the onset of nightfall. The next morning the Romans again assembled for battle but found the field abandoned, the Alammani having chosen to retreat under cover of darkness. German casualties amounted to 6,000 dead and 4,000 wounded, while Roman losses from the engagement totalled 1,200 killed and 200 injured.

Ammianus Marcellinus, *Res Gestae*, 27.2.1–8.

Catalunian Plains, AD 451 – In response to Attila's invasion of Gaul, the Western Roman *magister militum* Flavius Aetius assembled an army for the purpose of driving the Huns out of Western Europe. From the Rhenus (Rhine) River, Attila marched into portions of Germany, Belgium and Gaul, where he systematically reduced the cities of Durocortorum (Rheims), Moguntiacum (Mainz), Argentoratum (Strasburg), Colonia (Cologne), Borbetomagus (Worms) and Augusta Treverorum (Trier) before finally moving against Cenabum (Orleans). While the Huns prosecuted an investment of the city, Aetius advanced against the besieging army, forcing Attila to abandon his assault and withdraw into the open country of the Catalunian Plains outside the town of Durocatalaunum (Chalons-en-Champagne; arch. Chalons-sur-Marne). There, the Huns prepared to face their pursuer, an alliance army that included not only the Romans under Aetius, but Burgundians, Salian Franks and some of their Ripuarian kinsmen, Armorican Celts, Laeti, Olibreones and Saxons. In addition, Aetius was supported by a substantial formation of Visigoths led by their king, Theodoric. Less certain were the squadrons of Alani cavalry under King Sangiban, an ally of dubious loyalty who until recently had been actively treating with the Hunnic ruler. Opposing the coalition were Attila's Huns, together with additional forces drawn from

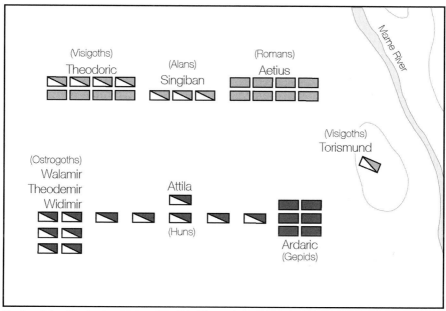

Battle of the Catalunian Plains, AD 451 (Phase 1)

the various German nations subject to the barbarian ruler. Among these were the Rugians, Thuringians, Heruli and Scirians. Most significant were the Gepidae, commanded by King Ardaric, and the Ostrogoths under the leadership of their three chieftains, Valamir, Thiudimer and Vidimer.

Despite the apparent readiness of both armies for action, Attila delayed the contest until mid-afternoon. When the two sides finally assembled for battle, Aetius arrayed the Alans in the centre of his line, with the stronger divisions of Visigothic cavalry and infantry situated on the right wing. On the left, he deployed his Roman infantry with Frankish and German allies. These troops were supported by detachments of Visigothic heavy cavalry under prince Thorismund and Roman horse-archers. On the other side, Attila positioned his Huns in the ecentre. He arranged the German allies on both wings; Ostrogoths on the left and Gepidae and other hosts on the right. Once the armies drew near to one another, a sharp skirmish quickly developed over control of a low ridge adjacent to the Roman left flank. Roman cavalry, accompanied by the Visigothic horsemen of Thorismund, moved swiftly to seize the crest of the hill as a band of Huns approached by means of the opposing slope. The ensuing melee remained undecided until Aetius reinforced his cavalry with Roman and Frankish infantry and seized the hill-top. His forces were now positioned to assault Attila's right flank. Despite this tactical setback, Attila recognized that his greatest threat came from the Visigoths and Alans, particularly their formidable squadrons of cavalry. Following an exchange of

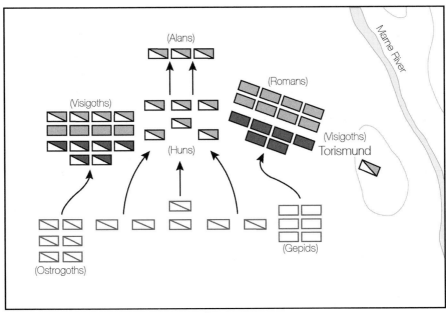

Battle of the Catalunian Plains, AD 451 (Phase 2)

missiles, the Huns launched a fierce attack into Aetius' centre. The Alans recoiled under the pressure of the charge, while, on the right flank, the Visigothic shield wall bore the full brunt of the Ostrogothic attack. The fighting quickly intensified as Attila's centre and left flank became fully involved in the struggle. As the Huns penetrated deeper into enemy ranks, Attila abruptly wheeled his centre to the left, driving into the flank of the Visigothic formation. The chaos of the engagement quickly produced a savage struggle between the cavalry and infantry of the opposing armies. Theodoric was killed during the onslaught; but the Visigoths successfully absorbed the attack, rallied, and then initiated a counter-assault that ultimately compelled Attila to abandon the field. Under cover of the gathering darkness, his army retreated to the nearby safety of the Huns' wagon *laager*. Aetius likewise elected to discontinue the main action, though sporadic fighting occurred for some time after sunset. Daylight revealed the extent of devastation. Thousands of casualties littered the battlefield. Unwilling to renew the contest, the Huns remained in their encampment for several days before finally withdrawing beyond the Rhine River.

Jordanes, *The Origins and Deeds of the Goths*, 36–41; Hydatius, *Chronicle*, 142 [Mom. 150]; Gregory of Tours, *History of the Franks*, 2.7; *Gallic Chronicler of 452*, c.139.

Chalons AD 273, see Catalunian Plains, AD 273.

Chalons, AD 366, see Catalunian Plains, AD 366.

Chalons, AD 451, see Catalunian Plains, AD 451.

Chrysopolis, AD 324, September 18 (Wars of Constantine I) – Near the community of Chrysopolis (Scutari) on the Thracian Bosphorus, legions of the Western *Augustus* Constantine defeated a Roman army under the Eastern Emperor Licinius. The turning point in the battle occurred when Constantine's forces completely routed the opposition with a single, massive assault. Licinius lost 25,000 men and the remainder of his army was put to flight. Constantine thereafter assumed control of the city.

> Eusebius, *Life of Constantine*, 2.17; Zosimus, *New History*, 2.26.1–3; Anonymous Valesianus, Pars Prior, *The Lineage of the Emperor Constantine*, 5.27; John Zonaras, *Epitome of Histories*, 13.5.

Cibalae, AD 316, October 8 (Wars of Constantine I) – Near the Pannonian hill town of Cibalae (Vinkovci), on a large plain between the Savus (Sava) and Dravus (Drava) rivers, the rival armies of the Roman co-emperors Constantine I and Licinius engaged in a day-long battle that resulted in the defeat of the Eastern *Augustus*. Constantine commanded 20,000 men, while Licinius possessed a larger army of 35,000, including armoured cavalry and Illyrian legions. The battle began with Constantine's forces firmly positioned within a defile near the slopes of an adjacent mountain. To guard his infantry from the danger of assault while on difficult terrain, the Western emperor deployed his squadrons of horse in a protective screen to the front. On open ground closer to Cibalae, Licinius arrayed his battle-line near the base of the hill in an effort to discourage attacks against his flanks. When all was in readiness, Constantine moved his formation onto the plain and advanced toward the awaiting enemy. As the distance between the armies narrowed, each was subjected to intense volleys of missile fire before the opposing legions joined in a fierce struggle. The contest remained undecided for several hours when, around sunset, Constantine led his right wing in a determined charge that finally routed the enemy formation. Shortly thereafter, Licinius, along with most of his cavalry, abandoned the field and withdrew under cover of darkness to the city of Sirmium (Mitrovica), having lost 20,000 infantry and a portion of his mailed horse.

> Anonymous Valesianus, Pars Prior, *The Lineage of the Emperor Constantine*, 5.16; Zosimus, *New History*, 2.18; Eutropius, *Abridgement of Roman History*, 10.5; Anonymous (Sextus Aurelius Victor), *Epitome of the Emperors*, 41.5 (T. Banchich, trans.).

Cibalis, AD 316, see Cibalae, AD 316

Cillium, AD 544 – In an attempt to suppress a regional insurrection in North Africa, a Roman army under the command of Solomon, *magister militum per Africam*, engaged a numerically superior Moorish force led by Antalas, tribal chieftain of the Frexi, near the city of Cillium (Kasserine). Initially, the battle proved to be evenly contested despite the refusal of some mutinous Roman troops to enter the struggle, but eventually the vast manpower advantage of the Moors overcame all resistance. As the Roman line collapsed, the *magister militum* made a last determined stand with some of his men, but was eventually forced to retreat. Near a creek in a small ravine, Solomon's horse stumbled, throwing its rider. Lifted into his saddle by members of his bodyguard, the badly injured general proved unable to flee and was quickly overtaken by pursuing enemy warriors. In the brief, uneven struggle which followed, Solomon, along with many of his guardsmen, was killed.

Procopius of Caesarea, *History of the Wars* (*The Vandalic War*), 4.21.23–28.

Colchester, AD 61, see Camulodunum, AD 61.

Corsica, AD 456 – The year after the Vandal assault on the city of Rome, the Western *magister militum*, Flavius Ricimer, defeated a Vandalic fleet of sixty ships off the coast of Corsica. This battle followed an initial Roman victory over King Gaiseric's forces at Agrigentium on the island of Sicily.

Hydatius, *Chronicle*, 169 [Mom. 176].

Corycus, AD 260 – Following the capture of the Roman Emperor Valerian by the Persian monarch Shapur I, the king's armies invaded Syria and Anatolia, capturing Antioch, Tarsus and Cappadocian Caesarea. After the loss of these territories, Valerian's principal general, Marcus Fulvius Macrianus, supported by the *praefectus* Callistus, rallied the region's Roman forces at Samosata (Samsat). At Corycus on the coast of Cilicia, the Romans defeated Shapur, forcing him to retreat eastward to the Euphrates River.

John Zonaras, *Epitome of Histories*, 12.23–24; *Scriptores Historiae Augustae* (*Tyranni Triginta*), 'Macrianus', 12.1–4.

Cremona, AD 69, 24 October, see Bedriacum, AD 69, 24 October.

Cremona, AD 69, 14 April (Year of the Four Emperors, Roman Civil Wars) – The death of Emperor Nero in early June of AD 68 resulted in open civil war throughout the Roman Empire. Following the assassination of the hastily chosen Emperor Galba, the armies of his successor, Marcus Salvius Otho, clashed with those of Aulus Vitellius, governor of *Germania Inferior* (Lower Germany), near the northern Italian communities of Cremona and Bedriacum (Calvatone). In a preliminary contest outside the village of Locus Castorum, an Othonian army led by the general Suetonius Paulinus defeated an inferior rival force commanded by Aulus Caecina Alienus. The defeated Vitellian troops fled to Cremona, where they were soon joined by an army under Fabius Valens. As the two sides prepared for the coming engagement, Otho's principal commander – his brother, Titianus, and the *prefectus*, Proculus – rejected the counsel of Paulinus and the *legatus* Marius Celsus to await reinforcements and instead elected to immediately force a major action outside of Cremona. The emperor withdrew to the safety of Brixellum (Brescello), accompanied by a strong force of his bodyguards, cavalry and Praetorian Guardsmen. The two armies arrayed for battle near Cremona. The forces of Vitellius possessed the advantage of both strength and numbers, and their greater morale permitted the legions to quickly form into orderly ranks, while confusion slowed the development of the Othonian line. The fighting concentrated along the raised causeway of the Via Postumia, a road situated on the left bank of the Padus (Po) River. In an open plain bounded by the river and road, intense fighting erupted between Vitellius' veteran *Legio XXI Rapax* from *Germania Superior* (Upper Germany) and the less experienced *Legio I Adiutrix*. The First Legion, consisting of marines levied from the fleet at Ravenna, inflicted heavy casualties on the leading ranks of the Twenty-first and temporarily captured its eagle before a ferocious counter-attack drove back the *Legio I* with heavy losses, including its legate, Orfidius Benignus. At the same time, Vitellius' *Legio V Alaudae* from *Germania Inferior* (Lower Germany) routed the *Legio XIII Gemina* based in Pannonia. On another part of the battlefield, the Vitellians attacked Otho's *XIV Gemina* after successfully isolating the legion with superior forces. The general struggle remained undecided for some time until Caecina and Valens reinforced their legions by the application of reserves. The Vitellian effort was further strengthened with the arrival of Batavian *auxilia* under Varus Alfenus. Fresh from their victory

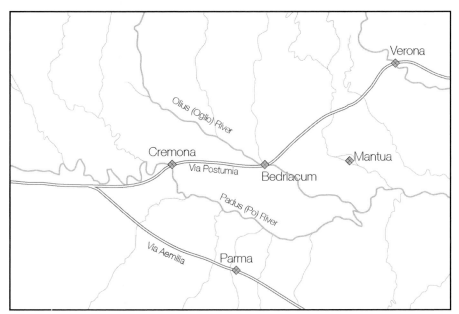

Cremona-Bedriacum Theatre, AD 69–70

over Othonian forces at the Padus, the Batavians immediately launched a concentrated assault against the enemy's flank. This attack, together with continued pressure brought against the opposing ranks by the Vitellian legions, caused Otho's centre to collapse. The loss of this central formation triggered a total rout. Both victors and vanquished were temporarily slowed by the carnage on the Via Postumia as each departed the field in the direction of Bedriacum, approximately 15 miles (24km) away. As the army of Vitellius reached the town's fifth milestone, Caecina and Valens ended the pursuit. Total Roman dead amounted to over 40,000.

> Publius Cornelius Tacitus, *The Histories*, 2.41–45; Dio Cassius, *Roman History*, *epitome*, 63.10.3; Plutarch, *Otho*, 8–14.

Crossfeld, AD 101, see Tapae, AD 101.

Ctesiphon, AD 363 (Persian Wars) – Shortly after crossing the Tigris River, a Roman army led by Emperor Julian was challenged by a formidable Persian force consisting of squadrons of *cataphractii* arrayed in close order, supported by formations of infantry and further strengthened with a contingent of war elephants. The Romans deployed into battle formation and advanced slowly against the enemy. When the armies were sufficiently near to one another, Roman skirmishers opened the battle with a discharge of javelins. Then, in order to reduce the number of casualties resulting from Persian arrows, the Roman heavy infantry surged forward in an effort to quickly close

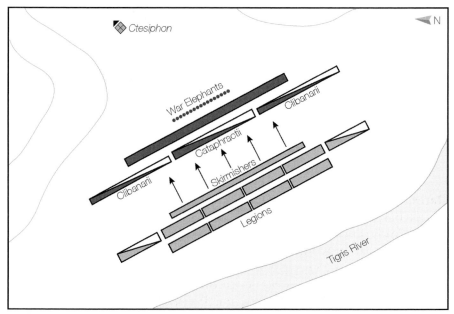

Battle of Ctesiphon, AD 363

with the enemy ranks. The fighting thereafter degenerated into an intense hand-to-hand struggle that only abated when the Persian front line wavered, and then broke, under the sustained pressure of the legions. In the subsequent rout the enemy fled in disorder toward the community of Ctesiphon, closely pursued by the victorious Romans, who ended the chase at the city's walls. Persian losses totalled 2,500, while Roman dead amounted to seventy men.

Ammianus Marcellinus, *Res Gestae*, 24.6.8–15; Zosimus, *New History*, 3.25.1–7.

Cyzicus AD 193 (Roman Civil Wars, Year of the Five Emperors) – The assassinaton of Emperor Didius Julianus in June of 193 once again plunged the Roman Empire into civil war. The general Lucius Septimius Severus, governor of *Pannonia Superior* (Upper Pannonia), secured control of both Rome and the imperial throne and then turned his Danubian armies eastward to challenge a rival claimant, the Syrian governor Caius Pescennius Niger, who possessed the support of all nine Eastern legions. Niger established his headquarters at Byzantium and Severus moved to place the city under siege. Meanwhile, near the Anatolian port of Cyzicus, Niger's lieutenant – the *pro-consul* of Asia, Asellius Aemilianus – was defeated in battle by some of Severus' generals. This battle proved inconclusive, and only served to set the stage for a more significant encounter near the city of Nicaea.

Dio Cassius, *Roman History*, 75.6.4; Herodian, *Roman History*, 3.2.1–2; *Scriptores Historiae Augustae* (*Severus*), 8.10.16.

Daphne, AD 272 (Palmyrene War, War against Zenobia) – On a steep hill overlooking the suburbs of Daphne (Harbiye), the Roman forces of Emperor Aurelian, having only recently departed the city of Antiochia (Antakya) in pursuit of the Palmyrene army under Queen Zenobia, encountered a detachment of enemy troops intent on delaying the Roman advance. The emperor's infantry formed a *testudo* and charged up the slope, shattering the Palmyrene formation and driving the fugitives from the knoll. Afterwards, the Romans resumed their march south toward Emesa (Homs), following the course of the Orontes River.

Scriptore Historiae Augustae (*Aurelianus*), 25.1; Zosimus, *New History*, 1.52.1–2.

Daras, AD 530 (Persian Wars, Wars of Justinian I) – Outside the Roman fortress of Daras in northern Mesopotamia, a Roman army of 25,000 engaged a numerically superior force of 50,000 Persians. Learning of the approach of a sizeable Persian army under the command of the *mihran* Perozes, Roman command-general Belisarius immediately began construction of a defensive trench outside the castle's walls. With the arrival of the Persian host, both armies assembled for battle. Arrayed in well-disciplined order along the entire length of the completed trench were detachments of Roman and allied

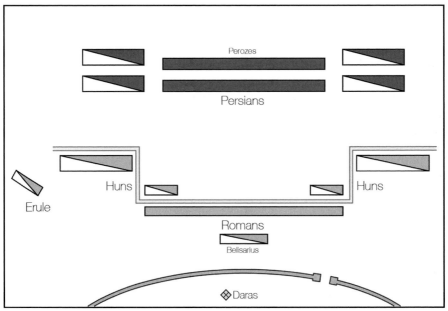

Battle of Daras, AD 530

cavalry, and placed in the centre directly behind the mounted squadrons was a strong formation of infantry commanded by Belisarius and his general, Hermogenes. Perozes deployed half his army only a few hundred yards in front of the Roman battle formation, retaining the remaining portion in the rear as a reserve. Because each commander hesitated to open the engagement, the two armies stood to arms until late afternoon, when all inactivity was momentarily broken by a cavalry skirmish. Thereafter, the armies resumed their stations until nightfall, when both elected to retire. The following morning, each army again took the field, the Persian general now determined to fully engage Belisarius' command before day's end. The battle began around midday with a heavy exchange of arrow fire from each side, before a sudden strong charge of Cadiseni infantry temporarily broke the Roman left wing. The momentum of this attack drove through the Roman line, but was abruptly checked by a dramatic counter-charge of Hunnic and Herulian cavalry. Observing this reverse, Perozes deployed his total force of 10,000 Immortals in a vain attempt to stem the retreat, which quickly preceded the total collapse of the Persian line. As the enemy turned in flight, the entire Roman line surged forward in pursuit; partially encircling thousands seeking escape and killing some 5,000 men. The Romans returned to Daras after a brief chase.

Procopius of Caesarea, *History of the Wars* (*The Persian War*), 1.13.9–39, 1.14; *Chronicle of Pseudo-Zachariah Rhetor*, 9.3.

Decimus, AD 533, see Ad Decimum, AD 533.

Deols, AD 469, see Vicus Dolensis, AD 469.

Dibaltum, AD 377 – Close to the Thracian community of Dibaltum, a Gothic army surprised several companies of Roman infantry and a detachment of Cornuti commanded by Barzimeres, a tribune of *scutarii*. The Roman force quickly assembled into battle formation and, having ensured the protection of his flanks, Barzimeres ordered an attack in an effort to turn the momentum of the engagement and compel the Goths to break off the assault. The tactic proved successful until the beleaguered Romans were surrounded by a large force of enemy cavalry. Exhausted from the protracted struggle, the Romans were unable to resist a final mounted charge by the Goths.

Ammianus Marcellinus, *Res Gestae*, 31.8.9–10.

Dolensis, AD 469, see Vicus Dolensis, AD 469.

Durocatalaunum, see Catalunian Plains, AD 366 and AD 451.

Duro-Catalaunum, see Catalunian Plains, AD 366 and AD 451.

Durocortorum AD 356 – In early summer, after wintering in Vienna (Vienne), the *Caesar* Julian assembled a sizeable force of unknown strength and marched northward toward the city of Durocortorum (Reims, Rheims), where his entire army was to rendezvous in preparation for an impending campaign against the Alamanni. On 24 June, he relieved the town of Augustudonum (Autun), which had until that time suffered under a protracted siege by German tribesmen. In order to complete his journey as quickly as possible, Julian reduced the size of his accompanying forces, electing to take only *cataphractarii* and *ballistarii*. He then chose to follow a shorter but more perilous track that eventually led the Romans through the towns of Autessiodorum (Auxerre) and Tricasae (Troyes). As the march progressed, the column was increasingly subjected to hit-and-run attacks by bands of tribesmen. These assaults and the resulting skirmishes persuaded Julian to strengthen his flanks and thoroughly reconnoitre the surrounding forests. Such preparations served the army well until it neared Durocortorum. While marching in a heavy mist under low cloud cover, the Alamanni attacked the rearguard of Roman column. The dense fog prevented detection of the ambuscade, permitting the German warriors to launch a powerful surprise assault against the two rearmost legions. Both were briefly in danger of being annihilated before reinforcements were able to reach the location of fighting and rescue the hard-pressed units. Roman losses resulting from the defeat are unknown.

Ammianus Marcellinus, *Res Gestae*, 16.2.1–10.

Edessa, AD 259 (Persian Wars, Wars against the Sassanids) – The resumption of Persian attacks along Rome's Syrian frontier compelled Emperor Valerian to respond with a massive counter-offensive. Leading a large army of some 70,000 men, the emperor advanced to the relief of the cities of Carrhae and Edessa. During this time, an outbreak of plague swept through the expeditionary force, killing many within its ranks and seriously undermining the overall vitality of the legions. Despite the poor health of his army, Valerian remained determined to force the Sassanid king, Shapur I, to abandon his campaign. The two sides met near Edessa. The resulting battle ended in the total defeat of the Romans, and the capture of the emperor, his *praefectus praetorio* and generals. Valerian died the following year, still a prisoner of the Persians.

> Zosimus, *New History*, 1.36.1–2; Lucius Caecilius Firmianus Lactantius (Lactantius), *On the Deaths of the Persecutors*, 5; *Res Gestae Divi Saporis*, 9–11 (inscription at Naqsh-i Rustam); Michaels Rostovtzeff, 'Res Gestae Diviv Saporis and Dura', *Berytus* 8:1 (1943), pp. 17–60; Eutropius, *Abridgement of Roman History*, 9.7; Georgios Synkellos (Syncellus), *Chronography*, c.466; Anonymous (Sextus Aurelius Victor), *Epitome of the Emperors*, 32.5 (T. Banchich, trans.).

Elegia, AD 162 – Following the provocative encroachment into the affairs of the Kingdom of Armenia by King Vologeses IV of Parthia; the Roman governor of Cappadocia, Marcus Sedatius Severianus, marched a legionary force south-eastward into the neighbouring realm in order to reassert Rome's presence in the region. At Elegia (Iz Oghlu) in Armenia, near the Cappadocian frontier, a Parthian army under the veteran general Chosrhoes trapped and destroyed the Roman legion. Severianus committed suicide.

> Dio Cassius, *Roman History*, 71.2.1.

Emesa, AD 272 (Palmyrene War, War against Zenobia) – A few miles north of the city of Emesa (Homs), near the banks of the Orontes River, a Roman army led by Emperor Aurelian engaged a massive force of 70,000 Palmyrenian and allied troops under the command of Septimius Zabdas, the leading general of Queen Zenobia of Palmyra. Opposing the Palmyrene divisions were the Dalmatian and Mauritanian light cavalry and an array of European and Asiatic light and heavy infantry, including veteran legions drawn from Moesia, Pannonia, Rhaetia and Noricum. When the battle opened, the Roman cavalry almost immediately gave way before the superior formations of Palmyrene armoured cavalry, the *clibanarii*. The Palmyrenians pressed their attack, inflicting heavy casualties among the Roman horse. The primary responsibility for combating the enemy now fell on the Roman infantry. Observing that the charge of the *clibanarii* had disrupted the ranks of the entire Palmyrene formation, the legions wheeled around and attacked. The assault caught the armoured squadrons scattered and in disorder after their pursuit of the Dalmatian and Mauritanian horsemen, unprepared to properly resist the sudden surge of heavy infantry. In the fighting that followed, the Palmyrenians suffered severe losses before abandoning the field. The fugitives that managed to escape the carnage fled to Emesa. Aurelian resumed his march toward Palmyra soon thereafter.

Scriptore Historiae Augustae (*Aurelianus*), 25.2–3; Zosimus, *New History*, 1.52–53.

Euphrates River, AD 231 – As part of his strategic plan to expand Sassanid territory, King Ardashir I of Persia invaded Roman Mesopotamia in 229 and threatened to overrun the provinces of Cappadocia and Syria. In response, Roman Emperor Severus Alexander led a large army to the East in an effort to repel the invaders. He implemented a large three-pronged invasion; sending one column through Armenia to attack the territory of Media, a second army into central Mesopotamia under his personal leadership and a third column southward along the Euphrates River toward its confluence with the Tigris River. The danger posed to the Sassanid capital of Ctesiphon by this last column of troops compelled Ardashir to retain only those forces in the north sufficient to combat the threat in Media, and then concentrate the remainder of his army to the south in the region of Mesene. Once there, the Persians intercepted the southern Roman column and, using large numbers of armoured cavalry and mounted archers, trapped and destroyed the legions. Despite the evident slaughter of Romans during this battle, Persian losses were apparently serious enough to discourage Sassanid aggression in the region for some seven years.

Herodian, *Roman History*, 6.5.4–10.

Euphrates River, AD 363, Spring (Persian Campaign) – The day following a successful two-day Roman siege of the city of Pirisabora, a Persian force attacked three squadrons of Roman scouts deployed to reconnoitre ahead of the imperial army. The unexpected assault resulted in the deaths of several cavalrymen, including a tribune, and the loss of a military standard. In response, Emperor Julian personally led an armed attack which routed the enemy and resulted in the recovery of the dragon standard.

Zosimus, *New History*, 3.19.1–2; Amminus Marcellinus, *Res Gestae*, 24.3.1–2; Libanius, *Oration*, 18.229–230.

Euphrates River, AD 363, Spring (Persian Campaign) – Following the Roman capture of the Persian towns of Dacira (Hit) and Ozogadana (Sari al-Hadd), a scouting patrol dispatched by Emperor Julian ahead of his advancing army encountered an enemy force under the command of the *Surena* and the *malechus*, Podosaces. The reconnaissance detachment, led by the fugitive Sassanid prince Hormizd, discovered the enemy and charged across the river in the company of the main army, inflicting a number of casualties and routing the remainder of the Persians.

Zosimus, *New History*, 3.15.4–6; Amminus Marcellinus, *Res Gestae*, 24.2.4–5.

Faesulae, AD 406 – In the autumn of 405, a large force of several thousand Ostrogoths, Vandals and other allied German tribesmen under the leadership of King Radagaisus crossed the Alps and descended into the eastern Padus Valley (Po Valley). For some six months thereafter, the band raided unchecked in northern Italy before the Roman *magister militum*, Flavius Stilicho, finally mobilized sufficient forces at Ticinum (Pavia) to effectively deal with the interlopers. In the summer, a Roman army consisting of thirty *numerii* reinforced by federate bands of Alans, Goths and Huns moved against the invaders, who were preoccupied with the investment of Florentia (Florence). After relieving the city, the Romans pursued Radagaisus' band into the nearby hills of Faesulae (Fiesole), approximately 5 miles (8km) away. There, Stilicho defeated the massive barbarian army. The Romans subsequently executed Radagaisus on 23 August 406.

Marcellinus Comes, *Chronicle*, 4th indiction, Arcadii VI et Probi, in year 406 (Croke); Zosimus, *New History*, 5.26.3–5; Olympiodorus, *fragment* 9 (Blockley); Aurelius Augustinus (Augustine of Hippo), *City of God*, 5.23; Paulus Orosius, *Seven Books of History against the Pagans*, 7.37; *Gallic Chronicler of 452*, c.50, c.52.

Fano, AD 271, see Metaurus River, AD 271.

Fanum Fortunae, AD 271, see Metaurus River, AD 271.

Fanum, AD 554, see Pisaurium, AD 554.

Faventia, AD 542, Spring (Gothic War, Wars of Justinian I) – Having failed to capture the Ostrogothic stronghold of Verona, the Roman generals Constantian and Alexander withdrew south across the Padus (Po) River and encamped on the banks of the Anemo (Lamone) River near the town of Faventia (Faenza) with an army of 12,000 men. The Ostrogothic King Totila marched in pursuit with a force of 5,000 infantry and cavalry. When the Goths neared the Anemo, he ordered 300 horsemen to ford the river some 2 miles (3.2km) away in an effort to move in behind the enemy camp undetected. The remainder of Totila's army then continued across the river and advanced against the Roman position, where they were immediately met by the assembled divisions of Constantian and Alexander. The two armies soon engaged each other in an intense contest which was only decided when Totila's 300-man detachment launched a sudden assault on the Roman rear. The attack panicked the unsuspecting soldiers and caused a rapid collapse of the formation. Most of the Roman army was destroyed in the resulting rout.

Thousands died on the field or were captured, while both generals succeeded in escaping the carnage in the company of only a few survivors.

> Procopius of Caesarea, *History of the Wars* (*The Gothic War*), 7.4.19–32.

Fields of Cato, AD 548, Spring – After the defeat of Roman forces at Gallica the year before, John Trogita, the *magister militum per Africam*, began amassing a new army in preparation for a renewal of hostilities against those Moorish tribes still hostile to Rome's presence in North Africa. He also entered into alliances with a number of other Moorish tribes, including those under the leadership of the powerful chieftain Coutzinas. Once preparations for the campaign were in order, John marched south from Carthage and temporarily encamped at Iunce near the coast before moving his army toward the Moorish camp, situated on an inland plain called the Fields of Cato. After drawing the enemy into a pitched battle, the Roman army and its tribal allies soundly defeated the rebellious Moors in what proved to be the final, decisive battle in the four-year Moorish uprising. In the pursuit which followed, the Romans and their allies killed large numbers of the enemy, while survivors fled into the interior wilderness. Among the dead were the insurgents' leader, Carcasan, and sixteen other Moorish chieftains.

> Procopius of Caesarea, *History of the Wars* (*The Vandalic War*), 4.28.50–51; Flavius Cresconius Corippus, *Iohannis*, 8.164–656.

Florence, AD 406, see Faesulae, AD 406.

Forum Julii, AD 69 (Year of the Four Emperors, Roman Civil Wars) – During the Roman civil war between Emperor Otho and Aulus Vitellius, governor of *Germania Inferior* (Lower Germany), envoys from Gallia Narbonensis appealed to the Vitellian general, Fabius Valens, for protection in the province from a marauding Othonian fleet. In response, he dispatched a force of *auxilia*, both infantry and cavalry, to secure the region, which had earlier declared its allegiance for Vitellius. A portion of these troops bivouacked at the port of Forum Julii (Frejus) to help secure the unprotected coast from indiscriminate raiding by the enemy. Upon the approach of an Othonian army, the Vitellians prepared for battle. They deployed twelve *turmae* of cavalry, including Trevirian horsemen, and a select detachment of infantry. These were reinforced by local auxiliaries, 500 Pannonian recruits not yet formally enrolled into service and one Ligurian cohort. Once the two armies began assembling for battle, the Vitellians, who were strongest in cavalry, formed two lines; the mounted squadrons in front, followed by the infantry in close ranks. The Ligurian auxiliaries were located on adjacent high ground. Opposing the Vitellians was a numerically superior army that included several cohorts of Praetorian infantry and a mixed contingent of marines and local militia. These were deployed over a level area extending inland from the coast. Nearby, the Othonian fleet was anchored close to shore, its ships facing the battlefield in order to better provide support for the army. The Trevirian cavalry opened the contest with an imprudent charge against the Praetorians, which not only failed to disrupt the formation of veteran infantry, but needlessly exposed their flank to the fire of slingers. While both armies were fully engaged in the struggle, the Othonian fleet attacked the enemy's rear. The action trapped the Vitellians, who were only able to avoid complete destruction with the onset of nightfall. The Othonians returned to camp following this victory, unaware that the enemy, though defeated, was prepared to regroup for a second battle. After receiving fresh reinforcements, including two cohorts of Tungarian *auxilia*, the Vitellians launched a surprise assault that penetrated their opponents' encampment and forced the Othonians to abandon their defences and rally on a nearby hill. The resulting struggle was long and stubbornly contested, and both sides accrued heavy casualties. The battle finally ended when intense missile fire overwhelmed the determined resistance of the Tungrian infantry and put the Vitellians to flight once again. An effort by the Othonians to underscore their victory with a vigorous chase was abruptly stopped when the enemy horse wheeled around and briefly surrounded their pursuers. Both armies thereafter withdrew, the Vitellians to nearby Antipolis (Antibes) and the emperor's forces further up the coast to Albingaunum (Albenga) in Liguria.

Publius Cornelius Tacitus, *Histories*, 2.14–15.

Forum Terebronii, AD 251, see Abrittus, AD 251.

Forum Trebonii, AD 251, see Abrittus, AD 251.

Frigidus River, AD 394, 5–6 September – In the spring of 392, 21-year-old Western Roman Emperor Valentinian II died from unknown causes. Control of the empire was almost immediately assumed by the powerful *magister militum*, Flavius Arbogastes, a Frank who had long served as the most potent authority in the West. With the death of the young emperor, Arbogastes appointed a *magister scrinorum* named Flavius Eugenius as a puppet to assume the imperial title, while continuing to retain actual management of the state himself. These circumstances ultimately proved intolerable to the Eastern Emperor Theodosius I, who soon began to formulate an invasion of the West. Two years later, in May 394, the Eastern imperial army departed Constantinople under the personal direction of the emperor. The massive expeditionary force moved easily through the northern Balkans and into Pannonia before reaching the slopes of the Julian Alps. The two armies met in the valley of the Frigidus (Vipava) River, some 30 miles (48km) east of the Roman city of Aquileia. Arbogastes commanded a smaller force consisting of Roman, Gallic and Frankish troops, while Theodosius led an army composed of both regular units and *auxilia*, including a sizeable band of 20,000 Visigoths. The emperor's principal generals included Flavius Stilicho and the *magistri militum*, Flavius Timasius. Theodosius assigned the leadership of the Gothic allies to his Armenian general, Bacurius, and the officers Gainas and Saulus. Eugenius deployed both his Frankish and Gallic auxiliaries before the battle commenced. Theodosius countered by placing his *auxilia* in front and ordering Gainas and the soldiers under his command to open the engagement, followed by additional detachments of allied cavalry, mounted archers and infantry. The initial struggle proved savage and resulted in heavy casualties on both sides, including the loss of some 10,000 Visigothic warriors along with their commander, Bacurius. The action finally ended after hours of fighting, Eugenius having won the first day's contest. At dawn, Theodosius again committed his forces to battle, now joined by additional troops led by Count Arbitio, who had defected from the opposing army the night before. The sudden attack was accompanied by a violent Alpine windstorm which blew directly into the faces of the enemy. The strong gale magnified the devastation wrought by Theodosius' archers, while proving equally detrimental to the work of Arbogastes' bowmen. The wind and dust also disrupted the cohesion of Eugenius' entire formation, causing the weakened line to completely collapse when struck by the first violent shock of the Eastern legions. Much of the Western army capitulated in the resulting rout. Eugenius was

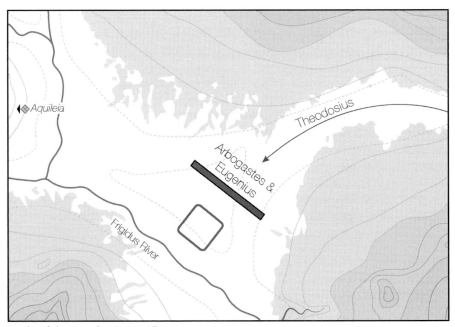

Battle of the Frigidus River, AD 394

captured and shortly thereafter put to death. Arbogastes fled into the surrounding mountains, but later committed suicide rather than surrender.

Zosimus, *New History*, 4.58.1–6; Paulus Orosius, *Seven Books of History against the Pagans*, 7.35; Socrates of Constantinople, *Ecclesiastical History*, 5.25; Jordanes, *The Origins and Deeds of the Goths*, 145; Aurelius Augustinus (Augustine of Hippo), *City of God*, 5.26; Marcellinus Comes, *Chronicle*, 7th indiction, Arcadii III et Honorii II, in year 394 (Croke); Anonymous (Sextus Aurelius Victor), *Epitome of the Emperors*, 48.7 (T. Banchich, trans.).

Gallica, AD 547, see Plain of Gallica, AD 547.

Gamala, AD 67 (First Jewish Revolt, Jewish Wars) – After conquering the city of Taricheae in Galilee, Roman general Titus Flavius Vespasianus prepared to reduce the remaining pockets of Jewish opposition in the region. Moving his army into the more rugged country east of the Sea of Galilee, he proceeded to invest the heavily fortified hill city of Gamala. The Romans were unable to thoroughly circumvallate the community, so Vespasian elected to build a siege ramp in order to breach the city's defences. Three legions led the assault, the *Legio X Fretensis*, *Legio XV Apollinaris* and *Legio V Macedonica*. The cohorts began the construction of the earthen works in an attempt to bring forward the machinery necessary to overwhelm the city's walls. Jewish opposition proved stubborn, forcing the Romans to first use artillery, including *ballistae*, to sweep the walls free of the enemy before concentrating battering rams at three separate locations. The legionaries were eventually able to enter the city through a destroyed section of the wall, but the resulting battle quickly degenerated into a congested and disorderly melee amidst the maze of narrow streets and adjoining houses. This irregular combat prevented the Romans from implementing their cohortal tactics to best advantage, and thereby created the conditions necessary for the Jews to successfully repulse the attack. Vespasian resumed the assault several days later, when the Roman army had rested and regained its confidence. The inhabitants of Gamala began to suffer from famine as the investment progressed, and many escaped the deteriorating conditions by fleeing into the countryside. The reinvigorated legions eventually overran the lower city, then captured Gamala's hilltop citadel a short time later. During this final attack, the Romans massacred 4,000 residents who had sought safety in the fortress. A further 5,000 Jews died in their attempt to escape the ongoing slaughter.

Flavius Josephus, *The Jewish War*, 4.1.1–10.

Gelduba, AD 69 (Revolt of Civilis, Batavian Revolt) – While legionary forces were encamped near the village of Gelduba (Krefeld), approximately 4 miles (6.4km) from the Rhenus (Rhine) River, the Germans attempted to steal a Roman grain ship that had run aground on a mud bar. On learning of this, Herennius Gallus, *legatus* of the *Legio XVI Gallica*, dispatched a cohort to intervene. The Germans soon received reinforcements, shortly followed by the arrival of more Romans. After each side had responded with additional forces, a pitched battle inevitably resulted. The Romans suffered heavy casualties and the Germans were able to successfully tow the ship to the eastern bank of the river.

Publius Cornelius Tacitus, *The Histories*, 4.26–27.

Gelduba, AD 69, December (Revolt of Civilis, Batavian Revolt) – While a German army led by a chieftain and former Roman auxiliary officer named Julius Civilis prosecuted the investment of Castra Vetera (Xanten), a Roman relief column, consisting of the *Legio I Germanica*, *Legio XXII Primigenia* and *Legio XVI Gallica* reached the village of Gelduba (Krefeld) approximately 25 miles (40km) to the south of the besieged fortress. The Romans were attacked by a substantial German force under the command of Julius Maximus and Claudius Victor. The legionary commander, Caius Dillius Vocula, hastily arrayed his battle line with the legions in the centre. Opposing the Romans were eight veteran cohorts of Batavian *auxilia*. The speed of the offensive prevented Vocula's auxiliary cavalry from properly assembling, and an opening charge was easily turned by the enemy horse. Once the infantry joined in, the Germans quickly scattered the cohorts of Nervian *auxilia* anchoring the Roman flanks and exposed the legions to attack from the sides. The momentum of the initial assault drove the Roman centre back against the camp palisade, and some fighting occurred inside the *castrum*. While Vocula's heavy infantry struggled to recover from the force of the Batavian onslaught, the entire German formation was abruptly taken in the rear by the unexpected arrival of Roman reinforcements. As the Batavians pressed their offensive, several cohorts of Vasconian auxiliaries, newly arrived to the battle, struck the enemy from behind. The force of the sudden attack panicked the tribesmen, who imagined that a second Roman army from Novaesium (Neuss) or Mogantiacum (Mainz) had arrived at Gelduba undetected. The appearance of the Vascones emboldened the flagging Roman legions. The entire German host was put to flight in the resulting counter-attack and the flower of the Batavian *auxilia* destroyed. The Romans suffered substantial battlefield losses.

Publius Cornelius Tacitus, *The Histories*, 4.33.

Genil River, AD 438, see Singilis River, AD 438.

Grampians, AD 84, see Mons Graupius, AD 84.

Grove of Buduhenna, AD 28, see Baduhennawood, AD 28.

Haemus Mons, AD 270 – Following the great Roman victory at Naissus (Nis), the remnants of the defeated Gothic army crossed the Nisava River and fled eastward into Macedonia, pursued by elements of Roman cavalry. Near the Haemus Mons (Balkan Mountains), south of the Ister (Danube) River, Roman horse finally clashed with Goths, killing many and delaying their escape until the arrival of imperial legions led by Emperor Claudius II. Surrounded and badly weakened by a shortage of food and provisions, the Goths suffered many casualties in the subsequent skirmishing but were unable to affect a successful breakout. When the emperor finally elected to resolve the matter by means of a decisive engagement led by the infantry, the Romans experienced a thorough defeat. The legions sustained considerable casualties in the unexpected reverse, but the presence of cavalry helped to avoid heavier losses and avert a more serious setback on the battlefield. Undeterred by the Gothic victory, Claudius immediately resumed the chase in an effort to force another contest with the invaders.

Zosimus, *New History*, 1.45.

Heiligenberg, AD 368, see Mons Piri, AD 368.

Helinium, AD 70, Autumn (Revolt of Civilis, Batavian Revolt) – Determined to end the revolt of the German Batavi once and for all, a Roman army invaded the Insula Batavorum (Betuwe), a large island between the Rhenus (Rhine) and Vacalis (Waal) rivers that served as the Batavian homeland. The legions' commander, Quintus Petilius Cerialis, chose to assault the island at two separate locations: near the confluence of the Vacalis and Mosa rivers, and further eastward along the north bank of the Vacalis. He dispatched a river fleet into the Helinium, the estuary of the Mosa (Maas, Meuse) River into which the waters of the Vacalis discharged, in order to prosecute a landing on the western shore of the island. The main Roman invasion force simultaneously crossed the Vacalis. As Roman vessels entered the waters of the estuary, they unexpectedly encountered a native flotilla commanded by Julius Civilis, a Batavian chieftain and former Roman auxiliary officer who was the prime instigator of the insurrection. Because of prevailing winds from the North Sea and strong currents in the estuary, the two fleets only briefly exchanged missile fire before each was carried away from the other. Following this aborted contest, Civilis steered his ships across the Vacalis, while Cerialis put his craft ashore. Once on the island, Roman armies proceeded to thoroughly devastate the countryside, but their progress was soon hindered by seasonal rains which swelled the river and inundated the low marshy ground. As the Romans prepared to press forward with their campaign despite the hardship, both belligerents secretly offered to negotiate peace. Faced with complete subjugation of the island and loss of their German and Gallic allies, Civilis and the Batavi chose to conclude the year-long rebellion.

Publius Cornelius Tacitus, *The Histories*, 5.23–26; Pliny the Elder, *Natural History*, 4.15.

Hellespont, AD 324, see Callipolis, AD 324.

Heraclea, AD 313, see Campus Serenus, AD 313, 30 April.

Hercynian Forest, AD 357 – The earlier success of Roman armies against the Alamanni at the Battle of Argentoratum moved the *Caesar* Julian to assemble a large army in preparation for invading Germanic territories across the Rhenus (Rhine) River. The enemy responded by amassing a considerable force of warriors, which prompted Julian to assume the offensive and launch a pre-emptive invasion before the Alamanni could themselves attack. After constructing bridges at Moguntiacum (Mainz), Julian crossed the river with his army and then dispatched a portion of his infantry under cover of darkness to effect a landing some 2½ miles (4km) upriver. Once Roman forces achieved the opposite bank they proceeded to devastate the countryside, sacking and burning the villages of the Alamanni. Julian then began to move eastward with his cavalry, while the infantry pushed deeper into German territory. After a brief show of resistance, the Germans fled toward the Menus (Main) River ahead of the advancing enemy. As Roman forces drove forward, they fought a running battle with retreating Germans that resulted in numerous Alamannic casualties. Some 10 miles (16km) from the river, the army reached the edge of the Hercynian forest, where they encountered large numbers of felled trees blocking all means of immediate entry. Judging the situation too dangerous to continue, Julian withdrew to an abandoned legionary fort and there prepared to gather materials for continuation of the campaign. This activity compelled the Alamanni to sue for peace rather than face the active resumption of hostilities.

Ammianus Marcellinus, *Res Gestae*, 27.1.1–11; Zosimus, *New History*, 3.4.1–2.

Hermaeum Promontorium, AD 468 – After a Vandal fleet under King Gaiseric raided into the Peloponnesus, Eastern Roman Emperor Leo III recognized that the North African kingdom threatened not only Italy and Sicily, but Roman commercial and economic interests throughout the Mediterranean region. Accordingly, he conspired with Western Roman authorities to organize a large naval and military expedition to topple Gaiseric from power and overthrow the Vandalic realm. The invasion force, which numbered over 1,000 vessels and several thousand combat troops, set sail from Constantinople (Istanbul) under the overall command of the emperor's brother-in-law, Basiliscus. The main target of this flotilla was Carthage, while a secondary invasion force, under the Eastern Roman general Heracleios, carried out a pre-emptive seizure of Vandal territories in Tripolitania before proceeding overland to reinforce Basiliscus' landing. At the same time, an Italian fleet led by Marcellinus captured the Vandal-controlled island of Sardinia off the western coast of Italy. Upon reaching the African coast, Basiliscus delayed his attack for five days following an appeal from envoys sent by Gaiseric. While the Roman vessels lay idle in a small port located on the Hermaeum Promontorium (Ras Addar, Cape Bon) west of Carthage, the Vandals took advantage of favourable winds to sail against Basiliscus. As the Vandal fleet neared the stationary enemy craft, Gaiseric ignited a number of fire-boats. Taken by surprise, and unable to suitably manoeuvre because of adverse winds forcing them against the coast, the Roman crews panicked at the sight of the fire-laden vessels bearing down on them. Because of the large number of ships present, Basiliscus' fleet could not properly take evasive action and many of the craft were either set ablaze by the boats or rammed by Vandal warships.

Procopius of Caesarea, *History of the Wars* (*The Vandalic War*), 3.6.1–27; Hydatius, *Chronicle*, 241 [Mom. 247]; Marcellinus Comes, *Chronicle*, 6th indiction, Anthemii Aug II solius, in year 468 (Croke).

Hippis River, AD 549, Summer (Lazic War, Wars of Justinian I) – The ongoing struggle for the Black Sea fortress of Petra led Sassanid King Chosroes I to send an additional Persian army into Lazica, reinforced by Alans. It was led by the veteran general Chorianes. Upon entering part of the Lazic kingdom called Mocheresis, the invaders camped near a shallow river called the Hippis (Tskhenistskali). In this vicinity, the Persians clashed with a combined Lazic and Roman army under the joint command of Goubazes, king of the Lazi, and Dagisthaeus, the *magister militum per Armeniam*. The battle began with a series of ineffectual cavalry skirmishes, followed by a major encounter between the opposing formations of infantry. After achieving little headway against their opponents in hand-to-hand fighting, both armies resorted to heavy concentrations of missile fire. As the contest intensified, the Roman shield wall provided critical protection from the amassed firepower of Persian and Alan bowmen. In the midst of this action, an arrow struck Chorianes in the neck, killing him. The sudden loss of their commander demoralized the Persian host, who fled in disorder to their camp. The Romans and Lazi took up the pursuit and, after a violent struggle at the main gate, managed to overrun the compound. The Sassanid army was largely destroyed by the end of the day.

Procopius of Caesarea, *History of the Wars* (*The Persian War*), 8.1.3–6, 8.8.1–38.

Hippo Regius, AD 430 (The Vandalic War) – Events in the Western Roman Empire during the early fifth century resulted in a Vandal invasion of North Africa in May 429. Because of an ongoing dispute between Bonifacius, the *comes Africae*, and the imperial court at Ravenna, the former arranged to receive military support from Vandal King Gaiseric and invited him to settle his peoples in the western provinces of Roman North Africa. The arrival of Vandalic forces was temporarily delayed by the unexpected invasion of Suevians into Baetica in the northern Iberian Peninsula, a situation that threatened the Vandal nation then residing in Spain. By the time Gaiseric and his subjects, together with a minority of Alans, crossed into Mauretania Tingitana, Bonifacius was reconciled with the court in Ravenna, and Romans now sought to stop Vandal migration from spreading to Eastern provinces. Frustrated by the turn of events, the king elected to lead his people from the Mauretanias into Numidia. There, the Vandals defeated a Roman army under Bonifacius and then besieged the governor in the port city of Hippo Regius (Annaba) in the early summer of 430. After several months, the Vandals abandoned the siege due to a shortage of provisions. Sometime later, Eastern Roman general Aspar arrived in Africa with reinforcements from Italy and Constantinople. Encouraged by this influx of fresh troops, Bonifacius decided to resume the war, but Gaiseric defeated both Roman commanders in a single decisive battle. Hippo Regius fell to the Vandals shortly afterwards. The Western Roman government granted all of Numidia and the Mauretanias to the German invaders in 435.

Procopius of Caesarea, *History of the Wars* (*The Vandalic War*), 3.3.14–36; Possidius, *Vita Augustini*, 28 (H. T. Weiskotten, trans., 1919 and 2008).

Idistaviso, AD 16, see Idistavisus, AD 16.

Idistavisus, AD 16 (German War) – On a river plain called Idistavisus, situated between a line of low hills and the Weser River, eight Roman legions under the regional governor Germanicus Caesar engaged a large force of Germans led by Arminius, chief of the Cherusci and a former auxiliary officer in the Roman army. The German formation occupied a significant portion of open ground with elements of infantry and cavalry, including the Cherusci, stationed immediately inside the treeline opposite the river and deployed along the adjacent slopes. In response, Germanicus arrayed his legions in a *duplex acies*, each formation consisting of four legions. Ahead of the first line of legionary troops were deployed units of Gallic and German auxiliaries accompanied by archers. Germanicus himself then followed in the company of two cohorts of Praetorian Guardsmen and a detachment of chosen cavalry. Directly behind the general's station was the second line of legionary cohorts, fully supported by auxiliary infantry and mounted bowmen to protect the army's tactical rear. As the Romans drew near the German position, the battle was opened by a spontaneous charge of the Cherusci. Germanicus quickly countered by ordering his best mounted squadrons to attack the enemy flank, while his remaining cavalry under Lucius Stertinius swung round to assault the German rear. At the same time, the legions advanced against the main formation of Arminius' army. The collective effect forced the collapse and rout of the primary German line. As the mass of fleeing warriors sought protection in the surrounding forests, German horsemen suddenly burst from

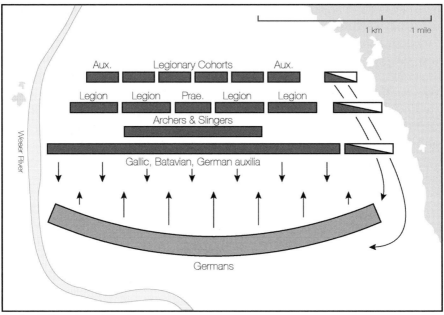

Battle of Idistavisus, AD 16

the treeline onto open ground, dislodged by the pressure of the Roman cavalry attack. In the midst of this confusion, Arminius and his Cherusci were driven from their elevated position directly into a formation of Roman bowmen. Here they sought to cut their way through the archers but were stopped in the attempt by the presence of Raetian, Vindelician and Gallic auxiliary cohorts. Trapped within the maelstrom and unable to recover control of the battlefield, Arminius elected to abandon the fight along with other fugitives, but the greater preponderance of the German army was unable to escape. The slaughter continued unabated from midday until sunset, and the weapons and bodies of the defeated were scattered for some 10 miles (16km) around the original site of the engagement at Idistaviso. The Romans suffered negligible losses in the struggle.

Publius Cornelius Tacitus, *Annals*, 2.16–18.

Immae, AD 218, 8 June – Near Antioch, Syria, the *Legio II Parthica* – which supported Elagabalus in his claim to the imperial throne – engaged a legion of Praetorians in the service of Emperor Macrinus, himself a former Praetorian *praefectus*. After an intense struggle, the Praetorians gained the advantage and forced the *II Parthica* into retreat; but Macrinus inexplicably panicked and fled the field, permitting Elagabalus to rally his forces and carry the battle.

Dio Cassius, *Historiae Romanae*, 79.37.3–4, 38.3–4; Herodian, *Roman History*, 5.4.5–11.

Immae, AD 272 (Palmyrene War, War against Zenobia) – After accepting the submission of the cities of Ancyra (Ankara) and Tyana, Roman Emperor Aurelian continued his march southward toward the city of Antioch (Antakya) in search of the Palmyrene army commanded by Septimius Zabdas. As they approached the city, the Romans observed the enemy arrayed in battle formation. The emperor quickly realized that the Palmyrene armoured cavalry, the *clibanarii*, were superior to his own mounted squadrons, and elected to send the legions across the Orontes River to the safety of the opposite bank while he prepared his Dalmatian horsemen for battle. When the Palmyrene horse opened the engagement with a strong charge, the Roman cavalry immediately fell back in feigned retreat, and repeated this ploy until the enemy eventually tired. The Dalmatians then turned and attacked the *clibanarii*. The spent riders and their mounts, exhausted by the day's heat and the weight of their own mail, were unable to resist the Roman assault and suffered heavy casualties. Following this defeat, the remainder of the Palmyrenians withdrew to Antioch.

Zosimus, *New History*, 1.50.2–4.

Insula Batavorum, AD 69, Summer (Revolt of Civilis, Batavian Revolt) – The Batavians of Lower Germany, led by a chieftain and former Roman auxiliary officer named Julius Civilis, initiated a revolt in the summer of 69 against Roman authorities in the region. After an initial defeat of auxiliary forces, and the loss of several outposts and forts in and around the Vacalis (Waal) and Rhenus (Rhine) rivers, the Roman governor of *Germania Superior* (Upper Germany), Marcus Hordeonius Flaccus, dispatched two legions under the *legatus* Munius Lupercus to end the rebellion. The Roman expedition consisted of the *Legio XV Primigenia* and *Legio V Alaudae* based at Castra Vetera (Xanten). They were joined by Ubian auxiliaries, a detachment of Treviran cavalry and one squadron of Batavian horse led by Civilis' personal rival, the *praefectus alae* Claudius Labeo. On a stretch of open ground in the eastern portion of the Insula Batavorum (Betuwe), a large island between the Rhenus and Vacalis rivers, the Romans engaged a significant force of German tribesmen. As the two armies positioned their lines for battle, the Batavian squadron stationed on the Roman left wing deserted to Civilis and then immediately turned around to face their former allies. This loss of cavalry badly exposed the Roman infantry on the left to attack, but the cohorts maintained their disciplined ranks and prepared to receive the enemy. Once battle was joined, the legions capably held their ground, but the Ubii and Treveri soon fled in disorder. When the Ubian and Treviran *auxilia* scattered over the countryside, the Batavians redirected their assault against the fleeing Gallic tribesmen, permitting the Romans time to withdraw toward Castra Vetera (Xanten).

Publius Cornelius Tacitus, *Histories*, 4.18.

Interamna Nahars, AD 253, Summer – After the Danubian legions proclaimed the *legatus* Marcus Aemilius Aemilianus emperor, he crossed into
Italy and marched southward toward Rome, intent on securing the imperial
throne. As his army advanced toward the capital, following the *Via Flaminia*,
reigning Emperor Trebonianus Gallus and his son, the *Caesar* Caius Vibius
Volusianus, advanced northward to block the usurper's approach to the city.
The two armies clashed some 45 miles (72.4km) north-east of Rome near
the Umbrian town of Interamna Nahars (Terni) in central Italy. Aemilianus
eventually won the contest, and father and son were afterward slain by the
defeated troops. The assassins then joined with the victor.

Sextus Aurelius Victor, *Liber de Caesaribus*, 31; John Zonaras, *Epitome of Histories*, 12.21;
Eutropius, *Abridgement of Roman History*, 9.5.

Isle of Mona, AD 61 – Caius Suetonius Paulinus assumed the governorship
of Britannia in AD 58, and the next year initiated a two-year campaign to
subdue all of northern Wales, including the Isle of Mona (Anglesey). Every-
thing was in readiness for an invasion by the early spring of 61. From the
Welsh coast the legions crossed the Menai Strait aboard a large concentration
of flat-bottom boats and landed on the southern shore of the island. Both the
narrowness of the channel and its shallow depth permitted the cavalry to wade
across at low tide, though they were forced to swim through certain areas of
deep water. Paulinus was particularly determined to seize control of Mona
because it served as a refuge for Welsh leaders seeking escape from Roman
authority and as a centre of druidism. The legionaries observed a large array
of warriors awaiting their arrival as the flotilla ground ashore on the beach.
Darting amidst the Celtic ranks were black-clothed women with disheveled
hair, carrying torches, and to one side stood a circle of druids uttering curses.
The Romans were momentarily taken aback by the unusual sight, but quickly
assembled for battle. The army began its assault when the cohorts were
properly organized. The attack proved devastating. Within a short time the
Celts were utterly defeated. Paulinus proceeded to destroy the oak groves
held sacred by the druidic cult after securing control of the island.

Publius Cornelius Tacitus, *Annals*, 14.29–30.

Issus, AD 194 (Roman Civil Wars, Year of the Five Emperors) – In a
move to further secure his claim to the imperial purple following the outbreak
of civil war, Lucius Septimius Severus, the Roman governor of *Pannonia
Superior* (Upper Pannonia), marched his Danubian legions against those of
rival claimant Caius Pescennius Niger, governor of Syria. After gaining victories at Cyzicus and Nicaea on the southern shore of the Sea of Marmara,
Severus' armies advanced into south-eastern Anatolia. The two armies met at
Issus in Cilicia. The generals Valerianus and Publius Cornelius Anullinus

commanded the forces of Severus, while Niger led the Syrian legions personally. Both armies were arrayed in three lines. Anullinus deployed his legions in the front line, followed by light-armed troops, including archers, who were arrayed in the rear in such a manner as to provide suppressive fire against the enemy once the heavy infantry engaged in fighting. Niger assembled his troops in like manner, positioning his Syrian legions in front, then contingents of light infantry and skirmishers, and lastly the bowmen. To protect his flanks, Niger relied on cliffs to his left toward the sea and a dense stand of woods on the right. Realizing that these natural obstacles would make it difficult to turn his opponent's flanks, Anullinus ordered Valerianus to take the cavalry and circumvent the forest in an effort to attack the enemy from the rear. The Severan legions then advanced against their adversary, forming a *testudo* as they approached the opposing line of cohorts in order to resist incoming flights of arrows. The struggle remained undecided for a long time before Niger's forces began to gain the advantage. The momentum of the match continued to favour the Syrian divisions until a sudden violent thunderstorm swept over the battlefield. The tempest, which blew from the northwest, threw Niger's legions into confusion, while causing minimum effect among the soldiers of Anullinus, whose backs were against the rush of wind and rain. The storm served to demoralize one army even as it worked to rally the other. The Danubian legions pressed forward with renewed vigour, causing the opposing line of heavy infantry to waver and then lose courage.

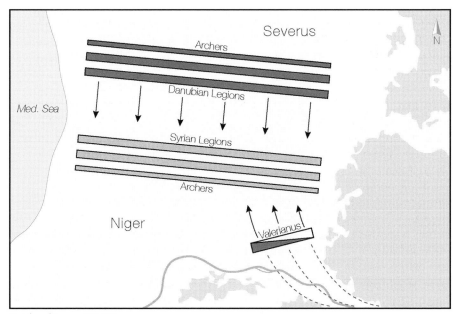

Battle of Issus, AD 194

As portions of Niger's men turned to flee, they suddenly encountered the mounted squadrons of Valerianus. This sight caused those in retreat to turn about in a futile attempt to again challenge the legions of Anullinus, but the cause was lost. With a final thrust, the Danubian cohorts irreparably ruptured the constitution of the opposing formation, and the rout was complete. Losses to the defeated Niger amounted to 20,000 dead.

Dio Cassius, *Roman History*, 75.7–8.1; Herodian, *Roman History*, 3.4.

Ister River, AD 166 – During the fifth year of the Roman emperorship of Marcus Aurelius, 6,000 Langobardi and Obii crossed the Ister (Danube) River, but were completely routed by the cavalry of Marcus Macrinus Vindex, supported by the infantry of Candidus. The defeat compelled the Germans to send peace envoys to Iallius Bassus, the Roman governor of Pannonia.

Dio Cassius, *Roman History*, Epitome of 72.

Ister River, AD 172, Winter – A Roman army engaged a large force of Sarmatian Iazyges on a frozen expanse of the Ister (Danube) River. As the tribesmen started across the river ahead of their pursuers, they suddenly stopped their flight and turned on the Romans, anticipating a tactical advantage on the ice by reason of their greater experience fighting under such conditions. Some of the warriors charged directly at the legionary formation, while detachments of horsemen swept around both flanks. Calmly observing the enemy's movements, the Romans formed into a defensive square and capably checked the initial attack. Thereafter the battle devolved into hand-to-hand fighting in which both sides were equally hampered by the icy surface underfoot. Locked in a protracted contest, and opposed by heavily armoured infantry, the more lightly equipped Iazyges were unable to overcome the enemy and eventually retreated, having suffered very heavy casualties in the encounter.

Dio Cassius, *Roman History*, Epitome of 72.

Ister River, AD 270 – Anticipating a Vandal invasion of Pannonia, Emperor Aurelian led an army northward out of Rome toward the city of Aquileia on the northern Adriatic coast before continuing his journey to the province. Once there, he ordered the rural population to seek protection in the surrounding cities and then prepared his legions for battle. Near Aquincum (Budapest) in *Pannonia Inferior* (Lower Pannonia), the Vandals, supported by Sarmatians, crossed the Ister (Danube) River where they were engaged by the imperial army. The struggle remained undecided when darkness finally put an end to the contest. However, the barbarians withdrew across the river that same night. At dawn, the Vandals sent representatives to Aurelian to sue for peace.

Zosimus, *New History*, 1.48.1–2; Scriptores Historiae Augustae (*Aurelianus*), 18.2.

Ister River, AD 270 – After receiving intelligence that the Juthungi and their Germanic allies intended to invade Italy, Emperor Aurelian left adequate forces in Pannonia to protect the province and then marched toward the peninsula. The Juthungi entered Italy, but upon learning of the emperor's approach they ended their depredations and withdrew toward their homeland. The Roman army encountered a sizable band of the German warriors near the Ister (Danube) River. Aurelian gained the victory in the resulting battle, and thousands of tribesmen died in the clash.

Zosimus, *New History*, 1.49.1.

Ister River, AD 322 (Wars of Constantine I) – Taking advantage of the ongoing civil war between Constantine I and Licinius, the Sarmatians crossed the Ister (Danube) River under the leadership of their king, Rausimodus, and proceeded to ravage the thinly defended Roman countryside. The Western emperor soon learned of these depredations and marched an army into the territory, where he suddenly fell upon the invaders in the midst of besieging a strongly fortified garrison town. The attack inflicted severe casualties and put the remainder of the enemy to flight. At the Ister, Rausimodus led the badly mauled remnants of his army across the river to safety on the northern bank; but contrary to the king's expectation, Constantine followed in pursuit. The Sarmatians were finally overtaken by the Roman army near a heavily wooded hill and again badly defeated. Among the many barbarians killed in this second encounter was Rausimodus himself. Survivors were taken captive.

Zosimus, *New History*, 2.21.3.

Ister River, AD 358 – Moved to action by the depredations committed in Roman territory by the Sarmatian Limigantes, Emperor Constantius II led an army into the Pannonian Plain (Vojvodina, Serbia) to the juncture of the Parthiscus (Tisa) and Ister (Danube) rivers. Late in the afternoon, near the Parthiscus, Roman efforts to parley failed and the two armies joined in battle. The Limigantes directed their assault against the emperor's position on a slight knoll. This thrust was capably turned by the Praetorian Guard. The legions then countered the general attack by forming a wedge-shaped formation called a *caput porcinum*, or *cuneus*, and driving into the enemy's formation. The tactic split the mass of Limigantes. On the right, the Romans shattered the bands of infantry, while to the left, the heavier Roman cavalry overwhelmed lighter squadrons of enemy horse. The barbarian horde broke in disorder under the weight of the legions' onslaught. The battle ended in the total defeat of the Limigantes.

Ammianus Marcellinus, *Res Gestae*, 17.13.8–11.

Ister River, AD 381 – A force of Sciri, Carpodaces and Huns crossed the Ister (Danube) River and entered imperial territory, where they were intercepted by a Roman army led by Emperor Theodosius I. The invaders were defeated and forced to withdraw across the river to their homelands. The victory was significant enough to temporarily restore peace to the entire region and permit the rural population to resume agricultural activity.

Zosimus, *New History*, 4.34.6.

Ister River, AD 386 – After assembling a large multi-tribal force, Ostrogothic leader Odotheus prepared to invade Roman territory south of the Ister (Danube) River. While the entire army was crossing the river, Roman forces under the command of Promotus, the *magister peditum per Thracias*, suddenly attacked the Gothic infantry and boats. The Ostrogoths retired from the field following extensive fighting, having suffered heavy casualties in the battle.

Zosimus, *New History*, 4.35.1; Claudian, *de quarto consulatu Honorii*, 623–635.

Jenil River, AD 438, see Singilis River, AD 438.

Jerusalem, AD 70, March–September (First Jewish Revolt, Jewish Wars) – In an effort to bring the Jewish uprising to a decisive conclusion, the Roman general Titus, oldest son of Emperor Vespasianus, besieged the city of Jerusalem with an army of 70,000 men. This force included four legions: the *V Macedonica*, *X Fretensis* and *XII Fulminata*, all from Syria, and the *XV Deiotariana* from Alexandria, Egypt. Titus approached the city from the north with the main body of the Roman command and ordered the Fifth Legion to join him en route by way of Emmaus. The *Legio X* was instructed to converge on the city from the east via Jericho. Once Roman forces reached Jerusalem, two camps were established on Mount Scopus, north-east of the city. The first was a double camp housing the Twelfth and Fifteenth Legions, and the second, placed approximately 700 yards behind the main encampment, contained the *Legio V*. With the arrival of the Tenth Legion, a third *castrum* was situated on the Mount of Olives, south of the main Roman position and some 1,300 yards east of the city walls. After securing Mt. Scopus, Titus elected to completely clear and level the ground between Jerusalem and the Roman encampments, preparatory to the relocation of the Fifth, Twelfth and Fifteenth Legions to two new camps west and north-west of the city. Upon securing this new position, the Roman army concentrated its first assault on the western wall, north of the Hippicus tower. Covered by their own artillery, the three redeployed legions began construction on an earthen siege ramp. Simultaneous with this action, the *Legio X* initiated a diversionary bombardment from the slopes of the Mount of Olives using *ballistae* and *scorpions*. Once the works were completed, battering rams were brought into action against the wall, and artillery on the adjacent slopes moved nearer the city to provide suppressive fire in support of the besieging forces. The sustained nature of the attack compelled the Jewish defenders to launch a series of sallies to destroy

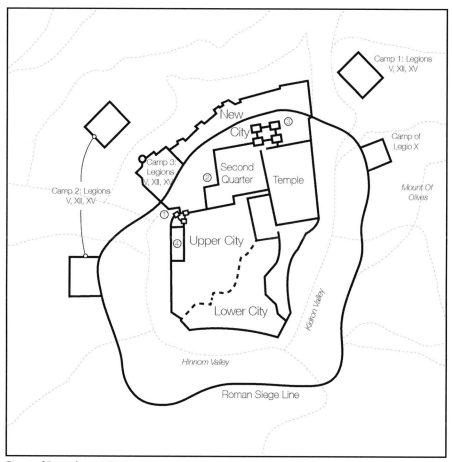

Siege of Jerusalem, AD 70

the siege works. These attacks were successfully turned by the cohorts, and a breach of the city defences was finally achieved on the fifteenth day of the assault. The acquisition of this line of defence by the Romans forced the Jews to abandon the northern suburb of Bezetha and retire to a second line of walls. Titus followed this retreat by establishing another camp inside the newly occupied zone, turning his siege machinery against the second wall. On 30 May, after five days, Roman forces succeeded in breaching the second line of fortifications, but were soon driven back by a counter-attack. This proved only a temporary setback. A subsequent Roman assault recaptured the second wall, forcing the Jewish defenders to retire to a third line of static fortifications and the fortress Antonia. Titus responded by dividing his legionary forces to simultaneously besiege the Antonia and the Upper City. The Fifth and Twelfth Legions were deployed to raise the fortress, and the Tenth and

Fifteenth concentrated on the reduction of the Citadel and the north-western defenses of the Upper City.

This effort experienced a catastrophic setback when Jewish sappers successfully undermined the earthworks erected against the Antonia, and a subsequent surprise attack destroyed the remaining ramp and siege machinery near the Citadel. These losses convinced Titus that a protracted siege was inevitable, and compelled him to initiate the construction of a wall of circumvallation some 5 miles (8km) in length to contain and isolate Jerusalem. From the main legionary base north-west of Middle Town, the wall extended eastward through the Bezetha suburb, across the Kedron Valley to the *castrum* of the Tenth Legion on the Mount of Olives. It then continued southward, following a line of hillcrests which lay to the east, south and west of the city before terminating at the Roman camp situated adjacent the Citadel. As further reinforcement, a series of thirteen forts were constructed along the length of the wall and garrisoned by auxiliary troops. Having completed this blockade in only three days, Titus now concentrated the full energy of the legions against the Antonia. After three weeks, a new ramp was completed and rams brought against the northern wall of the fortress. A sustained assault by siege engines breached the Antonia's defences, though a second wall, hastily erected inside by the defenders, temporarily stalled the Roman advance. This impasse was overcome through a covert night action by *auxilia* which secured the Antonia in Roman control and exposed the temple platform to assault. Two subsequent penetrations by auxiliary forces were driven back from the temple area by Jewish counter-charges. Because the large containing walls of the temple severely limited access to the platform, Titus was unable to inject troops *en masse* into the temple perimeter. In order to facilitate a massive assault, the Romans levelled the fortress Antonia, permitting the legions access to the temple platform by means of a ramp extending through the north-west angle of the temple compound. A second ramp was constructed to reinforce the first, with two more erected on the western side of the temple opposite the northern and western porticoes. When all was in readiness, a final decisive attack by Roman infantry and mounted elements completely shattered Jewish resistance in the temple area, the inner court and sanctuary being destroyed in the final conflagration. Following the destruction of the temple, the Lower City was reduced. The Romans then systematically sacked and destroyed all of Jerusalem.

Flavius Josephus, *The Jewish War*, 5.39–7.4.

Jotopata, AD 67, June–July (First Jewish Revolt, Jewish Wars) – As part of the Roman campaign to suppress an uprising in Judaea, the Roman general Vespasianus besieged the Galilean fortress of Jotopata in June of AD 67. Having previously received the surrender of the city of Sepphoris, reduced by force the community of Gabara and devastated the Galilean countryside, Roman forces moved into the vicinity of Jotapata. A blockade of the town was secured by an advance force of 1,000 cavalry, under the tribune Placidus and decurion Aebutius, before Vespasian began a more thorough investment with a Roman army of some 55,000 men. This force included three legions – the *XV Apollinaris* from Alexandria, Egypt, the *V Macedonica* and *X Fretensis* – and a sizeable contingent of auxiliary troops. The defence of the fortress was directed by the Jewish general Joseph ben Matthias (Flavius Josephus). Upon arrival at Jotapata, Vespasian deployed the legions and cavalry in a thorough cordon around the city. This action was soon followed by a series of unsuccessful assaults against the city's ramparts over a five-day period. Unable to take Jotapata through a general offensive, Vespasian then ordered a concentrated attack on the northern face of the city's defences using siege machinery. This effort devolved into a protracted siege, which was capably stalled by the Jewish garrison before legionary forces finally achieved a breach. Having now secured a means of ingress, Roman cohorts initiated an assault which was decisively repulsed with great loss, forcing Vespasian to temporarily resume the siege. Finally, after forty-six days, a pre-dawn surprise attack led by elements of the *Legio XV* penetrated the city's defences. Jewish resistance quickly collapsed. Jotapata was thoroughly sacked and destroyed in the occupation which followed. Of the city's population, 40,000 were put to the sword.

Flavius Josephus, *The Jewish War*, 3. 141–339.

Kalkrieser Berg, AD 9, see Teutoburg Forest, AD 9.

Kalkriese Hill, AD 9, see Teutoburg Forest, AD 9.

Krefeld, AD 69, see Gelduba, AD 69.

Lake Benacus, AD 268, November – In the early autumn, thousands of Alamanni warriors crossed the Alps through the Brenner Pass and threatened the Padus (Po) Valley with devastation. Within a short time, a legionary army under the leadership of Emperor Claudius II moved against the invaders in an attempt to block their further penetration into Italy. Some 65 miles (104km) east of Mediolanum (Milan), near Lake Benacus (Lake Garda), the Romans delivered a devastating defeat to the German army. Half of the Alamanni died in the fighting and the survivors fled north to their homelands.

Anonymous (Sextus Aurelius Victor), *Epitome of the Emperors*, 34.2 (T. Banchich, trans.).

Lake Briantia, AD 355 – After choosing to remain with a portion of the army in southern Raetia on the Plains of Cantini (near modern Bellinzona), Emperor Constantius II dispatched the rest of his legions and cavalry against the Alamannic Lentienses, a tribe responsible for repeated raids across the

Roman frontier. The *magister equitum*, Arbetio, commanded this second Roman force. As the deployed legions approached Lake Briantia (Lake Constance) from the south, the general failed to properly dispatch scouts ahead of his advancing column, permitting a substantial band of German warriors to surprise and overwhelm the entire Roman command near the shores of the lake. The flower of the army, including ten tribunes, fell in the ambuscade, and only Arbetio and a remnant of his men managed to escape the carnage. The following day, the Lentienses moved against the Roman encampment with apparent impunity, as the majority of the troops inside feared to again offer battle. While the Germans continued to assail the *castrum*, they were suddenly attacked by a detachment of Roman *scutarii* from within the camp. Though bold in execution, this modest cavalry sortie was soon spent and in danger of failure when another contingent of Romans unexpectedly launched a second assault against the massed ranks of the Lentienses. Within a short time, a series of melees involving both veteran and elite Roman units, cavalry and infantry, threw the entire German force into confusion. Emboldened by their comrades' actions, and observing the resulting disorder, the remainder of the Roman army soon sallied from the camp to aid in the fighting. In the general struggle which followed, the Romans largely destroyed the German horde.

Ammianus Marcellinus, *Res Gestae*, 15.4.1–13.

Langres, AD 298, see Lingonae, AD 298.

Laureate, AD 549 (Gothic War, Wars of Justinian I) – After capturing the Dalmatian coastal towns of Mouicurumn and Laureate, an Ostrogothic army led by Indulf, a former guardsman of Belisarius, engaged a Roman force under command of the general Claudian. Having arrived aboard a small fleet of *dromons* from the nearby port city of Salonae, the Romans attempted to defeat and drive off the Goths, but were instead thoroughly beaten and put to flight. Indulf and his troops thereafter sacked the harbour town and captured a number of abandoned Roman cargo vessels transporting grain and other provisions for the army.

Procopius of Caesarea, *History of the Wars* (*The Gothic War*), 7.35.23–30.

Leptis Magna, AD 543 – Angered by the treacherous murder of seventy-nine of their brethren while in Leptis Magna during a parley with Sergius, the Roman *dux Tripolitaniae*, the powerful Leuatha tribe of Tripolitania assembled a large army outside the city. In response, the Romans confronted the Leuathae in an engagement that resulted in significant battlefield losses for the Moorish tribe. Afterward, the Roman army plundered the Moors' encampment and enslaved a large number of women and children.

Procopius of Caesarea, *History of the Wars* (*The Vandalic War*), 4.21.12–14.

Licus River, AD 278 – Near the Licus (Lech) River, a tributary of the Ister (Danube) River in the province of Rhaetia, a Roman army under Emperor Probus intercepted a numerically larger force of Vandals and Burgundians raiding into imperial territory. While the two armies lay on opposite banks, the emperor provoked the barbarians to battle in an attempt to divide them by drawing a portion of the army across the river. A sizeable body of German warriors answered the challenge by rashly fording the Licus in an effort to engage the Romans. This action permitted the legions sufficient time to concentrate their assault against the approaching detachment before it could properly leave the water and assemble on open ground. In the ensuing struggle, the Romans routed the disorganized formation, forcing those Germans still across the Licus to sue for peace. The emperor granted the request, but shortly afterward the enemy violated the provisions of the treaty, compelling Probus to launch a second, more devastating attack which badly defeated the German host.

Zosimus, *New History*, 1.68.

Lingonae, AD 298 – While outside Lingonae (Langres) in eastern Gaul, the *Caesar* Constantius Chlorus and his army were forced to take refuge in the city by the sudden onset of the Alamanni. Because the city's gates were closed in fear of an impending attack, Constantius only gained entry into Lingonae after being lifted over the wall by a rope. He then rallied his army and launched an attack against the German tribesmen. Within six hours, the Romans caused some 60,000 Alamanni casualties.

Eutropius, *Abridgement of Roman History*, 9.23; John Zonaras, *Epitome of Histories*, 7.31; Theophanes, *AM* 5788, p.8.4–13.

Lingones, AD 298, see Lingonae, AD 298.

Lippe, 11 BC, see Arbalo, 11 BC.

Locus Castorum, AD 69 (Year of the Four Emperors, Roman Civil Wars) – The death of Roman Emperor Nero in the summer of AD 68 proved the catalyst for a violent power struggle in the Empire that eventually pitted various Roman legions against one another in open civil war. Following the demise of the Julio-Claudian dynasty, Servius Sulpicius Galba briefly served as emperor from June of AD 68 until the following January, before his assassination again plunged the Empire into chaos. Two other contenders now openly sought the emperorship: Marcus Salvius Otho, the former governor of Lusitania, and Aulus Vitellius, governor of *Germania Inferior* (Lower Germany). The contest between these two pretenders was ultimately decided in the Po Valley of northern Italy. The first clash occurred at Locus Castorum, a location some 12 miles (19.3km) from the town of Cremona.

Vitellian forces encountered an Othonian army led by the general Suetonius Paulinus. With the approach of Otho's troops, the *legatus* Aulus Caecina Alienus prepared an ambuscade for the enemy. Deploying auxiliary troops in some woods near the road, he sent his cavalry with instructions to provoke an engagement and then feign retreat in order to draw the Othonians into the trap. The opposing generals soon learned of the intended ambush and approached the location with caution, though still intent on pursuing battle. Paulinus immediately assumed command of the infantry, while Marius Celsus led the cavalry. Before reaching the location of Caecina, Otho's commanders assembled their army into battle formation. On the left flank, they positioned a vexillation of the *Legio XIII Gemina*, four cohorts of auxiliary infantry and 500 auxiliary cavalry. Opposite these troops, on the right flank, were arrayed the *Legio I Adiutrix*, a pair of auxiliary infantry cohorts and 500 horse. In the centre, spanning the road, were three praetorian cohorts. To the rear, Paulinus stationed a reserve of 1,000 Praetorian and auxiliary cavalry. As the Othonians advanced, a portion of the Vitellian line broke and fled. Celsus suspected a trick, and in turn initiated a feigned withdrawal which lured some of the enemy from cover. Caecina's troops gave chase and quickly found themselves constrained by legionary cohorts to their front and auxiliary infantry on the flanks. Before they could properly react, the prompt arrival of Celsus' cavalry closed any avenue of retreat toward Cremona. While the two sides faced one another, Paulinus paused long enough to redress his line and formulate a plan of attack. The delay offered Caecina's men opportunity to seek the relative safety of nearby vineyards and a small grove of woods. When the Othonian army was properly arrayed, Paulinus ordered his battle line to charge. The attack proved irresistible. Even with the piecemeal arrival of reinforcements, the auxiliary cohorts of Caecina were flushed from the tangle of vines and tree cover and completely routed. The defeated remnants of the army thereafter retreated to Cremona.

Publius Cornelius Tacitus, *The Histories*, 2.24–26; Caius Suetonius Tranquillus, *Otho*, 9.

Long Bridges, AD 15 (German War) – Having buried the remains of the three Roman legions destroyed in the disastrous defeat of Publius Quinctilius Varus at the Teutoburg Forest in AD 9, the army of Germanicus Caesar briefly pursued the German forces of Arminius, the architect of the victory six years earlier. Unable to achieve more than limited contact with the enemy, the Roman general finally elected to withdraw his forces to the Ems River. Transporting four legions out of the theatre by ships, Germanicus ordered a portion of the cavalry to return to the Rhenus (Rhine) River, following the North Sea coast. The remaining four legions, under the command of Aulus Caecina Severus, were to march overland by way of a narrow causeway called the Long Bridges, constructed years earlier by a Roman army under Lucius

Domitius Ahenobarbus. Surrounding the narrow land bridge was a vast bog, made more treacherous by intersecting streams and huge stands of forest on the slopes beyond. These woods were now occupied by heavy concentrations of Germans, who had already reached the location by forced marches in hopes of ambushing the approaching legions. On reaching the site, Caecina found portions of the causeway in need of repair, so elected to establish his camp before proceeding with any refurbishment. As a precaution he deployed a screen of troops for protection and then set parties to work reconstructing the roadway. These efforts compelled the Germans to initiate attacks against the Roman position. These continued throughout the day and only ended with the arrival of dusk. That night, the enemy flooded some of the recently completed work by diverting the flow of streams from their courses in the surrounding hills. This setback forced the engineering crews to redouble their labour the next day. In the meantime, recognizing the need to contain Arminius' forces in the woods until the wounded and heavier-laden troops in his column could pass, Caecina seized a narrow strip of level ground between the hills and swamp that was of sufficient size to permit the army to assemble into battle formation. He then posted the *Legio V* on the right flank and the *Legio XXI* on the left, while the *Legio I* served as the vanguard. The *Legio XX* was deployed to protect the rear. With this screen in place, Caecina hoped to move the more cumbersome elements of his army under cover of darkness, but daylight revealed the Roman position to be dangerously compromised. At dawn, the Fifth and Twenty-first Legions deserted their assigned stations

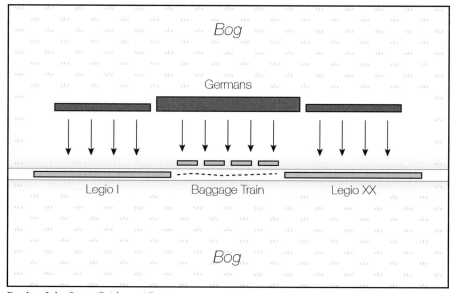

Battle of the Long Bridges, AD 15

and withdrew to a plain beyond the swamp, an action which jeopardized the integrity of the entire legionary formation. Equally serious, the army's heavy baggage was badly mired in mud, and the attending detachments of men and surrounding units were in disarray. Seeing the Romans' state, the Germans attacked. In the subsequent struggle, the muddy terrain badly hampered the legions' effectiveness on the battlefield, and the army was only able to recover the situation after the enemy abandoned the engagement to collect spoils. That evening, the exhausted cohorts, shaken by the day's action and made restless by the unseen presence of their enemy, were briefly panicked to the point of flight by an incident in the camp; but Caecina, with the aid of his tribunes and centurions, managed to recover the situation and rally the men's spirits in preparation for the coming battle. The following day, Arminius launched an assault against the Roman encampment. Anticipating an easy victory over a demoralized foe, the Germans reeled under an unexpected sortie by the reinvigorated legions. In the engagement which followed, the Roman army largely destroyed the force set against it.

Publius Cornelius Tacitus, *Annals*, 1.62–68.

Lugdunum, AD 197, 19 February (Roman Civil Wars, Year of the Five Emperors) – The ongoing struggle between Roman Emperor Lucius Septimius Severus and his rival Clodius Albinus reached a climax in southern Gaul on a plain north of the city of Lugdunum (Lyons). Because of the anticipated significance of the coming engagement, both leaders arrived at the head of massive armies numbering some 150,000 men each. Once the battle began, Albanus' left wing was the first to be defeated and driven from the field. At the same time, the right wing initiated a feint in an effort to compel Severus' men to counter-charge into a trap of concealed trenches and pits constructed immediately in front of Albinus' line. The ruse worked, and the leading rank of attackers stumbled into the excavations in a cascade of men and horses. In the unexpected confusion, the rearward ranks were suddenly pressed back into a natural ravine by the recoil of those seeking to avoid danger ahead. While these contingents were struggling to extricate themselves from the chaos between the ravine and trenches, they were suddenly exposed to devastating volleys of missiles and arrows from Albinus' archers and light infantry. Witnessing this struggle from another part of the field, Severus attempted to relieve the imperiled men with reinforcements of Praetorian Guardsmen, yet the elite body was almost destroyed when it became embroiled in the confrontation. Overwhelmed, the defeated wing began to retreat in disorder but was stopped when the emperor rode forward and successfully rallied the fugitives, who then turned to again face the enemy. In the clash which followed, the reconstituted line of Severan troops succeeded in routing their pursuers. As the legions of Albinus began to flee the fighting, they were immediately charged from one side by fresh cavalry under the command of Severus' lieutenant, Maecius Laetus. This unexpected attack assured victory. Albinus shortly thereafter committed suicide. Severus permitted his army to sack Lugdunum in the wake of the battle. Both armies suffered thousands of casualties in what proved to be not only a truly historic engagement, but one of the bloodiest fought in recent generations.

> Dio Cassius, *Roman History*, 76.6; Herodian, *Roman History*, 3.7.1–8; Eutropius, *Abridgement of Roman History*, 8.18; *Scriptores Historiae Augustae* (*Septimius Severus*), 11.1–7.

Lupia River, 11 BC, see Arbalo, 11 BC.

Main River, 9 BC, see Moenus River, 9 BC.

Maidens' Meadow, AD 16, see Idistaviso, AD 16.

Maiozamalcha, AD 363 (Persian Wars) – On reaching the Tigris River, Roman Emperor Julian ordered the construction of bridges in order to permit the army to cross over and lay siege to the Sassanid fortress of Maiozamalcha. Once imperial troops surrounded the city, the infantry began a general assault, but the heavily fortified battlements, rugged terrain and precipitous cliffs in the immediate area made the army's efforts largely futile. In addition, the Persian defenders offered stiff resistance while refusing to be drawn into open battle. After repeated attacks failed to breach the city's defences, Roman sappers were finally able to successfully mine the walls in preparation for a surprise assault. Following the completion of this work, Julian directed a night action against two sides of Maiozamalcha's defences as a diversion. Once battle was joined on the walls, a select force of soldiers secretly entered the city through the excavated tunnels and overwhelmed the watch. Shortly thereafter, the Romans gained entrance and thoroughly sacked the fortress, killing most of the inhabitants.

> Ammianus Marcellinus, *Res Gestae*, 24.4.1–25.

Mammes, AD 534 (Moorish War, Wars of Justinian I) – Shortly after his arrival in North Africa, the Roman general Solomon led an army from Carthage in an effort to stop the widespread depredations caused by Moorish tribes in the provinces of Byzacium and Numidia. At a place called Mammes in the mountainous border region of Mauretania, the imperial army encountered a force of tribesmen led by the chieftains Coutzinas, Esdilasas, Iourphouthes and Medisinissas. The Moors awaited the enemy on a small plain near the foothills of the mountains, their camels formed into a large defensive circle and all baggage and noncombatants gathered inside. With the Roman army in battle array, the Moors opened the engagement. As the armies drew together, Solomon's entire formation was quickly thrown into disorder by his own cavalry, whose horses abruptly panicked on first encountering the enemy's camels. The situation threatened to completely undo Roman resistance. The Moors persisted in their effort to press home the assault, even as the imperial units desperately worked to reconstitute their battle line. As the two sides settled into a protracted struggle, Solomon ordered a portion of his cavalry to dismount and reinforce the flagging infantry. He then led some 500 men in an attack on the Moorish rear. The Romans killed about 200 camels in order to breach enemy's defences and then penetrated into the vulnerable centre of the circle. Thrown into confusion by this sudden assault from an unexpected quarter, all Moorish resistance eroded. Approximately 10,000 Moors died in the fighting.

Procopius of Caesarea, *History of the Wars* (*The Vandalic War*), 4.11.14–56.

Maranga, AD 363, 22 June (Persian Wars) – After choosing to abandon the siege of Ctesiphon (Teq-e Kasara), Emperor Julian and a sizeable Roman army withdrew northward following the Tigris River toward Corduene. For several days during the march the Romans repeatedly skirmished with Persian elements before finally engaging a large enemy force in the district of Maranga, under the command of the Sassanid cavalry general Merena. The Persians assembled for battle, deploying formations of heavily armoured *cataphractarii* and mounted archers in the front line, supported from behind by a contingent of armoured war elephants. Julian arranged his legions and squadrons of cavalry facing the enemy in a concave formation, with the wings extending toward the Persian line. As the Romans advanced to within range of the opposing archers, the cohorts increased their speed and quickly closed with the Persian ranks in an effort to diminish the effect of the enemy's missiles. Once the two lines joined together, the fighting rapidly degenerated into a fierce struggle that lasted until the legions were finally able to disrupt the opposing ranks. As Merena's forces began to retreat from the field, the Romans were slowed in their pursuit by flights of arrows fired by Persian bowmen in an attempt to cover the withdrawal. Following the signal for recall, Julian's army ended its chase, the Persians having suffered the preponderance of casualties during the day's action.

Ammianus Marcellinus, *Res Gestae*, 25.1.1–19; Zosimus, *New History*, 3.27–28.2.

Marcianopolis, AD 376 – Poorly treated by Roman authorities and suffering from famine, the Theruingi – a Gothic tribe recently permitted by Emperor Valens to enter Thrace and settle inside the borders of the Empire – rose in revolt. A Roman army under the general Lupicinus intercepted the Goths 9 miles (14.4km) from the city of Marcianopolis (Devnya). Imperial forces were largely destroyed in the battle which followed. Lupicinus fled the field before the fighting ended.

Ammianus Marcellinus, *Res Gestae*, 31.5.9.

Mardia, AD 316, see Plains of Mardia, AD 316.

Mardis, AD 316, see Plains of Mardia, AD 316.

Margum, AD 285, see Margus River, AD 285.

Margus River, AD 285, May – The murder of Emperor Numerian by the *Praefectus praetorio*, Arrius Aper, again threw the leadership of the Roman state into jeopardy. His death left his older brother and co-emperor, Marcus Aurelius Carinus, the sole ruler of the Empire. The Eastern legions soon challenged this state of affairs when they proclaimed the general Diocles (Emperor Diocletian) the Eastern emperor to replace the deceased Numerian. Carinus, who was in Italy at the time, rejected this declaration and almost immediately moved his armies eastward to confront the pretender. The ensuing battle occurred in *Moesia Superior* (Upper Moesia), between the towns of Viminacium (Kostolacz) and Aureus Mons (Oresac), near the confluence of the Margus (Morava) and Ister (Danube) rivers. Carinus, who possessed the larger army, was on the verge of winning the struggle when his troops turned against him. He was slain by a tribune before the fighting ended.

> Eutropius, *Abridgement of Roman History*, 9.20; *Scriptores Historiae Augustae* (*Carus, Carinus, Numerian*), 18.1–2; Anonymous (Sextus Aurelius Victor), *Epitome of the Emperors*, 38.8 (T. Banchich, trans.); Sextus Aurelius Victor, *Liber de Caesaribus*, 39.

Marosch, AD 101, see Tapae, AD 101.

Marta, AD 547, see Plain of Gallica, AD 547.

Campus Mardiensis, AD 316, see Plain of Mardia, AD 316.

Masada, AD 73 (First Jewish Revolt, Jewish Wars) – Following the death of the *legatus* Licilius Bassus, the general Flavius Silva succeeded him as *procurator* of Judaea. A significant task still left to the Roman governor of the province was the reduction of Masada, a fortress built on a remote mountain plateau above the Judaean desert. After the earlier capture of the Jewish stronghold at Machaerus east of Lake Asphaltitis (Dead Sea), only Masada remained beyond Roman authority. By the spring of AD 73, the Jewish rebel Elazar ben Ya'ir and a sizeable band of *sacarii*, an extremist offshoot of the Zealots, controlled Masada, which was situated high in the mountains to the immediate south-west of the lake. In the early months of the year, Silva set out with his army to erase this last show of native defiance arising from the Jewish rebellion which began seven years earlier. The core of the Roman military forces employed on the campaign was the *Legio X Fretensis*, a veteran legion of the previous years' fighting. The elevation of Masada and the rugged nature of the terrain surrounding the site demanded that the legion first construct a wall around the base of the mountain to isolate the inhabitants from any possibility of receiving outside aid or escaping. The army then erected a

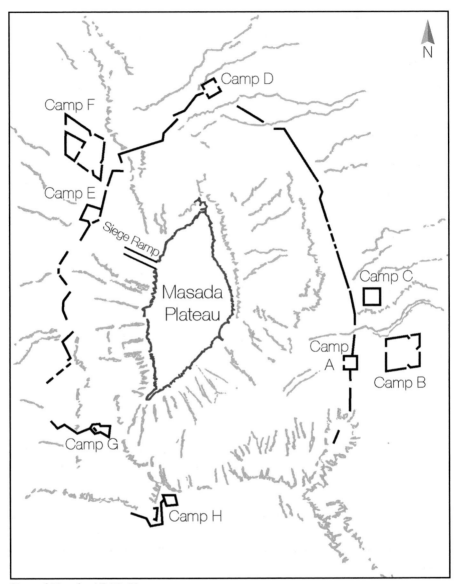

Siege of Masada, AD 72–73

large earthen siege ramp atop a spur of ground on the western side of the plateau. The ramp permitted Silva to raise the army's siege engines to a height sufficient to breach the fortress walls. Months of labour resulted in the completion of both the ramp and an accompanying siege tower. The Romans then subjected the fortress' defences to a battering ram. The wall was penetrated in late April or early May, but a hastily constructed secondary wall of timber temporarily blocked the legionaries' access to the citadel's compound. While the Jewish defenders retreated behind this makeshift barrier, Silva delayed the final assault for a day in order to destroy the wooden structure by fire. On the last morning of the siege, the cohorts finally broke through to the interior of fortress. Once inside they found only hundreds of dead bodies. After a search of the site, the soldiers discovered seven survivors: two women and five children. The remaining 960 Jews perished in a mass suicide.

Flavius Josephus, *The Jewish War*, 7.8–9.

Maurica, AD 451, see Catalunian Plains, AD 451.

Campus Mauriacus, AD 366, see Catalunian Plains, AD 366.

Campus Mauriacus, AD 451, see Catalunian Plains, AD 451.

Mediolanum, AD 259 – A confederation of German tribes called the Alamanni crossed the Alps and descended into the Padus (Po) Valley, invading as far south as the city of Ravenna. After ravaging northern Italy, the Germans marched against the city of Rome, but were forced to abandon their assault following a determined defence by a makeshift force of Roman soldiers and hastily conscripted plebeians. The invaders then withdrew northward. Near the city of Mediolanum (Milan), a 10,000-man Roman army under the command of Emperor Gallienus intercepted the Germans and delivered a shattering defeat.

John Zonaras, *Epitome of Histories*, 12.24.

Mediolanum, AD 268 – Soon after defeating the Goths at the Battle of Naissius in Moesia, Roman Emperor Gallienus faced a revolt led by his once loyal cavalry commander, Manius Acilius Aureolus, who was presently charged with defending the Italian peninsula against the usurper Postumus. Returning to Italy, the emperor confronted his rebellious lieutenant at Pons Aureoli (Pontiruolo) on the Addua (Adda) River. Aureolus' forces lost the battle and withdrew to the city of Mediolanum (Milan), some 20 miles (32km) to the south-west. Gallienus went in pursuit and promptly subjected the city to siege, but was assassinated in a *coup* before he could force the capitulation of Aureolus.

Scriptores Historiae Augustae (*Gallieni Duo*), 14.6–9; Scriptores Historiae Augustae (*Tyranni Triginta*) 'Aureolus', 11.4; Anonymous (Sextus Aurelius Victor), *Epitome of the Emperors*, 33.2 (T. Banchich, trans.); Zosimus, *New History*, 1.40–41; John Zonaras, *Epitome of Histories*, 12.25; Aurelius Victor and SHA *Tyranni Triginta* differ in the circumstances of Aureolus' death.

Medway River, AD 43 (Invasion of Britannia) – The arrival of a Roman invasion force in south-eastern Britannia heralded the beginning of a protracted campaign to reduce the southern portions of the island to imperial authority. As commander of the expedition, Aulus Plautius led a substantial army that included four legions: the *Legio XIV Gemina*, *Legio XX Valeria Victrix*, *Legio II Augusta* and *Legio IX Hispana*. Anticipating the possibility of native opposition, the Romans sailed from Gaul in three divisions and landed without incident along the Kentish coast. Those Celtic tribes that did not immediately ally with the Romans joined together under the leadership of two brothers, Caratacus and Togodumnus, who were members of the powerful Catuvellauni. Plautius defeated the enemy in two preliminary engagements before advancing further into the interior with the intention of provoking a major action. The Celts withdrew to the western bank of the River Medway, believing the Romans would not attempt a crossing without the aid of a bridge. Upon reaching the river, Plautius ordered detachments of *auxilia* to the opposite shore. The soldiers swam the river in full armour. Once these elements of light infantry were successfully across, the Roman commander dispatched the Second Legion with its general Titus Flavius Vespasianus. Fighting immediately erupted between the two sides, but the Romans were unable to achieve a victory before nightfall ended the struggle. The battle resumed the following day. Its outcome remained uncertain until legionary cohorts under Gnaeus Hosidius Geta were able to decisively defeat the enemy and put them to flight. Afterwards, the Celts retired to the north-west, crossing the Thames River at low tide. For his efforts, Geta was later accorded the rare honour of the *ornamenta triumphalia*, the Roman triumph.

Dio Cassius, *Roman History*, 60.19–20; Eutropius, *Abridgement of Roman History*, 7.13; Caius Suetonius Tranquillus (Suetonius), *Vespasian*, 4.

Melabasa, AD 527, August (Persian Wars, Wars of Justinian I) – Downstream from Amida, a Roman force approached the Melabasa Mountains for the purpose of constructing a fortress outpost in the area. The effort was decisively checked by a Persian army under Gadar the Qadishite.

Chronicle of Pseudo-Zachariah Rhetor, 9.5a.

Membresa, AD 536 – During Eastertide, a revolt erupted in North Africa within the ranks of the Roman army. A variety of factors fuelled the mutiny, including the soldiers' dissatisfaction with the army's general, Solomon, who was appointed two years earlier as *magister militum per Africam* to replace the previous commander, Belisarius. Following a failed assassination plot against him, Solomon temporarily charged his generals with maintaining authority in Carthage, and then departed amidst the growing disorder and violence in the city to acquire reinforcements from Belisarius, who was at that time completing a successful campaign in Sicily. Solomon soon returned to Carthage in the company of the celebrated general to find the city under siege by 9,000 rebel troops under the leadership of a junior officer named Stotzas.

Word of Belisarius' arrival proved sufficient to compel the mutineers to lift the siege and retire from the city. The present crisis extinguished, the veteran general immediately assembled a loyal force of 2,000 men and went in pursuit of the insurrectionists. Some 40 miles (64km) west of Carthage, near the city of Membresa, Belisarius intercepted the rebels. Because of the lateness of the day, both armies encamped for the evening; the smaller force near the Bagradas River and the larger, commanded by Stotzas, on higher, more difficult terrain. The two sides entered into battle the following day. As the armies prepared to engage, the mutineers quickly found themselves handicapped by a strong wind blowing directly into their faces. Hampered by dust and unable to use its archers and javelineers to best effect, the rebel army attempted to manoeuvre toward the flank for better advantage, but was immediately subjected to an unexpected attack which shattered all unit cohesion. The intensity of Belisarius' assault forced the rebels to abandon the field in total disorder and retreat toward Numidia. Casualties on both sides proved relatively light, since the imperial troops did not offer pursuit.

Procopius of Caesarea, *History of the Wars* (*The Vandalic War*), 4.14.7–4.15.47.

Mercurium, AD 468, see Hermaeum Promontorium, AD 468.

Meshike, AD 244, see Misiche, AD 244

Metaurus River, AD 271, Winter – After the defeat of a Roman army near Placentia (Piacenza) by a large band of Alamanni and Juthungi, Emperor Aurelian resumed his pursuit of the German invaders as they continued to move further south into the Italian peninsula along the *Via Aemilia*. The two armies again clashed near the Umbrian coastal town of Fanum Fortunae (Fano) on the Adriatic Sea. Fought west of the town on the banks of the Metaurus (Metauro) River, the battle remained undecided until the legions were able to successfully trap the Germans against the river. Many of the tribesmen drowned during the struggle or in the effort to ford the waters. Remnants of the invaders fled northward in the hope of reaching their homelands across the Alps.

Anonymous (Sextus Aurelius Victor), *Epitome of the Emperors*, 35.2 (T. Banchich, trans.).

Milvian Bridge, AD 312, 28 October (Wars of Constantine I) – As the *Augustus* Constantine I approached Rome from the north along the *Via Flaminia*, his imperial rival Maxentius led an army northward some 6 miles (9.6km) from the city and offered battle at the village of Saxa Rubra, on the far bank of the Tiber River near the Milvian Bridge. When Constantine reached the crossing, his army encountered the divisions of Maxentius already positioned on the open plain in front of the stone bridge, their ranks astride the highway and extending to the river's edge. After pausing to arrange his forces,

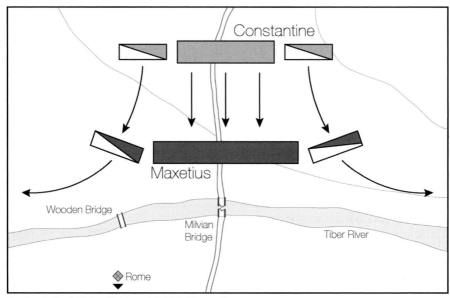

Battle of the Milvian Bridge, AD 312 (Phase 1)

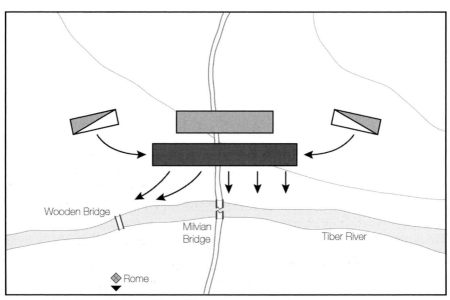

Battle of the Milvian Bridge, AD 312 (Phase 2)

Constantine opened the battle with a strong cavalry charge that threw the opposing mounted squadrons into complete disarray. The loss of cavalry on both wings suddenly exposed Maxentius' infantry formation to unrestrained assaults on its flanks. Once the opposing battle lines clashed, the contest quickly evolved into an intense struggle between the veteran legions and *auxilia palatina* of Constantine and the larger body of less experienced Roman and Italian troops from the city. Subjected to an unrelenting attack by both cavalry and infantry, and confined by the waters of the Tiber, Maxentius' army began to disintegrate. The defeat was temporarily prevented from becoming a total rout by the Praetorian Guard, who made a determined stand against the onslaught of Constantine's forces. While the remainder of the army rushed into the river or sought safety over the bridge, the Praetorians bravely faced their enemy and fell before the irresistible charges of heavy cavalry and mounted archers. In the crush to escape the carnage of the battlefield, thousands of men drowned in the flight across the river. Among the dead was the *Augustus* Maxentius.

Eusebius, *Ecclesiastical History*, 9.9.2–7; Eusebius, *Life of Constantine*, 1.38; Lucius Caecilius Firmianus Lactantius, *On the Deaths of the Persecutors*, 44; Zosimus, *New History*, 2.15–16; Anonymous, *Panegyrici Latini* [AD 313], 12.16–17; Anonymous Valesianus, Pars Prior, *The Lineage of the Emperor Constantine*, 4.12; Nazarius, *Panegyrici Latini* [AD 321], 4.28–30.1; John Zonaras, *Epitome of Histories*, 13.3; Sextus Aurelius Victor, *Liber De Caesaribus*, 40; Anonymous (Sextus Aurelius Victor), *Epitome of the Emperors*, 40.7 (T. Banchich, trans.).

Milvian Bridge, AD 538 (Gothic War, Wars of Justinian I) – Upon learning that a 2,000-man army under the Roman general John controlled the strategically important coastal city of Ariminum (Rimini), Vittigis and the Ostrogothic army immediately lifted the siege of Rome in preparation for withdrawing north-eastward across the Apennines toward Ravenna. After setting fire to their various encampments, the Goths began the long march northward along the *Via Flaminia*. The highway passed over the Tiber River at the Milvian Bridge immediately north of Rome. While the Goths were in the midst of crossing the river here, and one half of the great army still remained on the Latin side, Roman forces from the city suddenly struck the hapless column. Trapped between the river and the massed formations of Roman infantry and cavalry, the Goths fought desperately against the on-slaught but were eventually overwhelmed. As resistance collapsed, thousands of Vittigis' warriors died in the fighting, drowned in their attempt to ford the Tiber or were killed in the crush of humanity trying to flee across the bridge. Those Goths already on the far bank of the river could do little to aid their comrades while disaster unfolded. The Romans largely destroyed that por-tion of the Ostrogothic army still on the south bank of the river. Along with the remnants of the Gothic forces, Vittigis continued on to Ravenna. The Romans chose not pursue.

Procopius of Caesarea, *History of the Wars* (*The Gothic War*), 6.10.8–20.

Mindouos, AD 528 (Persian Wars, Wars of Justinian I) – In late summer of 527, Emperor Justinian ordered his general Belisarius, the Roman commander in Mesopotamia, to construct a fortress on the site of Tanurin in northern Mesopotamia. The proposed frontier outpost, situated between the strategically important Persian-controlled city of Nisibis and the formidable Roman fortress of Daras, almost immediately served as a provocative flash-point in the perennially unstable relationship between Byzantine Rome and Sassanid Persia. Despite Persian protests, building operations progressed un-abated at Tanurin, south of Nisibis, and at Mindouos, north of the city. Because of the acute danger of hostilities resulting from the forts' construction, Justinian deemed it prudent to dispatch two additional armies to the location under the Thracian generals Coutzes and Bouzes. The arrival of these reinforcements was soon matched by a commensurate build-up of Persian forces in the region, with the inevitable result that major fighting erupted between the two powers. In the ensuing struggle, the Roman army was almost completely destroyed at Tanurin while likewise suffering a defeat at Mindouos. Belisarius was able to escape with the cavalry, but most of the infantry were either killed in the clashes or captured. Shortly afterward, the Persian victors razed the partially completed fortress at Tanurin to the ground.

Procopius of Caesarea, *History of the Wars* (*The Persian War*), 1.13.1–8; *Chronicle of Pseudo-Zachariah Rhetor*, 9.2b. See also John Malalas 18.26.

Misiche, AD 244, Spring (Persian Wars, Wars against the Sassanids) – The Roman victory over Persian forces in Syria was followed by a campaign into Mesopotamia led by Emperor Gordianus III. In the region of Misiche, west of the Euphrates River, the expeditionary army encountered the Persians commanded by the Sassanid king, Shapur I. In the resulting battle, the Roman legions were defeated and forced to retire.

Res Gestae Divi Saporis, 3–4 (inscription at Naqsh-i Rustam); Michaels Rostovtzeff, 'Res Gestae Diviv Saporis and Dura'; *Berytus* 8:1 (1943), pp. 22–23.

Moenus River, 9 BC – As part of his continuing campaign to subjugate the German tribes between the Rhenus (Rhine) and Albis (Elbe) rivers, the Roman general Nero Claudius Drusus entered the lands of the Marcomanni, situated in the valley of the Moenus (Main) River. There he defeated the tribesmen in a decisive battle. Within the year the Marcomanni, under their new king Maroboduus, migrated eastward into the region of Boihaemum (Bohemia).

Lucius Annaeus Florus, *Epitomy*, 2.30.23; Strabo, *Geography*, 7.1.3.

Mona, AD 61, see Isle of Mona, AD 61.

Mons Colubrarius, AD 430, see Arelate, AD 430.

Mons Graupius, AD 84 – During his seventh year as Roman governor of Britannia, Caius Julius Agricola led his forces northward against the Caledonii and their allies in Scotland. After crossing the Firth of Forth, he moved through the valley of Strathmore, while simultaneously sending warships laden with additional troops north to reconnoitre the coastline as far as the Firth of Tay. After an initial engagement between Caledonian and Roman forces, Agricola advanced his column into the Grampians. At the same time, the Caledonii began to gather warriors in anticipation of a confrontation. Eventually some 30,000 men came together under the leadership of a capable chieftain named Calgacus. At a location north-west of the mouth of the Don River, the Romans and Caledonians clashed in a decisive battle. Agricola deployed his main battle line against the Caledonii and their allied tribesmen. Some 8,000 auxiliary infantry formed the Roman centre, with 3,000 cavalry posted on the wings. The legionary forces, numbering perhaps 15,000 men, assembled in front of their entrenched *castrum*. Facing the Roman line was the enemy formation, arrayed on high ground in a large convex crescent; the main van of warriors situated on the plain, with the remainder of the tribesmen drawn up on the slopes of the low hill. In an effort to avoid being outflanked by the enemy's superior numbers, Agricola lengthened the Roman front line, though the decision threatened to badly attenuate the ranks of his *auxilia*. The contest began with a series of chariot attacks by the Caledonii, followed by a mutual exchange of missiles. As the distance between the opposing

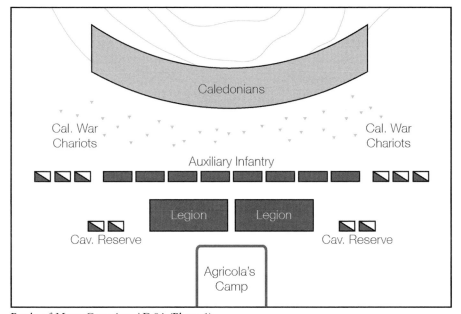

Battle of Mons Graupius, AD 84 (Phase 1)

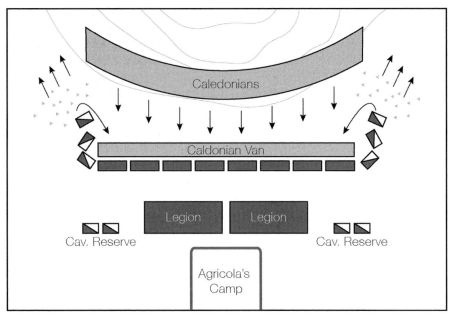

Battle of Mons Graupius, AD 84 (Phase 2)

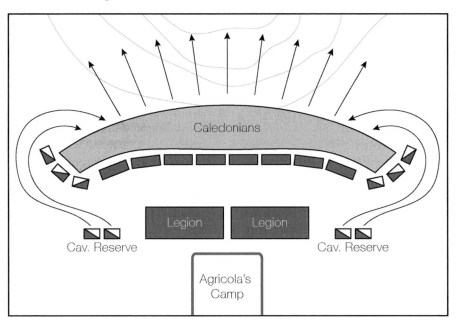

Battle of Mons Graupius, AD 84 (Phase 3)

lines narrowed, Agricola deployed his Batavian and Tungrian cohorts in an attempt to draw all of Calgacus' forces into a hand-to-hand struggle on level ground. Once the cohorts began to press their attack toward the hill, the remainder of the *auxilia* joined in the fighting. The intensity of the infantry battle steadily escalated until Calgacus was finally persuaded to commit the last of his reserves in an effort to envelop the Roman flank and rear. Anticipating such a move, Agricola sent four squadrons of cavalry in a fast sweep behind the enemy formation. The sudden attack disrupted the momentum of the barbarian counter-assault, and trapped the mass of warriors against the line of auxiliary infantry. Pressed from two sides, Caledonian resistance eventually collapsed. The resulting rout was total. Some of the fugitives briefly attempted to rally in a nearby stand of woods, but were driven from their cover and overwhelmed by Roman cavalry and *auxilia*. Nightfall finally put an end to the relentless pursuit. Approximately 10,000 Caledonii and their allies died in the battle, Agricola's legionary cohorts having never entered the day's action.

Publius Cornelius Tacitus, *Agricola*, 29, 35–37.

Mons Lactarius, AD 553, 1 October (Gothic War, Wars of Justinian I) – Following a protracted period of indecisive skirmishing between Ostrogothic and Roman armies on the banks of the Draco (Sarno) River near the Bay of Naples, the Gothic King Teias withdrew his army to the slopes of nearby Mons Lactarius (Monte Lettere). Temporarily protected from Roman attacks by the difficult terrain, the location nonetheless deprived the Goths of sufficient food supplies and soon forced them to take action. Descending the mountain, Teias assembled his army near the fortified encampment of the enemy and ordered his cavalry to dismount in preparation for the engagement. The Ostrogoths then advanced against the Roman position as a solid wall of infantry. The Romans likewise arrayed for battle, but elected to abandon their typical unit formation in order to permit the soldiers to repel the inevitable mass attack in whatever fashion the tactical circumstances of the moment demanded. Like their Gothic counterparts, the Roman cavalry also determined to fight on foot alongside the legionaries. The battle began in early morning and devolved into a furious trial of strength between the two armies. The fighting almost immediately focused around the Gothic leader and his personal retainers. With great battlefield skill, Teias resisted all attacks against his person throughout the morning, but was finally killed in the early afternoon by an enemy javelin. Despite the king's death, the engagement lasted until nightfall, when both armies decided to retire from the field. The following morning, the battle resumed with equal intensity and continued unabated until darkness again ended the contest. Undeterred by the savage struggle, the Romans confidently prepared for a third day of fighting, but the

Goths chose instead to send representatives to the Roman general Narses to conclude a peace settlement to the long war. As the main Ostrogothic army moved to abandon Italy, the victorious Romans advanced into the central portions of the peninsula and prepared to reduce by siege the last major Gothic garrisons at Cumae and Centumcellae.

Procopius of Caesarea, *History of the Wars* (*The Gothic War*), 8.35.1–33; Agathias, *The Histories*, 1.1.

Mons Piri, AD 368 – Because the Alamanni were again stirring up trouble, Emperor Valentinian I crossed the Main River at the head of a large army, which included Illyrian and Italian legions. When the Romans reached Solicinium (Schwetzingen), scouts reported the presence of the enemy atop Mons Piri (Heiligenberg). The emperor at once advanced cautiously to the base of the mountain and ordered the legions to prepare for battle, while he and a small party reconnoitred the terrain immediately around the enemy position. Following this survey, in which Valentinian at one point narrowly avoided capture, the army assembled into battle formation. Electing to ascend the mountain on a side other than the northern slope, which offered the most gentle approach to the summit and was therefore the most heavily defended, the legions pressed forward, led by two divisions of the elite *Scholae Palatinae*, the *scutarii* and *gentiles*. As the cohorts strove to climb the rugged, thicket-covered ground, they were met with heavy resistance; resulting in fierce hand-

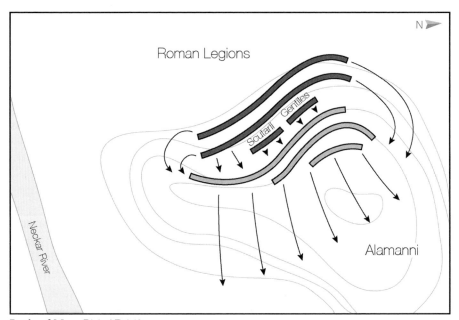

Battle of Mons Piri, AD 368

to-hand fighting. At last Valentinian extended the Roman line and enveloped both flanks of the Alamanni. This effort to encircle the Germans intensified the struggle, which lasted until the enemy formation was disrupted by an assault from the rear, precipitating a complete rout. As the German line collapsed in disorder, a reserve force led by the *comes* Sebastianus charged into the midst of the fugitives, devastating an exposed flank of the Germans and completely scattering all remaining resistance.

Ammianus Marcellinus, *Res Gestae*, 27.10.8–15.

Mons Seleucus, AD 353, August – At Mons Seleucus in Gallia Narbonensis, an army loyal to Roman Emperor Constantius II engaged forces commanded by the usurper, Flavius Popilius Magnentius. Magnentius' troops were completely routed in the resulting battle. With final defeat a certainty, Magnentius fled to the city of Lugdunum (Lyon) where he committed suicide.

Socrates Scholasticus, *Ecclesiastical History*, 2. 32; Anonymous (Sextus Aurelius Victor), *Epitome of the Emperors*, 42.6 (T. Banchich, trans.); John Zonaras, *Epitome of Histories*, 13.9. For an ancient visual reference to the location of Mons Seleucus, see the Antonine Itinerary.

Mount Bourgaon, AD 535 (Moorish War, Wars of Justinian I) – Undeterred by the Roman victory at Mammes the previous year, the Moors resumed their devastating raids into Byzacium. Once again assembling an army, the Roman general Solomon marched into the province with the intention of suppressing the tribal threat to the region. The Roman army discovered the enemy camp on Mount Bourgaon. Stung by their earlier defeat at Mammes, the Moors remained on the mountain, refusing to descend to level ground where the Roman cavalry could operate to best advantage. Toward late afternoon, Solomon resolved to dispatch the *excubitores*, an elite 300-man palace guard, and a detachment of 1,000 infantry to approach the mountain's eastern side and scale the more precipitous slopes under cover of darkness. The attempt was successful, and the following morning the Moors discovered that they were now trapped between Roman forces situated nearer the summit above them, and the larger formation approaching from below. The dire turn of circumstance inspired a sudden panic, which caused thousands of tribesmen to flee toward an adjacent vale and peak. Many were killed in the headlong press of humanity as all sought escape from the approaching Romans. By the end of the day some 50,000 Moors had perished in the flight.

Procopius of Caesarea, *History of the Wars* (*The Vandalic War*), 4.12.1–25.

Mount Melabason, AD 528, see Mindouos, AD 528.

Mount Pirus, AD 368, see Mons Piri, AD 368.

Mucellium, AD 542, Spring (Gothic War, Wars of Justinian I) – Embold-ened by his defeat of the Romans at the Anemo River near Faventia, Ostro-gothic King Totila sent an army south across the Apennine Mountains to attack the Tuscan community of Florentia (Florence) in north-western Italy. Once there, Gothic forces under the leadership of Ruderic, Vledas and Uliaris initiated a siege of the city, but were soon threatened by the approach of a large Roman army from Ravenna. The Goths promptly abandoned the assault and withdrew approximately 25 miles (40km) north to the valley of Mucellium (Mugello Valley) in the central Sieve River basin. When Roman forces eventually reached Florentia, the generals Bessas, Cyprian and John acquired additional soldiers from the local garrison and then turned north-ward to continue their pursuit of the Gothic army. As the Romans neared the entrance to the valley, John moved forward with the vanguard in a determined effort to make contact with the enemy ahead of the principal column of troops. This action alarmed the Goths, who abandoned their encampment in the valley and relocated to a nearby hill, where they awaited the arrival of the advancing army. In the struggle which followed, the final outcome remained bitterly contested for some time before a false report of John's death caused the Roman attack to flag. The demoralized vanguard was soon repulsed and began to retire toward the main body of Roman troops, which were arrayed in battle formation on the nearby plain. When the erroneous rumour of John's demise reached the assembled ranks of the army, the news disheartened the soldiers and undermined the resolve of Cyprian and Bessas to continue the engagement. What followed was a disorderly withdrawal that quickly degenerated into an uncontrolled flight as the Roman army lost all discipline and deserted the field, conceding victory to the Ostrogothic forces.

Procopius of Caesarea, *History of the Wars* (*The Gothic War*), 7.5.1–17.

Mulvian Bridge, AD 312, see Milvian Bridge, AD 312.

Mulvian Bridge, AD 538, see Milvian Bridge, AD 538.

Mursa, AD 259 – Ingenuus, the governor of Pannonia, led a rebellion in a bid for the imperial throne in the seventh year of the reign of Roman Emperor Gallienus. He was supported by the Roman legions stationed in both Pannonia and neighbouring Moesia. Near the city of Mursa (Osijek), situated on the south bank of the Dravus (Drava) River in Pannonia, an imperial army led by the emperor and veteran general Manius Acilius Aureolus defeated the pretender in battle. When all was lost, Ingenuus attempted to escape, but was captured and subsequently executed.

Scriptores Historiae Augustae (*Tyranni Triginta*) 'Ingenuus', 9.1–4; Eutropius, *Abridgement of Roman History*, 9.8.1; Anonymous (Sextus Aurelius Victor), *Epitome of the Emperors*, 33.2 (T. Banchich, trans.); John Zonaras, *Epitome of Histories*, 12.24; Paulus Orosius, *Seven Books of History against the Pagans*, 7.22.

Mursa, AD 351, 28 September – Near the Dravus (Drava) River in Pannonia, Emperor Constantius II defeated the usurper Flavius Popilius Magnentius in one of the most savage battles in Roman imperial history. After overrunning all of the lands near the Sava River, Magnentius attempted to capture Sirmium (Sremska Mitrovica), the capital of *Pannonia Inferior*. Lacking siege engines, he was repulsed by the inhabitants, who were joined by the local garrison. When Constantius learned that Sirmium was under attack, he immediately marched to the relief of the city. His approach persuaded Magnentius to withdraw to a position nearer the community of Mursa (Osijek) situated some 60 miles (96.5km) to the north-west on the southern bank of the Drava, where his army had access to the open plain beyond. As at Sirmium, lack of proper machinery denied him control of the city. Aware that the enemy was close at hand, Magnentius instead prepared an ambuscade from inside the local stadium using four companies of Celtae, but the plan was revealed to the emperor by the residents of Mursa. In response, Constantius dispatched a select detachment of archers and heavy infantry who trapped and destroyed the covert band. After this sharp but largely inconclusive skirmish, both armies withdrew to the adjacent plain, which offered each commander greater freedom to deploy troops to best advantage. Here, the two great armies finally clashed in a massive battle. The infantry of both armies were positioned in the centre, while the cavalry occupied the wings. When the battle opened, Constantius' forces on the left swept forward in a

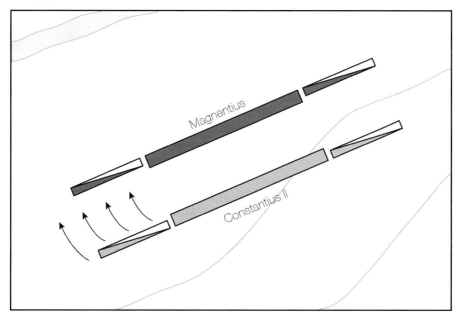

Battle of Mursa, AD 351

great envelopment which initially broke the enemy formation; but Magnentius' ranks soon recovered and the struggle continued unabated throughout the day and into the night. Finally, after hours of fighting, imperial forces succeeded in routing the divisions of Magnentius. Constantius' army slaughtered the defeated enemy in the pursuit which followed. Casualties on both sides were enormous, and included a number of high-ranking *legati*. Magnentius suffered 24,000 dead and wounded in the battle, and Constantius 30,000.

Zosimus, *New History*, 2.50.4–53.1; Eutropius, *Abridgement of Roman History*, 10.12; Anonymous (Sextus Aurelius Victor), *Epitome of the Emperors*, 42.4 (T. Banchich, trans.); Sextus Aurelius Victor, *Liber De Caesaribus*, 42; John Zonaras, *Epitome of Histories*, 13.8; Julian, *Oration I: Panegyric in Honour of Constantius*, 35D–37B.

Nacolia, AD 366, 26 May – At Nacolia (Seyyid el-Ghazi) in Phrygia, an army under Eastern Roman Emperor Valens engaged a sizeable force commanded by Procopius, a veteran general who proclaimed himself emperor the previous September while in Constantinople. As the two armies struggled to gain advantage on the battlefield, Agilo, a *magister militum* in the service of the usurper, suddenly switched sides at a critical moment in the contest and joined the emperor. His decision quickly turned the momentum of the battle against Procopius, as numerous troops also elected to abandon the fight and defect to Valens. This unforeseen turn of events soon forced Procopius to flee the field with the remnants of his army. The following day, he was betrayed by his soldiers and executed by order of the emperor shortly afterward.

Ammianus Marcellinus, *Res Gestae*, 26.9.7; Zosimus, *New History*, 4.8.3.

Naissus, AD 268 – After pillaging at length through the Balkans, a massive Gothic coalition army numbering perhaps 320,000 men marched into Moesia, where it clashed with a Roman army near Naissus (Nish), approximately 100 miles (161km) south of the Ister (Danube) River on the Nischava River. Both sides suffered heavy casualties before the Romans were able to trap the Goths in an ambuscade following a feigned retreat. The victory of Roman Emperor Gallienus proved complete. Gothic losses totalled some 50,000 dead and captured.

Zosimus, *New History*, 1.42–43, 45; *Scriptores Historiae Augustae* (*Claudius*), 1.6–12; *Scriptores Historiae Augustae* (*Gallieni Duo*), 13.

Narbo Martius, AD 436–439 – A Visigothic army under King Theodoric I besieged the city of Narbo Martius (Narbonne) on the south-eastern coast of Gaul. He was ultimately forced to withdraw following the arrival of the Roman general Litorius and a sizeable force of allied Huns.

Prosper of Aquitaine, *Chronicle*, c.1324, c.1326; Hydatius, *Chronicle*, 98 [Mom. 107], 101 [Mom. 110]; Sidonius Apollinaris, *Carmina*, 7.244ssq; Flavius Merobaudes, *panegyric*, frag. ii A 23 (or *pan.* i. 9, l. 23; *pan.* ii. 1. 16).

Narnia, AD 536 (Gothic War, Wars of Justinian I) – Faced with the approach of a large Ostrogothic army, the Roman general Belisarius ordered his commanders Constantinus and Bessas to garrison all of the Tuscan towns of strategic importance and then bring the remainder of their troops to his aid. While Bessas was in the process of securing the town of Narnia (Narni), some 40 miles (64km) north of Rome, his forces encountered a portion of the Gothic vanguard moving south along the *Via Flaminia*. After a sharp engagement, the Romans routed the enemy detachment and then deposited a garrison in the community before marching in support of forces in the capital.

Procopius of Caesarea, *History of the Wars* (*The Gothic War*), 5.17.1–6.

Nessos River, AD 267 – Departing the waters of the Lacus Maeotis (Sea of Azov) aboard 500 ships, the German Heruli crossed the Pontus Euxinus (Black Sea) and entered the mouth of the Ister (Danube) River in a significant invasion of Roman territory. The threat, though acute, could not be immediately addressed by the personal intervention of Emperor Gallienus since he was presently engaged in a war against Postumus. He therefore sent an army under the leadership of the eastern generals Kleodamus and Athenaeus. Despite the efforts of these commanders, the Heruli were able to penetrate into central Greece and the Peloponnesus, though their attempt to seize Athens ultimately failed. As the Germans retired northwards through Macedonia towards their homelands, they were met by a Roman army led by Gallienus near the Thracian frontier. The imperial divisions soundly defeated the Heruli on the banks of the Nessos (Nestos) River.

Scriptores Historiae Augustae (*Gallieni Duo*), 13; Georgios Synkellos (Syncellus), *Extract of Chronography*, *c.*467.

Nicaea, AD 194 (Roman Civil Wars, Year of the Five Emperors) – After defeating an army of the imperial challenger Caius Pescennius Niger near Cyzicus, the legions of Emperor Septimius Severus again engaged rival forces in the vicinity of Nicaea. The fighting occurred in the hill country between the port of Cius and the city of Nicaea, north-east of Lake Nicaea (Lake Iznik). The *legatus* Tiberius Claudius Candidus commanded the army of Severus, while Niger personally led his legions in the battle. The issue remained undecided for some time. The struggle initially turned to the advantage of Candidus, largely because his forces controlled higher ground; but the arrival of Niger to personally lead his troops in the fighting briefly shifted the engagement in favour of the Syrian legions. Finally, Candidus rallied his soldiers and they were able to turn the battle decisively in favour of the emperor. Only the onset of nightfall saved Niger from complete destruction. Afterward, the remnants of his tattered forces retreated south-eastward through Anatolia toward Antioch in Syria.

Dio Cassius, *Roman History*, 75.6.4–6; Herodian, *Roman History*, 3.2.10.

Nicopolis ad Istrum, AD 250 – Following reports of an invasion of Roman territory by a strong force of Goths under the leadership of King Kniva, Emperor Trajanus Decius left Rome and advanced into the province of Moesia with a strong army. In conjunction with the Gothic crossing of the Ister (Danube) River, the Carpi, a tribal people situated north of the Ister between the Hierasos (Sirat) and Porata (Pruth) rivers, penetrated into the Dacian provinces. With much of the eastern Danubian line ruptured, Decius dispatched a vanguard into the troubled region under the command of his son, *Caesar* Herennius Etruscus, and prepared to follow with the main body of troops. Once the Goths were in Roman territory, Kniva divided his army. While one division swept into the province of Thracia and besieged the city of Philippopolis (Plovdiv), a second column descended into Moesia. There, as a result of the diligent efforts of the local Roman governor Trebonianus Gallus, the invaders were forced to temporarily withdraw, allowing time for the *Caesar*'s reinforcements to arrive. Thwarted in his plan to sweep completely over the province, Kniva elected instead to invest the city of Nicopolis ad Istrum (Nikyup); but the attempt abruptly ended with the unexpected appearance of the Roman relief army. The resulting battle ended with a considerable Gothic defeat and forced Kniva to retreat after suffering heavy losses. The king then withdrew to Philippopolis.

> Sextus Aurelius Victor, *Liber De Caesaribus*, 29; Jordanes, *The Origins and Deeds of the Goths*, 101; Zosimus, *New History*, 1.23.

Nisibis, AD 217, Summer – Near the city of Nisibis in Mesopotamia, an army led by Parthian King Artabatus V clashed with the legions of Emperor Macrinus. Following a skirmish between opposing troops over control of a water source, the two armies assembled for battle. The Parthian host conisted of large formations of heavy cavalry – both *clibanarii* and *cataphracti* – light mounted bowmen and a contingent of armoured camel riders called *dromedarii*. Macrinus readied his army for battle across the plain: the legions deployed in the centre, with cavalry and Moorish troops placed on the flanks. Arrayed at intervals within the central formation were Moroccan *auxilia*. Once battle was joined, the Parthian heavy horse and mounted archers inflicted severe casualties on the Roman infantry, while the legionaries and light troops proved superior in all hand-to-hand action. As the contest wore on, the Romans found themselves increasingly at a disadvantage against the speed and manoeuvrability of the enemy cavalry. In an effort to disrupt these incessant attacks, the legions feigned retreat at one point so as to draw the horsemen onto ground littered with caltrops and other devices designed to cripple the horses. Fighting continued unabated until dusk. Battle resumed the next morning and lasted all day, but again ended at nightfall with no clear victor. On the third day, Artabatus attempted to use his superior numbers of

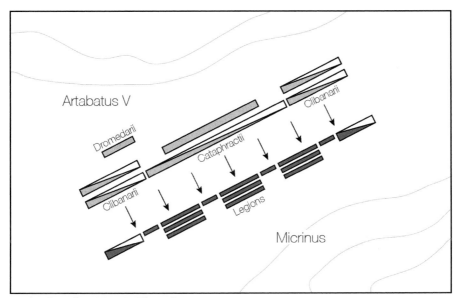

Battle of Nisibis, AD 217 (Phase 1)

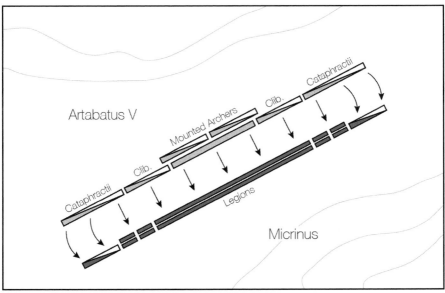

Battle of Nisibis, AD 217 (Phase 2)

cavalry to encircle the Roman formation by means of a double envelopment, but Macrinus extended his battle-line in order to thwart the Parthians' efforts. Toward late afternoon, the Roman emperor sent envoys to treat for peace, which was readily granted by the king. Artabatus afterward returned to Persia with his army, and Macrinus and his forces withdrew to the city of Antioch in Syria. To deter a resumption of hostilities, Macrinus presented the Parthian ruler with gifts amounting to 200 million sesterces.

Herodian, *Roman History*, 4.15.1–9; Dio Cassius, *Roman History*, 79.26.4–6, 27.1–2; *Scriptores Historiae Augustae* (*Opellius Macrinus*), 8.1–4.

Nisibis, AD 350 – During mid-April, Persian King Shapur II, aware that Roman Emperor Constantius II was distracted by imperial affairs in the west, launched a campaign into Roman Anatolia. His armies plundered the country-side and captured a number of outlying garrisons before finally besieging the city of Nisibis. Unable to breach the defences using conventional siege machinery, Shapur finally elected to divert the course of the Mygdonius (Jaghjaghah) River which flowed through the city. This exercise failed to force the population's capitulation. He next dammed the river and used water pressure from its sudden release to successfully collapse a portion of the walls. Now confident of victory, the king chose to delay the actual assault until the following day in order to rest his army. As his soldiers prepared to attack at dawn the next morning, Shapur discovered that residents of Nisibis had again fortified the location during the night by construction of a secondary wall. The Persians immediately resumed their investment but were ultimately forced to withdraw by late summer, having suffered several thousand casualties.

John Zonaras, *Epitome of Histories*, 13.7.

Novaesium, AD 69, December (Revolt of Civilis, Batavian Revolt) – During the Batavian Revolt of AD 69, a Roman army under the general Caius Dillius Vocula marched to the relief of the legionary fortress of Castra Vetera (Xanten) in the province of *Germania Inferior* (Lower Germany). After defeating an enemy force at Gelduba (Krefeld) and temporarily ending the siege at Castra Vetera, Vocula retraced his path through Gelduba before moving on to Novaesium (Neuss) some 13 miles (21km) to the south. Near this last town, German cavalry attacked the Roman column, which consisted of the *Legio XXII Primigenia*, *Legio I Germanica*, *Legio XVI Gallica*, detachments of the *Legio V Alaudae* and *Legio XV Primigenia*, and several auxiliary cohorts. The Romans defeated the enemy horsemen in the resulting engagement.

Publius Cornelius Tacitus, *Histories*, 4.36.

Noviodunum, AD 486 – In the fifth year of his reign, Merovingian King Clovis took the initial step in the consolidation of his overlordship among the Frankish and Gallic peoples. Gathering his military forces together, he moved against Syagrius, the *magister militum per Gallias*, and the last surviving repre-sentative of Roman authority in northern Gaul. The two armies met near the city of Noviodunum (Soissons), the seat of Roman authority in the region.

The battle ended in the crushing defeat of Syagrius, who quickly sought sanctuary in the Ostrogothic court of King Alaric at Toulouse. Fearing repercussions from the Merovingian ruling house should he elect to offer protection to his unwelcomed guest, the Gothic ruler promptly turned the visitor over to Frankish envoys. Clovis soon ordered the execution of Syagrius, thereby ending all vestiges of Roman political influence in the former province.

Gregory of Tours, *History of the Franks*, 2.18, 27.

Ocriculum, AD 413 – While imperial armies loyal to Western Roman Emperor Honorius were preoccupied with events in Gaul, Heraclianus, the *comes Africae*, initiated a revolt in North Africa and quickly proclaimed himself *Augustus*. He then threatened the Roman population with food shortages and famine by cutting off the supply of African grain to the city. This action was shortly followed by an invasion of Italy. Heraclianus assembled a large fleet and army in his province and sailed to the Italian peninsula with the intention of seizing the imperial throne. Near the Umbrian town of Ocriculum (Otricoli), some 42 miles (67.5km) north-east of Rome on the *Via Flaminia* leading to Ravenna, the invaders clashed with an imperial army led by general Marinus. Some 50,000 men died in a difficult struggle that ended with the defeat of Heraclianus. After the loss, the would-be usurper fled back to Carthage, but was subsequently assassinated by a band of soldiers.

Hydatius, *Chronicon*, 56; Paulus Orosius, *Seven Books of History against the Pagans*, 7.42; Zosimus, *New History*, 6.11.

Onoguris, AD 554 (Lazic War, Wars of Justinian I) – Near Archaeopolis (Nokalakevi), the primary city of the Lazi located on the banks of the Phasis (Rioni) River, a 50,000-man Roman army invested a Persian garrison at the fortress of Onoguris. While there, the Roman generals Rusticus and Buzes learned from a Persian captive that 3,000 cavalry reinforcements were expected from Mucheirisis. The Romans dispatched a detachment of 600 horsemen under the officers Dabragezas and Usigardus to intercept the relief column. The two sides clashed near Onoguris, and the Romans temporarily put their opponents to flight. When the Persians realized the inferior size of the attacking force, they quickly reformed their squadrons and responded with a strong counter-attack. The Romans fell back under the weight of the assault, resulting in both pursuers and fugitives reaching the Roman siege lines in total disarray. The chaos brought about by their swift and unexpected arrival caused wholesale confusion and panic among the Roman army, who, uncertain of the enemy's strength, fled the field. Observing all this from behind the defences of Onoguris, the beleaguered Persian garrison swept through the gates of the citadel and joined the chase. As the exodus of men reached the nearby Catharus River, the Roman cavalry easily escaped the onslaught, but thousands of their fellow infantrymen died in a desperate effort to cross a narrow bridge ahead of the charging Persian horsemen. Only a determined rearguard action by troops under Buzes slowed the enemy squadrons long enough to allow remnants of the Roman army to safely reach the opposite bank. After their victory, the Persians proceeded to plunder the Roman camp.

Agathias Scholasticos, *The Histories*, 3.5.6–3.7.

Pagyda River, AD 18 (Revolt of Tacfarinus) – At an outpost near the North African river of Pagyda, a band of nomadic warriors commanded by the Numidian rebel Tacfarinas, a leader of the Musulamian people and former Roman auxiliary soldier, attacked a Roman cohort. Decrius, the veteran commander of the Roman detachment, decided to engage the tribesmen on open ground and assembled his battle lines outside the encampment. When the Numidian horsemen charged the Roman position, the cohort immediately panicked and fled, leaving their officer to confront the attackers alone. Wounded in the chest and face, Decrius continued to fight until killed in the onslaught. The African *proconsul* Lucius Apronius ordered the unit punished by decimation because of their cowardice.

Publius Cornelius Tacitus, *Annals*, 3.20.

Palmyra, AD 272 (Palmyrene War, War against Zenobia) – The Roman victories at Emesa and Immae crippled the ability of Palmyrene Queen Zenobia to resist an assault of her capital by the armies of Emperor Aurelian. Imperial legions began the investment of the city once outside the walls of Palmyra. The emperor appealed to Zenobia to surrender following a protracted siege, but she rejected his request. To force the queen's capitulation, Aurelian employed both military force and diplomacy to deny Palmyra reinforcements from the Persians, Saracens and Armenians, while simultaneously using his army to completely sever the flow of goods and provisions into the city. With the capital's supplies exhausted, the queen left Palmyra to appeal for aid from the Persians, but was captured near the Euphrates River by Roman cavalry. Now without hope of succour, the Palmyrenes surrendered their city.

Scriptores Historiae Augustae (*Aurelian*), 26–28; Zosimus, *New History*, 1.54–56.2.

Panormus, AD 535 (Gothic War, Wars of Justinian I) – Following the decision of Emperor Justinian to invade Ostrogothic Italy, the Roman general Belisarius landed in Sicily at the head of a sizeable army of some 8,000 men, comprising 4,000 legionaries and *foederati*, approximately 3,000 Isaurians, 200 Hunnic horsemen, 300 Moorish cavalry and Belisarius' personal bodyguard. After securing control of the communities of Catana and Syracuse on the island's eastern coast, the Romans moved against the Gothic garrison at

Panormus (Palermo) in north-western Sicily. Unable to capture the port from the landward side because of the city's defences, Belisarius decided to sail his fleet into the unfortified harbour. Once the assaulting ships were moored against the city wall, the general noted that the vessels' masts extended above the parapet and ordered small boats hoisted to the tops of the vertical spars to serve as platforms, from which archers could direct their fire inside the ramparts. This exposure to attack quickly demoralized the Gothic defenders, who shortly surrendered the city, removing the last major obstacle in the restoration of the island to Roman imperial authority in Constantinople.

Procopius of Caesarea, *History of the Wars* (*The Gothic War*), 5.5.12–16.

Pavia, AD 271, see Ticinum, AD 271.

Perinthus, AD 193, see Cyzicus AD 193.

Perusia, AD 536 (Gothic War, Wars of Justinian I) – Upon learning that the Romans had secured control of a number of communities in Tuscany, Ostrogothic King Vittigis dispatched an army against Perusia, the leading city in the region and primary base for a Roman army under the general Constantinus. The two armies met in battle on the outskirts of the city. The Goths' superior numbers caused the battle to remain undecided for a time, before the Romans finally turned the momentum of the struggle and routed the enemy with very heavy losses. Among the Goths captured were the army's commanders, Unilas and Pissas.

Procopius of Caesarea, *History of the Wars* (*The Gothic War*), 5.16.5–7.

Phasis River, AD 550 (Lazic War, Wars of Justinian I) – Having encamped along the banks of the Phasis (Rioni) River near the frontier of Lazica, a 5,000-man Persian army under the command of Phabrizus began plundering the surrounding countryside. The force was soon intercepted by some 14,000 Lazic and Roman troops led by Goubazes, king of the Lazi, and Dagisthaeus, the Roman *magister militum per Armeniam*. While still some distance from the enemy position, the army surprised and destroyed a 1,000-man advanced patrol deployed to guard the Persian encampment. After learning from captives of the size, strength and location of the main enemy force; the Lazi and Romans advanced undetected against the Persian army and attacked in the early dawn, overrunning the camp and killing most of Phabrizus' command. As the cavalry ranged a considerable distance away from the battlefield in pursuit of survivors, they unexpectedly came upon a third contingent of Persian troops and inflicted an additional defeat on the enemy. These losses compelled the Persians to abandon Lazica and withdraw their forces from the immediate region.

Procopius of Caesarea, *History of the Wars* (*The Persian War*), 2.30.30–48.

Phasis River, AD 555, Spring (Lazic War, Wars of Justinian I) – During the spring of 555, a large Persian army under the command of Nakhoragan besieged Roman forces inside the town of Phasis (Poti), located at the mouth of the Phasis (Rioni) River on the eastern Black Sea coast. The river and coastline protected the town on three sides, allowing only a landward approach from the south. The Romans constructed an earthen rampart and water-filled moat. Against the shoreline and at the mouth of the Phasis, merchant vessels rode at anchor close to the town walls. From atop these ships, groups of Roman and allied archers occupied boats suspended from the mastheads. Distributed around the entire southern perimeter of the town's fortifications were additional detachments of allied troops: Moorish light infantry, Tzanian heavy infantry and Isaurian slingers and dart-throwers occupied the centre, facing south; soldiers under Martin, the Roman *magister militum per Armeniam*, and his general, Justin, were deployed on an elevated point near the sea to the west; and a force of Heruli and Lombards guarded the defences on the east side of the town. Lastly, a contingent of Eastern Roman infantry held a position on the extreme right. Opposing these defenders was Nakhoragan's army, which heavily outnumbered the forces of Martin by perhaps three to one. In the following weeks both armies settled into the business of the siege. After the investment had been going on for a while, Martin circulated a false story proclaiming the imminent arrival of a large Roman relief force. The deception, which was partially intended to embolden the Roman troops with false hope, eventually reached the ears of the Sassanid general, who then mobilized his whole army in an attempt to seize Phasis before the arrival of the anticipated reinforcements. At about this same time, Justin and a cavalry force numbering over 5,000 riders managed to escape the town undetected in order to visit a nearby Christian holy site. Shortly afterwards, the entire complement of the Persian army gathered below the citadel's fortifications, unaware of Justin's temporary departure. Once the Persians were assembled outside Phasis, they stormed the walls in a determined effort to overrun the Roman defences. This preoccupation by the enemy allowed Justin's returning cavalry opportunity to launch a destructive charge against one flank of Nakhoragan's formation. The strength of this unexpected attack reverberated through the enemy's ranks, creating confusion that quickly gave way to panic. As the Persian infantry on the left began to retreat, Nakhoragan's Dilimnite auxiliaries redeployed from their position near the centre of the wall to reinforce the collapsing flank. This sudden reduction of troops at the south wall was immediately exploited by the Romans, who initiated a strong sortie from that position. Seeing this, the Dilimnites swiftly retraced their steps, a manoeuvre misconstrued by their Persian comrades as flight, and the entire Sassanid left wing promptly broke apart as a result. The Roman counter-attack which inevitably followed simultaneously struck the entire enemy line from different directions, with differing effect. Persian resistance on the left completely disintegrated, while the Persian right wing absorbed the assault and remained intact. This situation on the right partially resulted from a formidable line of war elephants, whose presence served to dissipate the energy of the Roman left and whose charges continually disrupted the ranks of Roman infantry as they attempted to press their attack. Maddened by his wounds, an injured elephant broke free from his handlers in the midst of this fighting. The actions of the enraged animal destroyed the cohesion of the Persian formation, just as Roman reinforcements arrived on the scene to redress the flagging Roman left. Martin's infantry, now re-formed behind a solid wall of shields, overwhelmed the last pockets of Persian resistance and drove the enemy from the field. Persian losses from the battle included some 10,000 dead. When he learned of the defeat, Sassanid King Chosroes I ordered the execution of Nakhoragan.

Agathias Scholasticos, *The Histories*, 3.20–27.

Philippopolis, AD 251 – After the defeat of a Roman army under Emperor Trajanus Decius at the town of Augusta Traiana (Boroa; Stara Zagora), King Kniva led the victorious Goths to rejoin their countrymen in the ongoing investment of the Thracian provincial capital of Philippopolis (Plovdiv). The long siege finally ended with the capture and sacking of the city, and the murder of the Roman governor, Titus Julius Priscus.

Jordanes, *The Origins and Deeds of the Goths*, 101–103; Zosimus, *New History*, 1.24.

Pincian Gate, AD 537, see Porta Pinciana, AD 537.

Piri Mons, AD 368, see Mons Piri, AD 368.

Pisaurium, AD 554, Spring (Gothic War, Wars of Justinian I) – In the spring of 553, an army of 75,000 Frank and Alamanni warriors invaded Italy, led by the Alamannic chieftains Leutharis and Butilinus. The Germanic army subsequently pillaged throughout the northern and central portions of the peninsula before dividing into two armies near Rome. Leutharis moved his forces toward the Adriatic coast and marched southward to the port of Hydruntum (Otranto), while Butilinus moved south along the western coast of Italy, plundering the regions of Campania, Lucania and Brutium, before reaching the Straits of Messina. After pillaging the territory of Calabria in southern Italy, Leutharis turned his army north, intent on returning to his homeland over the Alps with a rich store of booty. Not far from the city of Pisaurium (Pesaro), a Roman army led by the general Artabanes surprised the Franks while they marched along the shore of the Adriatic. Trapped against the sea, the Frankish infantry was caught at the mercy of the Romans and their Hunnish allies. Some of the men attempted to flee by climbing the steep cliffs along the coastline, but most of the advanced guard was unable to escape and perished on the spot. After this defeat, Leutharis cautiously moved his army into the relative safety of the Apennine Mountains to the west, and then continued on to the Padus (Po) Valley in northern Italy. The army was devastated by a pestilence while encamped in the town of Ceneta (Ceneda). Leutharis himself was counted among the dead.

Agathias Scholasticos, *The Histories*, 2.2.1–7.

Placentia, AD 69 (Year of the Four Emperors, Roman Civil Wars) – The power struggle between Marcus Salvius Otho, the former governor of Lusitania, and Aulus Vitellius, governor of *Germania Inferior* (Lower Germany), was the latest chapter in the Roman civil war which followed the death of the Julio-Claudian Emperor Nero in the summer of AD 68. The assassination of his immediate successor, Galba, the following January signalled the beginning of a months-long internecine struggle between these two men. The contest between Otho and Vitellius was decided in the Padus (Po) Valley in northern Italy. The first significant clash came at Placentia (Piacenza). Here, the legions of Vitellius' lieutenant, Caecina, besieged the city in an attempt to force the capitulation of the resident Othonian forces led by Vestricius Spurinna. Once his army was across the Padus River, Caecina's legions attacked the community, but were unsuccessful in breaching its walls and suffered heavy losses by the end of the day's action. His army resumed the investment the next morning, this time with the aid of siege-works – fascines, manlets and sheds to mine the walls – but still failed to make progress against the defenders. Unable to overcome the city's defences by storm, Caecina ultimately abandoned the assault, re-crossed the river and marched against Cremona some 20 miles (32km) away.

Publius Cornelius Tacitus, *Histories*, 2.20–22; Plutarch, *Otho*, 6.1–2.

Placentia, AD 271 – Joined by the Alamanni, the Juthungi crossed the Alps and descended into the Padus (Po) Valley. When Emperor Aurelian learned of this invasion, he marched from Pannonia, where he was fighting the Vandals, and entered northern Italy with a substantial army. Having concealed themselves in some nearby forest, the Germans trapped the Romans in an ambuscade and inflicted a devastating defeat near the city of Placentia (Piacenza).

Scriptore Historiae Augustae (*Aurelianus*), 18.3–4, 21.1–4; Anonymous (Sextus Aurelius Victor), *Epitome of the Emperors*, 35.2 (T. Banchich, trans.).

Placentia, AD 456, 16 October – Growing turmoil within the Western Roman leadership eventually led to civil war in the early autumn of 456. With the support of the Roman Senate, Flavius Ricimer, the *magister militum* of the Western Empire, initiated a rebellion against Emperor Avitus. He was joined in the insurrection by Julius Valerius Maiorianus, commander of the *Domestici*, or imperial guard. The revolt forced the emperor to abandon Rome and withdraw to northern Italy. At Placentia (Piacenza), Avitus' forces attacked Ricimer's troops in the city, but were heavily defeated. The following day the *magister militum* forced the emperor to relinquish his title and accept the bishopric of Placentia. Avitus died a short time later.

> Hydatius, *Chronicle*, 176 [Mom. 183]; Priscus, *fragment 32* = John of Antioch, *fragment 202* (Blockley). See also *Fasti vindobonenses priores*, 579,580, in Theodor Mommsen. 1892. *Consularia italic.* Berolini: [s.n.].

Plain of Gallica, AD 547 – Faced with an uprising of the Leuathae, the largest of the Moorish tribes in Tripolitania, a Roman army under the leadership of John Troglita, the *magister militum per Africam*, moved against the insurgents and their leader, Carcasan. In response, the tribesmen withdrew into the desert, where the harsh conditions proved debilitating to both armies. At last the Romans encountered the Moors on the plain of Gallica. Hesitant to engage the Leuathae at that precise moment, John was eventually persuaded by his troops to enter battle, a rash decision which resulted in the total defeat of the Roman forces.

> Procopius of Caesarea, *History of the Wars* (*The Vandalic War*), 4.28.47–49; Flavius Cresconius Corippus, *Iohannis*, 6.472–773.

Plain of Mardia, AD 316 (Wars of Constantine I) – Following his defeat at Cibalae (Vinkovci) in early October, the Eastern *Augustus* Licinius fled south-eastward some 50 miles (88.5km) to the Pannonian town of Sirmium (Mitrovica), where he regrouped his army before undertaking a long march into Thracia. In pursuit were the victorious legions of Western Emperor Constantine I. After a journey of some 300 miles (483km), Constantine crossed through the Haemus Mons (Balkan Mountains) and established his army at Philippopolis (Plovdiv) on the banks of the Hebrus (Maritsa) River. Encamped to the south-east on the plain of Mardia (Harmanli) were the veteran Illyrian legions of Licinius, now reinforced by a second army commanded by the recently appointed co-*Augustus*, Caius Aurelius Valerius Valens. The resulting battle proved a long and bitter contest between opposing heavy infantry. While the legions were fully engaged, Constantine deployed a force of 5,000 cavalry to attack Licinius' rear in an effort to decide the battle; but the move was observed by the Illyrian troops, who then formed a double front and capably repulsed the assault, though suffering heavy casualties. Fighting continued unabated until nightfall, when both commanders elected to withdraw their forces from battle. In negotiations the next day, Licinius relinquished control of the Danubian and Balkans provinces to Constantine, but retained authority over Thracia and the eastern provinces of the Empire.

> Anonymous Valesianus, Pars Prior, *Origo Constantini Imperatoris*, 5.17; Zosimus, *New History*, 2.19.1–3.

Poetovio, AD 388, Summer – Emperor Theodosius' victory over the Western Roman usurper Magnus Maximus at Siscia in the summer of 388 was quickly followed by a second battle some 65 miles (105km) north-west, near the town of Poetovio (Ptuj) in the province of Noricum Mediterraneum. There, the usurper's brother, Marcellinus, and several cohorts of select troops, perhaps the primary core of Maximus' army, engaged Theodosius' forces. Following a hard-fought struggle in which Marcellinus' battle-line was ultimately ruptured and the front ranks driven backward into his reserve, the entire formation disintegrated. In the resulting pursuit by Theodosius' cavalry, the beaten army was all but destroyed.

Pacatus, *Panegyrici Latini* 2 [AD 389], 35; Ambrose, *Epistulae*, 40.23.

Pollentia, AD 403, 6 April – A Roman army led by the *magister militum* Flavius Stilicho defeated a Visigothic force under King Alaric at Pollentia (Pollenzo) on the Tanarus River. While the Gothic host was preoccupied by Easter services and unprepared for hostilities, the Romans launched an assault against the enemy encampment. Stilicho opened the battle with a cavalry charge by his Alan *feoderati*, led by King Saul. The attack initially threw the Goths into disarray, but Alaric was able to restore order and assemble his warriors for battle. While the Visigoths struggled to organize their ranks, the Alans delivered a series of assaults that only ended when their leader fell during fighting. The death of Saul demoralized the Alani, who prepared to withdraw from the field. Stilicho, recognizing that their departure would endanger his right flank, quickly redeployed a single legion in order to both protect the exposed flank and embolden the flagging Alans. With the Roman line fully restored, Stilicho subjected the Goths to a frontal attack by his entire army. The force of the charge drove the Visigoths back into their encampment. Savage fighting immediately erupted around the *laager* and within the confines of the encampment, and continued until the legions and *feoderati* were finally able to force a retreat of the enemy. The Roman victory was not decisive, though Stilicho managed to seize the Gothic camp. Both sides suffered very heavy casualties. Following the battle, the Visigothic army departed south-eastward toward Etruria, too badly mauled to contest the loss of either its rich store of booty or many of its people. Among the captives was Alaric's family. The battle likewise left Roman forces severely battered, making it impossible for Stilicho to immediately resume his pursuit of the enemy; a situation that later exposed him to hostile political accusations of duplicity with the Visigothic king.

Claudius Claudianus (Claudian), *Gothic War*, 550–647; Jordanes, *The Origins and Deeds of the Goths*, 154–155; Aurelius Prudentius Clemens, *Liber Contra Symmachus*, 2.694–719; Paulus Orosius, *Seven Books of History against the Pagans*, 7.37.

Pons Aureoli, AD 268, see Mediolanum, AD 268.

Ponte Salario, AD 537, 22 February (Gothic War, Wars of Justinian I) –
When the Ostrogothic army under King Vittigis reached the Anio River
outside Rome it prepared to cross over the *Ponte Salario*, but was hindered by
the presence of a small, gated fortlet which controlled access to the bridge.
This obstacle soon proved to be only temporary as the attending garrison of
soldiers, alarmed by the size of the enemy force, abandoned the position
during the night. The Goths were then able to secure control of the bridge
the following day. Unaware of these proceedings, the Roman general
Belisarius approached the crossing with 1,000 cavalry, only to find himself
challenged by a contingent of Goths already across the river. A sharp engagement between opposing horsemen quickly resulted. Conspicuously exposed
on his horse in the midst of the fighting, Belisarius drew the attention of
enemy riders, who soon directed their attack at the general personally. As
the Goths pressed their assault, the entire struggle gradually concentrated
about the Roman commander and his bodyguard, resulting in approximately
1,000 dead on each side. Through sheer valour, the Romans finally routed the
larger force of Ostrogothic riders. The enemy horsemen were then chased by
Roman cavalry before the pursuers were in turn driven off by the main
formation of Gothic infantry. As the Romans fell back, fresh detachments of
enemy cavalry broke away from the main body and resumed battle. After
extended fighting, Belisarius was finally able to withdraw from the mêlée and
retreat toward the *Porta Salaria*. When he and his small force of riders reached
the walls of Rome around nightfall, they were unable to gain immediate entry
through the gate because the frightened sentinels failed to distinguish the
general and his followers from the approaching Gothic horsemen in their
train. The delay continued while the enemy drew rapidly closer, and the
Romans, confined by the wall on one side and the moat on the other, found
themselves crowded together without room to manoeuvre their horses.
Unwilling to be trapped against the city's fortifications, Belisarius suddenly
ordered his cavalry to charge the Goths. Already disorganized from the pursuit, the enemy was thrown into further confusion by this unexpected attack
from the darkness. Thinking the audacious counter-charge to be the work of
fresh reinforcements from inside the city, the Gothic cavalry broke and fled in
panic. Instead of giving chase, the small band of Romans returned to the city
gate, where they were able to finally gain entry into the city, both sides having
accrued considerable casualties during the day's protracted struggle.

Procopius of Caesarea, *History of the Wars* (*The Gothic War*), 5.18.1–28.

Pontiruolo, AD 268, see Mediolanum, AD 268

Porta Pinciana, AD 537 (Gothic War, Wars of Justinian I) – At dawn, the
Roman general Belisarius dispatched a detachment of 1,000 cavalry through

the Pincian Gate on the north side of Rome, instructing the commanders Trajanus and Diogenes to harass the nearest Gothic camps, provoke the enemy into giving pursuit and draw their horsemen toward the walls of the city, where additional cavalry would be waiting. The mounted contingent carried out the plan as instructed, and when they drew near the *Porta Pinciana*, the second force of riders came to their relief. As the combined squadrons of horse charged the approaching Goths, an additional Roman force suddenly sallied out through the Flaminian Gate to the west. A portion of these men initiated an unsuccessful assault against the enemy camp near the *Via Flaminia*, while the remainder attacked the rear of the Gothic band still fighting the Roman cavalry outside the Pincian Gate. Trapped between the two forces, almost all of the Goths were killed in the engagement.

Procopius of Caesarea, *History of the Wars* (*The Gothic War*), 6.5.9–24.

Porta Salaria, AD 537 (Gothic War, Wars of Justinian I) – Over the course of several days, the Roman general Belisarius launched a series of three cavalry attacks against Ostrogothic forces besieging the city of Rome near the Salarian Gate. In the first action, 200 mounted bowmen under Trajanus rode near the Gothic encampment and were immediately set upon by enemy cavalry. Withdrawing to a predetermined knoll, the Romans halted and then turned on their pursuers with showers of arrows. When the supply of missiles was exhausted, the small force speedily retired toward the protection of the city walls, with the Goths giving chase. As Trajanus' command approached the gate, hotly pressed by the enemy cavalry, two arrow-firing catapults suddenly began discharging projectiles from atop the fortifications. The concentrated missile fire from the engines quickly drove off Gothic riders and ended the day's engagement. This tactic was successfully employed two more times over the following days, using detachments of 300 riders in each instance. Ostrogothic losses incurred in these clashes amounted to some 4,000 men. Roman casualties are not recorded but appear to have been minimal. Two subsequent attempts by the Gothic king, Vittigis, to duplicate the Roman actions ended in disaster for barbarian forces.

Procopius of Caesarea, *History of the Wars* (*The Gothic War*), 5.27.1–14.

Pselchis, 24 BC – While Aelius Gallus, the Roman prefect of Egypt, was campaigning in Arabia with a portion of his forces from the province, a 30,000-man Kushite army attacked into Thebais, the far southern district of Egypt. Led by Queen Amanirenas of Kush, the invaders defeated three Roman cohorts garrisoned at Syrene (Aswan) and then seized the nearby islands of Elephantine and Philae. Gallus' successor, Caius Petronius, soon responded by marching against the Kushites with a force of 800 cavalry and less than 10,000 infantry. Despite the larger size of the opposing army, the

Romans succeeded in driving back the Kushites to the city of Pselchis (Dakkeh), some 60 miles (96.5km) south of Syene. There, following three days of failed negotiations, Petronius launched an attack, forcing Amanirenas into battle. The Romans smashed the Kushite formation in the brief struggle. Thousands of enemy warriors died in the fighting, or were afterwards captured and sent to Alexandria. Petronius swiftly followed this victory with the assault and occupation of Pselchis. Then, ignoring the entreaties of the Kushite queen, he marched against the royal capital of Nabata and promptly destroyed it. Petronius garrisoned the fortified city of Premnis (Qasr Ibrim) before withdrawing. Amanirenas subsequently attempted to capture this Roman outpost using a force of several thousand men, but was thwarted in her efforts by the unexpected return of the prefect's army. Unwilling to risk a second major contest with Petronius' divisions, the Kushites sought a negotiated settlement.

Strabo of Amasya, *Geography*, 17.53–54.

Ravenna, AD 432, see Ariminum, AD 432.

Reims, AD 356, see Durocortorum, AD 356.

Resaena, AD 243, see Rhesaena, AD 243.

Resaina, AD 243, see Rhesaena, AD 243.

Rhesaina, AD 243, see Rhesaena, AD 243.

Rhesaena, AD 243 (Persian Wars, Wars against the Sassanids) – After the reign of Emperor Maximinus, Rome gradually lost a number of eastern cities and territories to Persian aggression. In 243, following an invasion of Syria by armies under the Sassanid ruler Shapur I, Roman military forces advanced east to push the intruders out, secure Antioch and recover the cities of Carrhae (Harran) and Nisibis. Near the Syrian community of Rhesaena (Ras-al-Ain), Shapur lost to a Roman army commanded by the *Praefectus praetorio*, Caius Furius Sabinius Aquila Timesitheus. The victory proved decisive and permitted Roman Emperor Gordian III to re-establish control over much of the provincial territory previously acquired by Persia.

Scriptores Historiae Augustae (*Gordiani Tres*), 26.5–6; Ammianus Marcellinus, *Res Gestae*, 23.5.17.

Rhandeia, AD 62 (Parthian Wars) – During the fourth year of war between Rome and Parthia for control of Armenia, Parthian King Vologeses I suddenly renewed hostilities in the spring of 62 after negotiations in Rome failed to settle the conflict. Marching north-westward with a large army to again assert Parthian authority over Armenia, Vologeses faced only two legions, the

Legio IV Scythica and *Legio XII Fulminata*, and supporting *auxilia*. The unexpected approach of Parthian forces caught the Roman commander, Lucius Caesennius Paetus, ill-prepared to oppose the invasion. With his armies still scattered in winter quarters and his officers furloughed, Paetus managed to hastily retrieve the Twelfth Legion and some cavalry, but his response to the approaching threat was both overly cautious and poorly judged. After suffering the defeat of a reconnaissance force dispatched to locate the enemy, Paetus refused to assume the offensive against the advancing enemy. Instead, he unwisely chose to scatter his already meagre command in an attempt to block the approach of the Parthians. Three thousand selected infantry were dispersed to guard nearby passes through the Tarsus Range, while several squadrons of Pannonian cavalry patrolled the local plain. In the encounters which followed, Vologeses' forces easily overwhelmed the Romans. The Parthian army thereafter besieged the defeated enemy within their encampment at Rhandeia, located on the banks of the Arsanias (Murad) River. Unable to escape and unaware of an approaching Roman relief force, Paetus surrendered. The defeated legions were permitted to withdraw, but not before their camp was plundered and the troops stripped of their arms and clothing. In a final act of humiliation, the Parthian king forced the Romans to pass under the yoke.

Publius Cornelius Tacitus, *Annals*, 15.9–15; Dio Cassius, *Roman History*, 62.21.

Rhenus River, AD 69 (Revolt of Civilis, Batavian Revolt) – During the course of the civil war between Vitellius and Vespasianus, a native rebellion erupted in the province of *Germania Inferior* (Lower Germany). The uprising was led by the Batavi, a German tribal people long recognized for loyal military service to Rome but lately dissatisfied by Vitellius' demands in the summer of AD 69 for additional levies of troops. A Batavian chieftain, bearing the adopted Roman name of Julius Civilis, took advantage of the widespread dissatisfaction among his people to organize an insurrection against Roman authority in Lower Germany. The uprising soon included the Frisii and Canninefates. These latter tribes, under the command of a chieftain called Brinno, initiated hostilities when their warriors attacked two unsuspecting cohorts of Roman *auxilia* stationed near the Rhenus (Rhine) River. Taken by surprise, the auxiliaries were ill-prepared to repel the numerically superior enemy force and were overwhelmed. Following their victory, the Canninefates plundered the Roman camp.

Publius Cornelius Tacitus, *Histories*, 4.15.

Rhenus River, AD 69 (Revolt of Civilis, Batavian Revolt) – Immediately after the revolt of the Batavi began in the late summer of AD 69, the Germans attacked a number of Roman forts in the province of *Germania Inferior*

(Lower Germany). Near the Rhenus (Rhine) River, a sizable force of Roman *auxilia* clashed with a coalition force consisting of the Canninefates, Frisii and Batavi. The German tribesmen, led by a Batavian chieftain bearing the adopted Roman name of Julius Civilis, attacked the Roman battle line, which was assembled a short distance from the river. The contest had barely begun when a cohort of Tungrians suddenly defected to Civilis. This unexpected betrayal by an allied detachment so demoralized the remaining Roman units that Civilis' warriors were quickly able to defeat the enemy formation. At the same time, desertions by Batavian oarsmen serving aboard nearby Roman ships resulted in the surrender or seizure of all twenty-four vessels in the river fleet. When the battle ended, Civilis allowed the Roman auxiliaries and their praefects the option of either returning to their homelands in peace or joining with his forces.

Publius Cornelius Tacitus, *Histories*, 4.16.

Rhenus River, AD 378 – A sizable force of Lentiensian Alamanni crossed the frozen Rhenus (Rhine) River in the winter of 378 and attacked into Roman territory, but its success proved short-lived. The *Celtae* and *Peutantes*, two units of *auxilia palatina*, camped in the vicinity of the Rhenus, and attacked and defeated the raiders. The Germans suffered significant losses in the battle, and the Romans likewise incurred casualties, though the specific numbers of dead and wounded for each side are unknown.

Ammianus Marcellinus, *Res Gestae*, 31.10.2–4.

Rhodanus River, AD 471 (Visigothic War, Gothic Wars) – Faced with the Visigothic occupation of Gaul, Roman Emperor Anthemius continued his efforts to restore the region to imperial authority. Placing his son, Anthemiolus, in overall charge of a campaign to relieve the besieged city of Arelate (Arles), the emperor also sent the generals Thorisarius, Everdingus and Hermianus to assist the prince in the recovery of the province. A Gothic army under King Euricus heavily defeated the Roman relief force near the Rhodanus (Rhone) River. Afterward, the Visigoths laid waste to the Rhodanus Valley. The battle not only ended Anthemius' efforts to reclaim southern Gaul, but essentially marked the permanent contraction of Roman power in Western Europe.

Gallic Chronicle of 511, no. 649, *s.a.* 471.

Rigodulum, AD 70, Summer (Revolt of Civilis, Batavian Revolt) – After assembling a sizeable Roman army at Mogontiacum (Mainz) in *Germania Superior* (Upper Germany), the general Quintus Petilius Cerialis marched his forces 35 miles (56km) west-south-west to the village of Rigodulum (Riol) on the banks of the Mosella (Mosel) River. On the south-western side of the river, legionary forces attacked a Treviran army led by Julius Valentinus.

The fighting was concentrated near the village, on the lower slopes of a hill adjacent to the main road leading to Augusta Treverorum (Trier), approximately 9 miles (14km) away. Cerialis assaulted the enemy fortifications with his heavy infantry while simultaneously deploying auxiliary cavalry up the hill. The infantry's ascent was temporarily slowed by missile fire before the cohorts were finally able to overrun the position and rout the Treviri. Among the enemy captured by Roman horsemen was Valentinus himself.

　Publius Cornelius Tacitus, *Histories*, 4.71.

Rimini, AD 432, see Ariminum, AD 432.

Rome, AD 69, 20–21 December (Year of the Four Emperors, Roman Civil Wars) – The Roman civil war that followed the death of Nero in the early summer of AD 68 climaxed eighteen months later in the autumn of 69 with an intense struggle between the armies of Emperor Aelius Vitellius and his challenger, the veteran *legatus*, Titus Flavius Vespasianus. Following the victory of Flavian legions at Bedriacum (Calvatone) in northern Italy, Vespasian's lieutenant, Marcus Antonius Primus, marched south toward Rome with the intention of finishing the conflict. Advancing along the *Via Flaminia*, Antonius' army arrived in late evening at Saxa Rubra, a village located some 6 miles (9.6km) north of the capital. Here he learned that a 1,000-man cavalry detachment, dispatched by him earlier under the command of Quintus Petilius Cerialis, had been defeated on the *Via Salaria* near Rome. Further, it appeared the preponderance of popular support in the city was for Vitellius. While the army halted temporarily on the far side of the river, a senatorial delegation arrived with a peace proposal for Antonius, soon followed by Vestals bearing letters from Vitellius requesting the Flavians delay their march until the next day. The general was inclined to accede to the request and camp near the Milvian Bridge, but the legions refused to stop their advance and demanded Antonius continue on despite the late hour. Once the Flavians resumed their march, they divided into three columns: one force continuing along the Flaminian Way, a second to the right of the highway following the banks of the Tiber and a third approaching the Colline Gate on the north-eastern side of the city. The Vitellians countered by deploying troops ahead of each of these columns. As a result, widespread fighting occurred near the northern and north-eastern walls of the city, on the Campus Martius and in the Sixth, or *Alta Semita*, Region of the city. In addition, Antonius' legions encountered particularly stiff resistance at the Castra Praetoria, which only ended after the complete destruction of the veteran praetorian cohorts of the emperor. After hours of combat, the Flavian divisions finally gained control of the city in late afternoon. By that time Vitellius was dead, murdered by soldiers earlier in the day.

　Publius Cornelius Tacitus, *Histories*, 3.79–85.

Rome, AD 410, 24–26 August – The failed relations between the Visigothic king, Alaric, and Western Roman Emperor Honorius, which had earlier resulted in brief Gothic sieges of Rome in 408 and 409, culminated in a third investment of the city in late August of 410. When political negotiations between the two leaders reached an impasse, the Gothic army drew near the walls of Rome and encamped on the north-eastern side of the capital near the Salarian Gate. While the emperor remained safely within the protected confines of the city of Ravenna some 180 miles (128km) away, thousands of Visigothic troops turned their might against the Eternal City. Alaric's forces surrounded Rome and then proceeded to starve the population into submission. On 24 August, accomplices inside the city overpowered the Roman guards at the *Porta Salaria* and opened the gates to the Visigoths. The invaders set about plundering the entire city. Pillaging was widespread but physical damage remained moderate, confined to only a few areas inside the city, including the residential properties around the Salarian Gate. The Visigoths seized numerous people in the city before departing, including the emperor's half-sister, Aelia Galla Placidia. Alaric and his army abandoned Rome after three days.

> Procopius of Caesarea, *History of the Wars* (*The Vandalic War*), 3.2.14–24; Hydatius, *Chronicle*, 35 [Mom. 43], 36 [Mom. 44]; Jordanes, *The Origins and Deeds of the Goths*, 156.

Rome, AD 472, July – The tumultuous relationship between the powerful Western *magister utriusque militum*, Flavius Ricimer, and Western Emperor Anthemius finally erupted in civil war in early 472. Ricimer marched on the capital with his army and invested the city for five months. While the siege continued, the emperor summoned military forces from Gaul under the command of the *rector Galliarum*, Bilimer. Bilimer drew up his army near Rome in an attempt to block Ricimer's forces from entering the central part of the city. In the resulting battle, Ricimer defeated Bilimer, who died during the course of the fighting.

> Priscus, *fragment* 64 = John of Antioch, *fragment* 209.1 (Blockley); Paul the Deacon, *Historia Romana*, 15.4.

Rome, AD 537 (Gothic War, Wars of Justinian I) – In an effort to bring an end to Emperor Justinian's invasion of Italy, the Ostrogothic army of King Vittigis began a siege of Rome in February. Defending the city was a force of 5,000 Roman troops, led by the general Flavius Belisarius, which was reinforced in April with the arrival of 1,600 Huns, Antae and Sclavenes under the commanders Martinus and Valerian. The new squadrons of horse soon proved their value by winning a series of cavalry engagements near the Salarian Gate on the north-eastern side of the city. Emboldened by these successes, and made increasingly desperate by the shortage of available provisions, both the army and civilian population in Rome soon demanded

Belisarius engage the besieging army in open battle. In answer, Belisarius led out the army, dispatching the bulk of his mounted troops through the Pincian and Salarian Gates on the northern side of the city near the primary Gothic encampments. In order to prevent the enemy troops camped on the nearby Plains of Nero to the north-west from participating in the coming battle, he deployed a sizeable force of civilian volunteer infantry through a western gate of the city, located across the Tiber River, with orders not to attack. In so doing, Belisarius hoped to prevent the Goths on the plain from coming to the aid of their brethren to the north for fear of a rear assault. Immediately outside the northern gates he stationed a small force of regular infantry to cover the withdrawal of the cavalry should they be defeated and seek protection inside the city. He positioned a second reserve of foot-soldiers directly behind the squadrons of horse to provide active support. In response, Vittigis assembled the entire Ostrogothic army opposite the Romans, ordering only those troops on the Plain of Nero to maintain their position in order to serve as a deterrent to an enemy attack from the west. He placed the infantry in the centre of the battle line and the cavalry on the wings. The engagement began in the early morning, and the battle immediately favored Belisarius as the Gothic cavalry suffered extensive casualties from the concentrated fire of Roman archers. Despite this initial success, the numerical superiority of the Gothic host prevented a quick end to the contest, though by midday the Romans had pushed the fighting back as far as the enemy encampments. While these events unfolded to the north of the city, the opposing troops near the Plains of Nero declined to engage until midday, when the Roman volunteers near the western gate suddenly launched an assault that routed the unsuspecting Goths. When the undisciplined attackers inexplicably stopped to plunder the Gothic camp, Vittigis' troops were given adequate time to recover from the confusion caused by the offensive, assess the situation and launch a furious countercharge that scattered the irregulars. This action was soon accompanied by a concerted charge of the Gothic right wing, whose cavalry shattered the smaller force of horsemen on the Roman left and initiated a general rout of the entire Roman army.

Procopius of Caesarea, *History of the Wars* (*The Gothic War*), 5.28.15–29–5.29.1–44.

Rome, AD 546, May (Gothic War, Wars of Justinian I) – Shortly after the departure of Totila and his Ostrogothic army from Rome in the spring of 546, the eastern Roman general, Flavius Belisarius, led a detachment of 1,000 men to survey the condition of the city. Learning of this, the Gothic king sent part of his army back to lay several ambuscades for the unsuspecting force. Belisarius and his men were ambushed by some of these troops near Rome. After a fierce engagement, the Romans routed the enemy with heavy losses.

Procopius of Caesarea, *History of the Wars* (*The Gothic War*), 7.23.8–11.

Rome, AD 547, May (Gothic War, Wars of Justinian I) – In the winter of 547, the Ostrogoths abandoned their occupation of Rome and marched into southern Italy in an effort to restore suzerainty over that portion of the peninsula. The Eastern Roman general, Flavius Belisarius, took advantage of his enemy's departure to relocate his army from Portus to the city. Finding Rome almost completely desolate and its defences in severe disrepair, he set his army to hastily reconstruct the city walls and re-excavate the surrounding trenches. This work was still in progress when the Gothic army under King Totila suddenly reappeared in May. Though large sections of the walls were already crudely rebuilt, the city was still extremely vulnerable to attack because it lacked gates. The Goths encamped near the Tiber River and launched a massive assault at sunrise the following day. Fighting was particularly savage near the gateless entries. Belisarius stationed his best troops at each location and they refused to yield to the foes' determined onslaught. The battle finally ended at night, the Goths having suffered heavy casualties during the day's action. The Ostrogoths again stormed the city's defences the next morning, but the Romans remained steadfast throughout, even growing confident enough to make a sally against the enemy in late afternoon. Totila then retired for several days to rest his army before resuming his attack against the city. This time the Romans assembled in battle formation outside the walls. Following intense hand-to-hand fighting, the sudden death of the king's standard-bearer resulted in a vicious struggle for ownership of the corpse. The Goths at last recovered the standard, but abandoned the field in disorder, having suffered significant losses during three days of combat. Afterward, Belisarius completed the restoration of Rome's defences.

Procopius of Caesarea, *History of the Wars* (*The Gothic War*), 7.24.1–26.

Salarian Bridge, AD 537, see Ponte Salario, AD 537.

Salarian Gate, AD 537, see Porta Salaria, AD 537.

Salarian Way, AD 69, see Via Salaria, AD 69.

Salices, AD 376 – While the Goths were fully involved in ravaging Thrace, Western Roman Emperor Gratian dispatched a small army under the command of the general Richomeres to aid Valens, his co-emperor in the east, in suppressing the revolt. Richomeres advanced into the Balkans with a force of under-manned cohorts, and Pannonian and Transalpine auxiliaries. Near Salices, he joined with Eastern Roman commanders Profuturus and Trajanus, whose legions were encamped outside the town, and learned that a large Gothic wagon *laager* was also situated in the vicinity. At dawn the following day, both armies assembled into battle formation. Each body of troops issued their war cry and then advanced against the enemy, their approach preceded by flights of javelins and other missiles. The two front lines quickly collided as both armies sought to force their way into the enemy's ranks. After intense fighting, the Goths finally broke through the Roman left wing, which was at the point of collapse when the arrival of a contingent of reserves redressed the line. The struggle continued unabated until nightfall finally ended the contest. Both armies suffered heavy casualties in the day-long engagement, but the battle ultimately proved inconclusive; each side electing to withdraw from the field before fighting could be resumed the following morning.

Ammianus Marcellinus, *Res Gestae*, 31.7.12–15.

Salonae, AD 535 (Gothic War, Wars of Justinian I) – Instructed by Emperor Justinian I to invade Dalmatia on the eastern Adriatic coast, Mundus, the *magister militum per Illyricum*, engaged Ostrogothic forces near the port of Salonae. The Romans occupied the city after defeating the Goths in battle.

Procopius of Caesarea, *History of the Wars* (*The Gothic War*), 5.5.11.

Salonae, AD 535 (Gothic War, Wars of Justinian I) – Soon after occupying the Dalmatian port of Salonae, Roman forces under Mundus, the *magister militum per Illyricum*, faced a major threat from an approaching Ostrogothic army commanded by generals Asinarius and Gripas. A Roman scouting expedition led by Mundus' son, Mauricius, unexpectedly encountered the Goths near the city. A violent struggle followed in which the entire Roman detachment was overwhelmed. Word of the defeat and death of his son alerted Mundus to the presence of the invasion force, and he immediately moved his entire army against the enemy. The battle which followed was stubbornly contested by both sides. After intense fighting, the Romans finally triumphed and the Goths were decisively routed from the field with heavy losses. Despite its victory, misfortune quickly befell the Roman army when Mundus was killed in the pursuit that followed. With the death of their commander, the Romans determined to immediately abandon Salonae and return home. The remnants of the Gothic force, having suffered the complete loss of their leadership, also elected to forgo the occupation of the city.

Procopius of Caesarea, *History of the Wars* (*The Gothic War*), 5.7.1–6.

Samarra, AD 363, 26 June (Persian Wars) – After their defeat at the Battle of Maranga, Persian forces resumed their harassment of the Roman army as it attempted to retire northward toward the region of Corduene, following the course of the Tigris River. Emperor Julian hoped, by his retreat away from the central Mesopotamian basin, to induce the Sassanid army under King Shapur II to abandon the fortified city of Ctesiphon (Teq-e Kasara) so that the Persians might then be forced into a decisive set-piece battle. The decision to withdraw was likewise motivated by the Roman army's need to replenish its depleted supply of grain and fodder. Local reserves were unavailable because the Persians had largely destroyed the region's agricultural resources as part of a scorched-earth campaign. While the army continued to progress along the Tigris, the Persians repeatedly laid ambuscades and otherwise subjected imperial forces to periodic skirmishes at every opportunity. These constant attacks forced the Romans to assume a defensive posture and advance in square formation, with each legion in open order. The rearguard suddenly came under attack near the city of Samarra. As the emperor rode back to restore order at the end of the column, a force of Parthian *cataphractarii* launched an assault against the centre of the main formation and then quickly overran the Roman left wing, which collapsed under the pressure. This action was soon turned by a counter-attack of Roman light infantry, but in the chaos Julian was seriously wounded and carried from the field. Aggrieved by the loss of their commander, the legions launched an aggressive attack against the enemy, which was swiftly met by an intense shower of arrows from Persian archers. At the same time, a number of war elephants pushed forward in an effort to further disrupt the Roman formation. With both armies now fully committed, the struggle intensified into a fierce melee that lasted until nightfall put an end to the fighting. Persian losses were heavy. Among the dead were numerous Sassanid nobles, including the generals Merena and Nohodares. Roman casualties, though lighter, included Emperor Julian, who succumbed to his injuries several hours after the battle ended.

Ammianus Marcellinus, *Res Gestae*, 25.3.1–14, 23; John Zonaras, *Epitome of Histories*, 13.13; Zosimus, *New History*, 3.28.3–29.1.

Samarra, AD 363, 27 June (Persian Wars) – The death of his predecessor Julian the day before persuaded the new Roman emperor, Jovian, to abandon the present campaign. As the Roman army prepared to depart from the vicinity of Samarra, a city on the banks of the Tigris River, it was attacked by a Persian army reinforced with a corps of royal cavalry dispatched by the Sassanid king, Shapur II. The Roman column, some 4 miles (6.4km) in length, was just beginning its march when it was struck by the Persians, whose attack was reinforced by a detachment of war elephants. The Roman cavalry and infantry were initially thrown into confusion by the charge of pachyderms; but two legions, the *Joviani* and *Herculiani*, held their ground, killing a number of the animals and successfully resisting attacks by *catafractarii*. Two additional legions, the *Jovii* and *Victores*, moved in to support the beleaguered legionaries, slaying two more elephants along with a substantial number of men. After successfully thwarting the assault and driving off the Persians with great loss, the army continued its withdrawal from Mesopotamia.

Ammianus Marcellinus, *Res Gestae*, 25.6.2–3.

Satala, AD 297 – Following the defeat of Roman forces by a Persian army near Callinicum in 296, Diocletian dispatched a second Roman army to redress the loss. This army, under the command of the *Caesar* Galerius, consisted of some 25,000 men, including troops from Illyricum and Moesia. In a major confrontation near the strategic city of Satala in Armenia, the Romans overran the Persian encampment, badly defeated the opposing army and put the Sassanid ruler, Narses, to flight. As a result of the victory, Galerius captured a large store of the king's treasure, numerous members of the Persian nobility and members of Narses' family, including his wife and daughters. The two powers subsequently concluded a treaty at Nisibis. The city of Satala thereafter became an important trading centre between the empires.

Eutropius, *Abridgement of Roman History*, 9.25; Festus, *Breviarium rerum gestarum populi Romani*, 25.2–3; Paulus Orosius, *Seven Books of History against the Pagans*, 7.25.

Satala, AD 530, Summer (Persian Wars, Wars of Justinian I) – As part of the ongoing struggle between the Eastern Roman and Sassanid empires in the regions of Armenia and the Caucasus, King Kavadh I sent an army of 30,000 men into Roman Armenia led by the general, Mermeroes. The force included Persarmenians, Sunitae and some 3,000 Sabiri Huns. Near the community of Satala in eastern Anatolia, south of the Black Sea coast, the Persians encountered a Roman army under the command of Sittas, the *magister militum praesentalis*. While the Romans occupied the city, Mermeroes encamped his forces approximately 6 miles (9.6km) away at Octava. Certain that an engagement was imminent, Sittas led 1,000 cavalry into the hills surrounding the city and ordered the army's regional general, Dorotheus – the *magister militum per Armeniam* – to maintain the rest of the troops inside the fortifications of Satala. Because the Roman army was roughly half the size of the Persian host, Sittas sought to avoid needlessly exposing his entire command to a decisive contest on the open plain outside the city. On the following day, Mermeroes began an investment of Satala when he was suddenly surprised by a charge of Sittas' mounted squadrons from the high ground behind his position. Unsure as to the size of the approaching force, the Persians quickly abandoned the siege and turned in an attempt to resist this new threat, but Sittas anticipated Mermeroes' response and abruptly divided his complement of riders. As the Persians manoeuvred to redress their formation in anticipation of the inevitable impact, both detachments of Roman cavalry swept in to the attack. When the Romans inside Satala witnessed the collision of the two armies, they eagerly rushed from the fortifications. Trapped between the forces of Sittas and Dorotheus, the integrity of the Persian line weakened, but their sheer numerical superiority ensured that the struggle devolved into an intense and protracted battle. While the fighting continued at close quarters, a detachment of Roman horse under the command of Florentius charged the enemy centre and pulled down Mermeroes' standard. The sudden absence of the banner confused the Persians and prompted a spontaneous retreat from the battlefield. The next day, the army of Kavadh I elected to entirely abandon the campaign and evacuate Roman territory.

Procopius of Caesarea, *History of the Wars* (*The Gothic War*), 1.15.9–17.

Sava, AD 388, see Siscia, AD 388.

Saxa Rubra, AD 312, see Milvian Bridge, AD 312.

Scalae Veteres, AD 537 – Following the defeat of a mutinous army at Membresa, Roman general Belisarius returned to Italy while Emperor Justinian appointed his own nephew, the patrician Germanus, as *magister militum per Africam*. Once in North Africa, the new commander prepared to end the insurrection. After securing the loyalty of the men under his command, Germanus set out in pursuit of the rebellious troops. The Imperial army overtook the insurgents in a place called Scalae Veteres. To prepare for battle, the *magister militum* arrayed his army in a relatively orthodox manner, marshalling the infantry in the centre and placing the army's supply wagons behind the formation as a deterrent to any assault from the rear. He then deployed strong concentrations of horsemen on each flank, including squadrons of Byzantine cavalry on the left wing and three divisions on the right under the command of the officers Ildiger, Theodorus and John. Opposite the Roman position, the mutineers assembled in a somewhat disorderly fashion, backed by thousands of Moors of dubious loyalty who secretly planned to declare their allegiance for whichever side won the day. When the battle commenced, the rebel leader Stotzas launched a strong attack against the Roman right, which threw the mounted squadrons under John into confusion and partially disrupted the nearest ranks of infantry. Having been alerted to the fact that his line was compromised on the right, Germanus – with great effort – routed the enemy opposing him and then wheeled his forces in an attempt to advance against the insurgent leader, even as the remaining two divisions of cavalry on the right, under Ildiger and Theodorus, turned in support of their general. As Stotzas continued his pursuit of the defeated John, the combined forces of Germanus suddenly overtook and drove in the rebel rear. The battle thereafter devolved into a protracted struggle, which finally ended with a Roman victory. As the remnants of the defeated mutineers fled the field, they were chased by Moorish cavalry now committed to the Roman cause. After making a last attempt to turn and engage the enemy, the remainder of Stotzas' troops were repulsed, bringing the mutiny to a decisive end.

Procopius of Caesarea, *History of the Wars* (*The Vandalic War*), 4.16–17.

Scardona, AD 536 (Gothic War, Wars of Justinian I) – An Ostrogothic army led by Uligisalus was defeated by a Roman force near the city of Scardona (Skradin) in western Dalmatia. Following this loss, the Goths retreated inland to the community of Burnum and awaited the arrival of reinforcements under the command of Asinarius.

Procopius of Caesarea, *History of the Wars* (*The Gothic War*), 5.16.12–13.

Sena Gallica, AD 551 (Gothic War, Wars of Justinian I) – In an attempt to capture the strategically valuable Picene port of Ancona in eastern Italy, King Totila of the Ostrogoths dispatched military and naval forces under the command of the generals Scipuar, Gibal and Gundulf. As the Goths began a siege and blockade of the city, a Roman fleet assembled in the Dalmatian port of Scardona (Skradin) for the purpose of assisting the beleaguered community. The flotilla consisted of thirty-eight *dromons* from the Italian port of Salona and twelve additional warships from Ravenna led by the general Valerian. The two squadrons joined forces and crossed the Adriatic Sea, making landfall approximately 16 miles (25.7km) north-east of Ancona at an anchorage called Sena Gallica. When the Gothic commanders learned of this, they immediately dispatched their entire complement of forty-seven ships in a bid to defeat and drive off the relief force. The vessels were placed under the leadership of Gibal and Gundulf, while Scipuar remained ashore to continue the investment of the city. When the Gothic fleet drew near the Roman

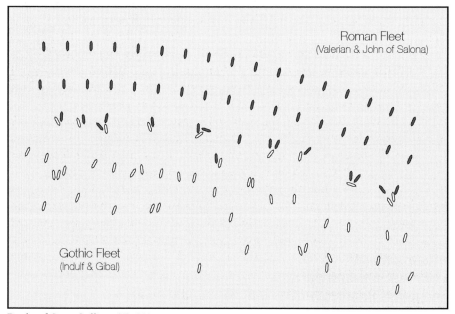

Battle of Sena Gallica, AD 551

warships, it immediately moved to attack. As the two battle lines closed to within missile range, flights of arrows were suddenly exchanged between the ships, shortly followed by numerous individual deck actions once the general melee began. In intense ship-to-ship fighting, the experienced Roman crews handled their vessels with efficiency, while the Gothic ships failed to maintain their tactical stations and were allowed to drift away from the main formation or collide with neighbouring craft. Consequently, many of the ships became scattered among the Roman vessels, isolated and then seized. The Goths eventually broke off the engagement and retreated with a loss of thirty-six ships captured. Gundulf managed to escape with the remaining eleven ships, but Gibal was taken prisoner. Most significantly, the defeat forced Totila to abandon the siege of Ancona and withdraw his forces from Picenum.

Procopius of Caesarea, *History of the Wars* (*The Gothic War*), 8.23.1–38.

Senonae, AD 356 – An under-strength army led by the *Caesar* Julian was present in Senonae (Sens) when a strong band of Alamanni chose to attack the city. The Germans, encouraged by the absence of the Roman *scutarii* and foreign cavalry called *gentiles*, assaulted the town for a month, but were unable to overcome its defences.

Ammianus Marcellinus, *Res Gestae*, 16.4.1–2.

Severn River, AD 50 – After several years of ongoing trouble from Caratacus, a powerful Celtic chieftain of the Catuvellauni tribe, the Romans finally brought him to battle in central Wales near the Severn River in the tribal lands of the Ordovices. In preparation for the coming engagement, Caratacus gathered his forces on a steeply inclined hill and fortified the few approaches that provided access to the summit. When the Romans arrived, their general Publius Ostorius Scapula examined the enemy position and determined that the only means to engage the Britons was to attempt an ascent at one of these points. The army then forded the river and re-assembled on the opposite bank in preparation for an assault. The Romans accrued a number of casualties from missile fire once they began their attack. In order to better force their way through the British defences, legionaries resorted to the use of a *testudo* to provide protection while they demolished the stone barrier. When this was done, Romans spilled over the destroyed breastworks, forcing the tribesmen to retreat to hilltops. The hasty withdrawal left the Britons badly disorganized and they were unable to resist being trapped between the advancing *auxilia* and the legionary cohorts. The defeat proved decisive. Caratacus fled the disaster, but his wife, daughter and brothers fell captive to Scapula.

Publius Cornelius Tacitus, *Annals*, 12.33–35.

Shropshire, AD 50, see Severn River, AD 50.

Siccaveneria, AD 545 – Faced with an ongoing Moorish insurrection in Africa, Emperor Justinian dispatched the senator Areobindus to lead Roman forces in the province of Byzacena while Sergius, the *dux Tripolitaniae*, was retained in command of an Imperial army in Numidia. Once in North Africa, Areobindus attempted without success to persuade his counterpart to unite the two Roman armies against their common enemy. Sergius adamantly refused to consider such a request and continued to pursue a separate campaign in Numidia. Such a decision proved devastating for Areobindus' command. Near the city of Siccaveneria (El Kef), approximately 100 miles (161km) west-south-west of Carthage, a small Roman army led by Areobindus' lieutenant – the very capable general John, son of Sisiniolus – engaged a numerically superior tribal force led by Antalas – chieftain of the Frexi – and the Roman rebel Stotzas. Predictably, the Romans were easily routed from the field. Following this defeat, the emperor recalled Sergius, who was soon sent to Italy with an army, and extended Areobindus' command to include all of Libya.

> Procopius of Caesarea, *History of the Wars* (*The Vandalic War*), 4.24. See also the Battle of Thacea in the *Chronica* of Victor Tonnennensis.

Silchester, AD 296, see Calleva Atrebatum, AD 296

Singara, AD 344, Summer (Persian Wars, Wars against the Sassanids) – Near the fortified city of Singara in northern Mesopotamia, the Sassanid army of King Shapur II clashed with the legions of Emperor Constantius II in an epic contest. The two armies briefly skirmished on the open plain near the city before the Sassanid ruler withdrew with a portion of his cavalry toward the Persian encampment located near the village of Eleia some 12 miles (20km) away. The remainder of the army then fought a rearguard action against the pursuing legions. The battle reached the outskirts of the Persian camp by late afternoon. Once there, the Roman infantry launched a strong frontal assault that drove the enemy within their defences. The emperor then reluctantly acquiesced to an imprudent demand by the army that they be permitted to storm the enemy barricades, even though it was almost nightfall. The resulting attack successfully breached the earthen fortifications and overran the camp, inflicting heavy casualties on the occupants and putting the king and his army to flight. While the exhausted legionaries recovered within the camp, Sassanid archers, slingers and javelineers suddenly delivered a heavy barrage of missiles from the darkness beyond in advance of a general assault by Persian forces. In the ensuing counter-attack, the Roman legions, thoroughly spent by the day's fighting, were unable to properly resist the Persian assault and suffered massive losses in the night battle which followed.

> John Zonaras, *Epitome of Histories*, 13.5; Ammianus Marcellinus, *Res Gestae*, 18.5.7, 18.9.3; Julian, *Oration I: Panegyric in Honour of Constantius*, 23–25B; Eutropius, *Abridgement of Roman History*, 10.10; Festus, *Breviarium rerum gestarum populi Romani*, 27 (T. Banchich, trans.); Libanius, *Oration 59*.

Singara, AD 360 (Persian Wars, Wars against the Sassanids) – As part of his continuing effort to wrestle control of more territory from the Romans, Sassanid King Shapur II moved with a sizeable Persian army against the fortified town of Singara, located in northern Mesopotamia. Defending the walls of the fortress was the *Legio I Flavia* and *Legio V Parthica*, with a detachment of auxiliary cavalry and a portion of the city's residents. After a failed attempt to reach a negotiated surrender, the Persian ruler resorted to a siege. The investment continued for days without resolution before a large battering ram succeeded in toppling a turret located at a vulnerable point on the walls. Once the Persians breached the outer defences, the town was shortly captured. The loss of Singara also resulted in the surrender of the city's defenders, including the entire complement of the Roman garrison.

Ammianus Marcellinus, *Res Gestae*, 20.6.1–8.

Singilis River, AD 438 – A Suevic band led by King Rechila encountered a Roman army in Baetica under the command of Andevotus, the *comes Hispaniarum*. The Suevi soundly defeated the provincial force in the resulting battle, fought near the Singilis (Jenil) River.

Hydatius, *Chronicle*, 106 [Mom. 114]; Isadore of Seville, *History of the Gothic, Vandal, and Suevic Kings*, 85.

Siscia, AD 388, Summer – In 387, the sudden invasion of Italy by Western Roman armies under the usurper Magnus Maximus provoked the outbreak of civil war between the Western and Eastern Roman empires. As Maximus' Gallic and German troops streamed into the northern regions of the Italian peninsula, 12-year old Western Emperor Valentinian II fled the imperial court at Mediolanum (Milan) and travelled to the Aegean coastal city of Thessalonika, where he received the protection of the imperial court at Constantinople. The following year, Eastern Emperor Theodosius I assembled a military expedition in Thessalonika for the purpose of restoring Valentinian to power. The army was composed largely of non-Roman soldiers, including sizeable formations of Goth, Alan and Vandal allies. Accompanying the emperor on his Western campaign were two talented Eastern Roman generals,the *magister peditum* Flavius Timasius and Promotus, the *magister equitum*. These were joined by a pair of loyal Frankish commanders, the *magister militum per Orientum*, Flavius Richomeres, and his nephew, the Western *magister peditum*, Flavius Arbogastes. The Eastern army's line of march eventually carried it to the northern Savus basin in the province of *Pannonia Superior* (Upper Pannonia). The two armies clashed near the town of Siscia (Sisak), located at the confluences of the Savus (Sava), Colapis (Kupa) and Odra rivers. Maximus' divisions were drawn up on the western bank of the Savus. As Theodosius' forces approached the location of the enemy, the

Hunnic cavalry immediately forded the river and charged the awaiting ranks. The Huns were soon joined by mounted squadrons of Alani and Gothic archers. The attack quickly routed the Gauls and Germans, who were inexperienced in dealing with the agile tactics of the Asiatic horsemen. After driving off any opposing squadrons of cavalry, the bowmen concentrated their assault against the fleeing infantry. Some were pursued as they sought safety in their nearby camp, while others were overtaken on open ground. Near the river, where banks proved impassable, the Eastern cavalry trapped the core of Maximus' army in a dense mass and proceeded to slaughter the hapless troops. The battle was over within a short time, Theodosius having achieved a complete victory.

Pacatus, *Panegyrici Latini* 2 [AD 389], 34; Ambrose, *Epistulae*, 40.23; Zosimus, *New History*, 4.42–45.

Soissons, AD 486, see Noviodunum, AD 486.

Solicinium, AD 367 – Following repeated Alamannic raids into Roman territory, Western Emperor Valentinian I assembled a sizeable army from throughout the empire, including Illyrian and Italian legions, and then set out to confront the interlopers north of the Rhenus (Rhine) River. In an effort to avert a surprise assault, the Romans advanced in square formation along a wide front, with the emperor commanding the centre and his generals, Jovinus and Severus, leading the flanks. Since the legions were unable to make immediate contact with the enemy, Valentinian deployed cohorts into the countryside to devastate the region's grain fields. When the army reached the vicinity of Solicinium, approximately 60 miles (96.5km) north of the Rhenus, scouts reported the presence of the enemy at some distance ahead of the Roman vanguard. The legions then moved forward in an attempt to bring the Alamanni to battle. The German tribesmen were situated atop a mountain, whose rugged terrain retarded an attack at all points except on the northern side, where a gentle slope made the summit more accessible. Drawing his forces into battle array, the emperor dispatched *comes Italiae* Sebastianus to secure control of the northern side of the mountain, and then set out with a small party of riders to reconnoitre the enemy's position. While preoccupied in traversing some marshy ground, the group was ambushed by a band of Germans and only narrowly escaped. Satisfied that he was properly apprised of the tactical situation, Valentinian ordered a mass assault. The attack demanded the legions charge the enemy uphill, resulting in a savagely contested action by both sides. As the momentum slowly appeared to shift in favour of the Romans, the emperor ordered his battle line to extend in an effort to encircle the German flanks. The dire turn of circumstance compelled the tribesmen to offer more determined resistance, resulting in heavy casualties all around. The unrelenting pressure of the Roman attack at last caused the Alamannic formation to collapse. As the exhausted Germans fell back in complete disorder, they suddenly encountered the fresh reserves of Sebastianus. Unable to offer proper resistance, the Alamanni were slaughtered.

Ammianus Marcellinus, *Res Gestae*, 27.10.15.

Sufetula, AD 547 – With the departure of Artabanes to Constantinople, Emperor Justinian appointed experienced general John Troglita as *magister militum per Africam* for the purpose of ending the Moorish insurrection which had plagued the North African provinces for the previous four years. Shortly after assuming command in Carthage, the new *magister militum* prepared to initiate a campaign against tribes in the provinces of Numidia and Byzacena still resistant to Roman authority. John moved against the Frexi, under the leadership of their chieftain Antalas, and the other confederate tribes in Byzacena. The two armies clashed south of the town of Sufetula (Sbeitla), approximately 150 miles (80km) south-west of Carthage. After a long and difficult struggle, the Romans finally succeeded in routing the Moors and overrunning their encampment. As a result of the victory, Imperial forces were able to recover the military standards captured in the defeat of Solomon at Cillium three years earlier.

Procopius of Caesarea, *History of the Wars* (*The Vandalic War*), 4.28.45–46.

Strasbourg, AD 357, see Argentoratum, AD 357.

Suma, AD 363, see Sumere, AD 363.

Sumere, AD 363 (Persian Wars) – The death of Emperor Julian at Samarra in late June abruptly ended Rome's Persian campaign in 363. His hastily chosen successor, Jovian, immediately began preparations for withdrawing the army from Mesopotamia. Near the fortress of Sumere, Sassanid King Shapur II ordered his cavalry to attack the departing Roman column. At the approach of the enemy, the legions formed into battle lines and were soon pressed by a strong charge of Persian war elephants. The assault initially threw the Roman right wing into confusion, but the *Joviani* and *Herculiani* legions held their ground in the midst of the chaos, killing some elephants while simultaneously resisting the repeated charges of Persian *clibanarii*. As a portion of the battered wing fell back in disorder, the momentum of the attack carried the fighting near some high ground, where the Roman baggage carriers were positioned. These soldiers joined in the struggle and succeeded in wounding some of the elephants with missile fire from above. The injured animals became uncontrollable and badly disrupted ranks of the nearby Persian cavalry. At that same time, the *Jovii* and *Victores* legions arrived on the right wing to aid their companion units in redressing the forward line. With the Roman formation now largely restored and his own army in disarray, Shapur elected to break off the action.

Ammianus Marcellinus, *Res Gestae*, 25.6.2–3; Zosimus, *New History*, 3.30.2–4.

Sura, AD 531, see Callinicum, AD 531.

Tabraca, AD 398 – In the twelfth year of his appointment as *comes Africae*, and also bearing the official designation *magister utriusque militia per Africam*, Gildo led a rebellion against Western Emperor Honorius. The uprising was accompanied by the very real danger that the *comes* might enter into an alliance with the Imperial court at Constantinople and elect to join his province with the Eastern Roman Empire. Such an act would jeopardize the security of Rome's food supplies from North Africa. Accordingly, the Western *magister militum*, Flavius Stilicho, deployed a military expedition to thwart the threat. Five thousand Roman troops from Gaul landed in Africa under the leadership of Mascezel, the brother of Gildo. Once ashore, the force marched inland and established a camp near the Ardalio River, located between the cities of Theveste (Tebessa) and Ammedera (Haidra). Mascezel's legions prepared to engage a much larger army, totalling 70,000 men, that included both Roman units and native allies. A skirmish erupted at a preliminary parley between the two sides. In the midst of the fighting, Mascezel struck the arm of a leading *signifer*, forcing the man to lower his banner. Gildo's remaining cohorts misconstrued this sight as a surrender, and immediately withdrew their loyalty to the *comes Africae*. The mass desertion of the Roman troops quickly persuaded the attending barbarian allies to likewise abandon Gildo's cause, and they retreated from the field. Defeated and abandoned by his army, Gildo fled to the coast, but was unable to escape by ship. Rather than fall into the hands of Western imperial authorities, the *comes* hanged himself. Mascezel returned to Ravenna in triumph.

Paulus Orosius, *Seven Books of History against the Pagans*, 7.36; Zosimus, *New History*, 5.11; Claudius Claudianus (Claudian), *War against Gildo*, 437–443; Claudius Claudianus (Claudian), *The Consulship of Stilicho*, 1.345–377.

Tadinae, AD 552 (Gothic War, Wars of Justinian I) – Near the Apennine village of Tadinae (Gualdo Tadino), a Roman army under the command of Narses engaged a large force of Ostrogoths led by King Totila. The two armies amassed for battle in the early morning. Narses arrayed his forces across the *Via Flavia* on a line perpendicular to the highway. He assembled Roman infantry on both flanks, and in the centre placed his entire force of mounted *feoderati*, including the Lombards and Heruli, who were ordered to dismount for action. Supporting this main formation of Roman and federate troops were some 8,000 archers positioned on both wings, and to the extreme left was a reserve force of 1,500 cavalry. Totila placed his army in a similar

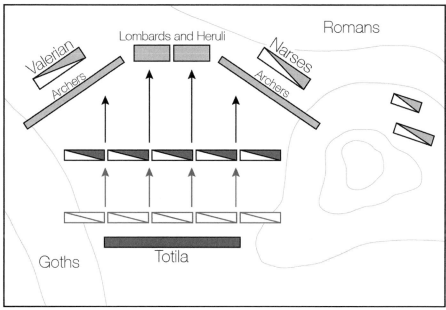

Battle of Tadinae, AD 552 (Phase 1)

manner opposite the Romans. Throughout the morning, both armies faced one another in silence, Narses waiting for Totila to commit his forces to battle, and the king delaying the struggle long enough to permit the antici-pated arrival of an additional 2,000 Gothic horsemen. Toward late morning, the Goths retired from the field, but Narses ordered the Romans to remain in arms. When the armies reassembled for battle in the early afternoon, Totila adjusted the arrangement of his forces by placing the Ostrogothic infantry behind the line of cavalry and instructing the Gothic troops to employ only their spears in the coming engagement. Narses also took the opportunity to implement some final tactical modifications, moving both wings of bowmen forward of his front line so that the overall shape of the formation now formed a crescent. The battle opened with a strong charge of Gothic horse toward the Roman centre. As the horsemen pulled away from the Gothic infantry and bore down on the Roman front line, they failed to realize until too late that the speed and direction of their attack carried them between the two formations of bowmen. The riders were instantly subjected to the amassed crossfire from 8,000 Roman archers. By the time the attack reached the forward line of *foederati*, the Gothic cavalry had suffered severe losses. The fighting continued until sunset, when the Romans finally succeeded in routing the enemy from the field in great disorder. As the defeated cavalry retreated in headlong flight, they struck their awaiting infantry with such force that it threw the entire Ostrogothic army into confusion. In the general

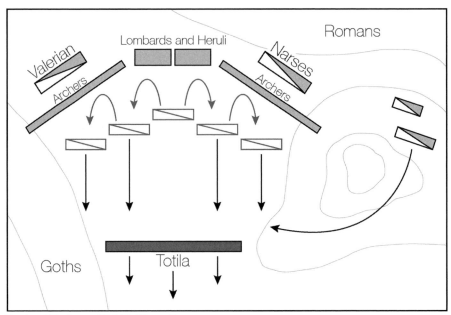

Battle of Tadinae, AD 552 (Phase 2)

panic which followed, the pursuing Romans overran the shattered remnants of Totila's force. Six thousand Goths died in the battle and large numbers were taken prisoner. All captives were later slain by the Romans.

Procopius of Caesarea, *History of the Wars* (*The Gothic War*), 8.31–32.1–21.

Tadinum, AD 552, see Tadinae, AD 552.

Taginae, AD 552, see Tadinae, AD 552.

Tanurin, also **Tannurin, Tannuris, Thannuris, AD 528**, see Mindouos, AD 528.

Tapae, AD 87 (Dacian Wars) – A Dacian army raided the Roman province of Moesia during the winter of AD 86. This attack proved the catalyst for a major Roman counteroffensive the next year that was personally led by Emperor Domitianus. That summer a Roman expeditionary army commanded by Praetorian prefect Cornelius Fuscus crossed the Ister (Danube) River and entered Dacia, intent on reaching the enemy capital of Sarmizegetusa. The Dacians ambushed the Romans at a narrow mountain pass called Tapae (Iron Gate Pass), inflicting heavy casualties on the unsuspecting legions. The defeat resulted in the loss of arms and catapults, the destruction of a legion (the loss of a legionary standard) and the death of Fuscus.

Dio Cassius, *Roman History*, 67.6.5; 68.9.3; Eutropius, *Abridgement of Roman History*, 7.23.

Tapae, AD 88 (Dacian Wars) – The Dacian defeat of a Roman army under Cornelius Fuscus in AD 87 failed to deter Emperor Domitianus from pressing forward with a second offensive the next year. Again moving northward from the province of Moesia along the same line of march used by Roman forces during the previous campaign, the emperor's newly appointed general, Tettius Julianus, encountered the Dacians at Tapae (Iron Gate Pass). The legions soundly defeated the enemy in the clash which followed. King Decebalus' chief lieutenant, Vezinas, only managed to avoid capture by pretending to be one of the countless Dacian dead lying on the battlefield. The Roman advance toward the enemy capital of Sarmizegetusa stalled after the victory. This delay permitted the Dacian king time to sue for peace.

Dio Cassius, *Roman History*, 67.10.1–2.

Tapae, AD 101 (Dacian Wars) – Just as Roman armies did two decades earlier during the Flavian campaigns, Emperor Trajan advanced with his legions across the Ister (Danube) River from Viminacium. From the north bank of the river, the Romans marched north-north-eastward toward the Dacian capital of Sarmizegetusa. Trajan's forces encountered the Dacians assembled in battle formation near the entrance to a narrow mountain pass called Tapae (Iron Gate Pass). The legions finally put the enemy to flight after a difficult struggle that resulted in heavy casualties on both sides.

Dio Cassius, *Roman History*, 68.8.1–2.

Tarbesium, AD 540 (Gothic War, Wars of Justinian I) – Near the northern Italian town of Tarbesium (Treviso), approximately 15 miles (24km) north of the Venetian Lagoon, Roman general Vitalius engaged an Ostrogothic army under Ildibadus. Roman forces were decisively defeated in the resulting battle. Most of Vitalius' army was destroyed, including a large number of German *feoderati*, the Heruli. The Herulian chieftain, Visandus, was among the dead.

Procopius of Caesarea, *History of the Wars (The Gothic War)*, 7.1.34–36.

Tarsus, AD 276, Summer – The death of Emperor Tacitus at Tyana in the summer of 276 was quickly followed by the rule of his half-brother, Marcus Annius Florianus, who immediately proclaimed himself the imperial heir without the approval of the Senate in Rome. At about that same time, the legions of Syria, Phoenicia, Palestine and Egypt declared in favour of the current *Dux totius orientis*, Marcus Aurelius Probus, prompting Florianus to march against his rival claimant in the East. The two armies met near the coastal city of Tarsus in south-eastern Anatolia. Aware that he was opposed by a much larger army consisting primarily of European legions unaccustomed to the Mediterranean climate, Probus deliberately avoided a pitched battle in order to prolong the enemy's discomfort in the oppressive conditions. The summer heat gradually weakened Florianus' army, which was further debilitated by the outbreak of sickness in camp. Probus soon thereafter subjected the exhausted legions to constant harassment, while denying his opponent any opportunity to fight a decisive action. Eventually, the machinations of Probus reduced the tactical advantage previously held by the larger force, compelling Florianus to abandon the struggle and withdraw. The European troops soon murdered Florianus and joined with Probus.

Zosimus, *New History*, 1.64.2–3.

Taurinorum, AD 312, see Augusta Taurinorum, AD 312.

Tebesta, AD 544 – Led by the Leuathae, an uprising of native tribes in Tripolitania quickly forced the *dux Tripolitaniae*, Sergius, to deploy troops in an effort to restore order. Despite achieving an initial victory over tribal forces outside the regional capital of Leptis Magna, discontent continued and soon spread to the neighbouring province of Byzacena, where Antalas, the powerful chieftain of the Frexi, joined the Moorish tribes to the west in opposing Roman authority. The growing insurrection finally persuaded Solomon, the *magister militum per Africam* in Carthage, to deploy his army in an effort to end the unrest once and for all. Marching southward from the capital, the Romans defeated a force led by Antalas near the city of Tebesta (Tebessa) in eastern Numidia. After the day's fighting ended, Solomon refused permission for his soldiers to personally retain any of the battlefield plunder. The decision demoralized the army. When Solomon again prepared to enter battle at Cillium (Kasserine) some 30 miles (48km) south-east of Tebesta, he was badly outnumbered by the enemy, in part because the disaffected troops within his command refused to participate in the confrontation. The Roman army was badly defeated in the battle which followed.

Procopius of Caesarea, *History of the Wars* (*The Vandalic War*), 4.21. See also the Battle of Cillium in the *Chronica* of Victor Tonnennensis.

Tegesta, AD 544, see Tebesta, AD 544.

Telephis, AD 552, see Ollaria, AD 552.

Forum Terebronii, AD 251, see Abrittus, AD 251.

Teutoburg Forest, AD 9, September – During the early empire, Roman campaigns into various German territories progressed successfully, particularly under the leadership of Nero Claudius Drusus and Tiberius. Following the outbreak of the Pannonian Revolt in AD 6, Tiberius was charged with ending the uprising, while the senator and *legatus*, Publius Quinctilius Varus, received the governorship of Germania. This latter appointment eventually generated unrest in the region, due in part to the new governor's callous treatment of the local population, particularly in matters of tax collection. The resulting discord further aggravated latent hostilities already present among the German tribes toward growing Roman authority throughout their lands. In late summer, rumours of an uprising compelled Varus to lead his army west from its summer base near the Visurgis (Weser) River into an un-familiar expanse of thickly-wooded forest east of the Hase River. The Roman column consisted of three legions, the *Legio XVII, XVIII* and *XIX*, plus six cohorts of *auxilia* and three cavalry squadrons. The surrounding woods and rugged terrain restricted the army's ability to adopt an effective defensive posture while on the march, and the situation was made more perilous by the presence of numerous wagons and camp-followers mixed among the troops. Stormy weather further compounded hardships on the journey, creating a treacherous, rain-soaked footpath littered with broken branches. As the governor's army attempted to transverse a narrow corridor of land between a large bog and a steep hill called the Kalkreiser Berg, a massive force of German warriors suddenly launched a ferocious assault against their un-suspecting foe. The attack was led by Arminius, a German prince and former commander of Roman *auxilia*. Spread out for several miles along the narrow track, Varus' legions were unable to assemble into battle formation and quickly found themselves completely surrounded and subjected to repeated volleys of missiles. The fighting gradually moved to close quarters, and the enemy's superior numbers offered the Romans no opportunity to attain a

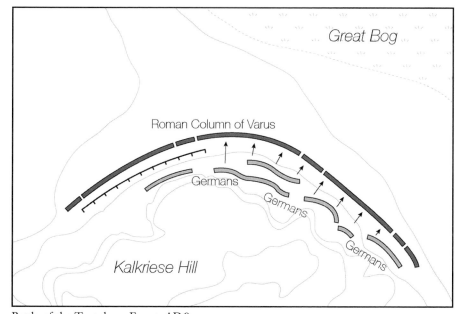

Battle of the Teutoburg Forest, AD 9

tactical advantage anywhere along their entire front, resulting in heavy casualties. Caught in such dire circumstances, Varus elected to encamp on the site for the evening. The next day, the cohorts advanced northward into a more open expanse, but suffered additional deaths in the running battle. On the third day, the army was forced to again enter the forest, an action easily anticipated by the German tribesmen. In the dense woods, the infantry and cavalry jostled for space, the trees allowing no room to respond to the enemy's incessant attacks. As a result, the legions accrued their gravest losses to date. Recognizing that the army's only hope lay in escaping the confines of the forest, the governor kept the troops moving throughout the night. The remnants of the Roman force were still advancing at dawn on the fourth day. A resumption of heavy rain and wind magnified the harsh conditions encountered by the already exhausted men, and following the arrival of fresh German reinforcements it quickly became apparent that the depleted legions, *auxilia* and *alae* faced a far larger opponent. With no hope of escape, Varus and his officers committed suicide to avoid capture. The amassed German host shortly overran and destroyed the remainder of the Roman expedition.

> Lucius Annaeus Florus, *Epitomy*, 2.30; Dio Cassius, *Roman History*, 56.18–24; Velleius Paterculus, *Roman History*, 2.117–120; Ovid, *Sorrows* (*Tristia*), 4.2. Also see Tacitus' description of a visit to the battlefield made by Germanicus Caesar during the Roman campaign of AD 15.

Teutoburger Wald, AD 9, see Teutoburg Forest, AD 9.

Thacea, AD 545, see Siccaveneria, AD 545.

Thala, AD 19 (Revolt of Tacfarinas) – The failure of Roman military forces in North Africa to permanently end a regional guerrilla war inevitably led to another hostile encounter, this time at Thala. A band of nomadic warriors commanded by the Numidian rebel Tacfarinas, a leader of the Musulamian people and former Roman auxiliary soldier, attacked a fortress containing a 500-man garrison of Roman veterans. The assault failed and the raiders withdrew.

> Publius Cornelius Tacitus, *Annals*, 3.21.

Thorda, AD 101, see Tapae, AD 101.

(Battle of) Thundering Legion, AD 174 – During the Antonine campaign to stop German incursions into the Roman Empire, a legionary army under Emperor Marcus Aurelius engaged the Quadi, a powerful southern German tribe responsible for penetrating imperial defences along the central region of the Ister (Danube) River. In the course of the expedition, the *Legio XII Fulminata* was trapped on unfavourable ground by a numerically superior enemy force. After intense, protracted fighting, a significant portion of the

Quadi disengaged from the action in expectation of the legion's imminent capitulation. While the majority of the warriors withdrew from the battle to await Roman surrender, tribal commanders retained sufficient forces in place to successfully contain the exhausted legion, now badly debilitated by heat and thirst. Surrounded in the open by the enemy, weakened by fatigue, denied access to water and fully exposed to the unrelenting heat of the day; the plight of the Romans' position appeared at the point of collapse when a sudden thunderstorm disrupted the stand-off and completely altered the situation. Heavy rain provided the legionaries unexpected relief, and a violent hailstorm and numerous lightning bolts created confusion and effectively ended the battle.

Dio Cassius, *Roman History*, 72.8–10; Paulus Orosius, *Seven Books of History against the Pagans*, 7.15.

Thyatira, AD 366 – On the plains near the community of Thyatira (Akhisar) in Phrygia, a Roman army under the command of Emperor Valens clashed with rebel forces in the service of the usurper Procopius. When it appeared that troops under general Hormisdas were on the verge of overpowering those of the emperor, another of Procopius' commanders named Gomoarius suddenly declared in favour of the *Augustus* and crossed the field, followed by most of the soldiers then opposing the imperial standard. The mass defection assured Valens the victory.

Zosimus, *New History*, 4.8.1–2; Ammianus Marcellinus, *Res Gestae*, 26.9.2–6.

Tiber River, AD 546 (Gothic War, Wars of Justinian I) – In the latter months of 545, Ostrogothic King Totila initiated a siege of Rome in an attempt to reassert Gothic control in central Italy. This effort was challenged by the arrival of imperial forces under the leadership of the Eastern Roman general, Flavius Belisarius. The siege inevitably led to a shortage of foodstuffs in the city, which the Roman army sought to redress by attempting to provision the population. Since his troops were too few to successfully challenge the Gothic army to a decisive battle, Belisarius elected to resupply the city via the Tiber River in an effort to delay its capitulation until his needed reinforcements arrived. In order to stop any such waterborne shipments of goods, the Ostrogoths had earlier built a barrier across the Tiber approximately 10 miles (16km) to the south of the city. The obstruction consisted of a number of very long timbers, which spanned the river between two wooden towers constructed on either bank. Each tower housed a garrison of troops to guard the entire structure. As an additional deterrent, a large chain was extended across this same narrow location in the river. So as to thwart the Gothic barricade, the Romans manufactured a wooden tower of greater height than those supporting the boom, and placed it on two barges which were lashed together. Atop the tower was suspended a small boat filled with combustible materials. When Belisarius' small flotilla was ready, including warships called *dromons*, all advanced from the harbour of Portus toward the city. As the vessels reached the site where the river was blocked, the Romans adroitly overcame the chain, pulled their tower within range of the wooden obstacle, ignited the flammable contents of the boat and dumped it over one of the enemy's towers. The resulting conflagration destroyed both the edifice and the entire 200-man garrison within. At the same time, archers firing from the *dromons* delivered flights of missiles into the ranks of Ostrogoths gathered near the river. Once the enemy was put to flight, Romans proceeded to wreck the boom. While this was going on, Belisarius received information that a detachment of Roman cavalry, deployed on the Isola Sacra to protect his flank, had been defeated by Gothic forces in a skirmish. Word of this loss, including the capture of his subordinate general, Isaac the Armenian, compelled him to abandon the attempt to reach the city. Totila eventually captured Rome in mid-December of 546.

Procopius of Caesarea, *History of the Wars* (*The Gothic War*), 7.19.1–22; Marcellinus Comes, *Chronicle*, 10th indiction, Post consulatum Basili anno VII, in year 547 (Croke).

Ticinum, AD 271 – In northern Italy near the community of Ticinum (Pavia), a Roman army led by Emperor Aurelian destroyed a band of Alamanni intent on plundering the region. The German survivors withdrew to their homelands across the Alps. This victory climaxed Aurelian's efforts to drive the Alamanni and Juthungi out of Italy, and was only made possible by his earlier defeat of the tribesmen at the mouth of the Metaurus (Metauro) River.

Anonymous (Sextus Aurelius Victor), *Epitome of the Emperors*, 35.2 (T. Banchich, trans.).

Tigris River, AD 359 (Persian Wars) – After receiving reports of Persian activity to the west, a Roman force led by the general Ursicinus marched toward the city of Samosata, situated on the west bank of the Euphrates River. Shortly after the Roman column crossed the Tigris River, approximately 100 miles (161km) east of the city, it unexpectedly observed the approach of a numerically superior Persian army from the west. The nearness of the enemy forced the Romans to quickly assemble into a defensive battle formation. While the two armies manoeuvred closer to each other in preparation for battle, the Roman troops stationed to the rear on higher ground observed the rapid approach of a second enemy division, consisting of *cataphracts*. The disparity in size and composition between the two armies, compounded by the imminent arrival of heavily armoured cavalry, finally moved the Romans to abandon their position. The withdrawal quickly degenerated into a disorderly flight, made more chaotic by the weight of the enemy formation pressing forward. As the Romans scattered in confusion toward the Tigris, pockets of fighting erupted between pursuers and fugitives, even as the overall momentum of the retreat carried both armies to the banks of the river. Here, some Roman soldiers turned in a last desperate effort to offer resistance before being overwhelmed, while most simply plunged headlong into the water in order to reach the safety of the far shoreline. The engagement proved a complete victory for the Persians.

Ammianus Marcellinus, *Res Gestae*, 18.8.

Tigris River, AD 363, see Ctesiphon, AD 363.

Timavus, AD 401, November – While a Vandal incursion in the region of Raetia preoccupied the Roman general Flavius Stilicho, a Visigothic army under King Alaric crossed the Julian Alps and entered Italy after plundering Illyricum to the east. The Goths defeated a Roman force of unknown strength near the Timavus (Timavo) River.

Claudius Claudianus (Claudian), *Gothic War*, 550–647; Jerome, *Apology against Rufinus*, 3.21.

Tinurtium, AD 197, see Lugdunum, AD 197.

Tolosa, AD 439 – After defeating the Visigoths at Narbo (Narbonne) in south-eastern Gaul, the Roman general Litorius drove the Gothic army back to the city of Tolosa (Toulouse). Once there, Romans placed the city under siege, but Visigoths led by King Theodoric I defeated the Romans in battle outside the city walls. Litorius was wounded in the engagement and captured. He died several days later while still in Gothic hands.

St Prosper of Aquitaine, *Epitoma chronicon*, *c.*1335, AD 439; Hydatius, Chronicle, 108 [Mom. 116]; Salvianus (Salvian), *The Government of God*, 7.9, 10; Hydatius 108 [Mom. 116] says that Litorius 'was wounded, captured, and then put to death a few days later'. (Burgess, p. 95).

Trachea, AD 551, Spring (Lazic War, Wars of Justinian I) – While Romans grappled with Persians over control of Lazica on the eastern Black Sea coast, Sassanid intrigue inspired a revolt among the Abasgi, a Roman subject tribe whose lands were located north of the region of Apsilia. In response, Roman Emperor Justinian ordered Bessas, the *magister militum per Armeniam*, to end the uprising by military force. Accordingly, he dispatched a strong army under the command of Uligagus and John of Armenia. After departing Phasis by boat, the Romans made an amphibious landing on the Apsilian coast and proceeded overland to Abasgia. Anticipating the arrival of imperial forces, the Abasgi gathered near a formidable defile called Trachea. The Romans found the narrow pass guarded by the tribesmen. Since passage through the gorge could not be achieved except by travellers marching single file, the Romans declined to challenge the Abasgi in a frontal contest. Instead, while Uligagus remained with a portion of the army at Trachea, John led the remainder of the soldiers back to the coast where they re-embarked aboard the boats and sailed north along the coast. The Roman flotilla then came ashore at a location that allowed the soldiers to circumvent the mountain pass and attack the enemy from the rear. When the Abasgi realized that enemy forces were behind them, they quickly withdrew to a nearby mountain fortress, closely followed by the Romans. The retreat soon turned into a running battle, and both fugitives and pursuers were thoroughly intermingled by the time the struggle reached the citadel. Both parties simultaneously rushed through the gates, and the battle resumed within the walls of the redoubt. Once inside the compound, numerous private homes presented the Romans with a further obstacle. From their rooftops, the Abasgi offered stout resistance, finally compelling the Romans to set fire to the structures. In the resulting conflagration many of the Abasgi died, including women and children, while others fell captive to the Romans. Among the few survivors of the holocaust was the tribal king, Opsites, who fled with some of his men into the Caucasus Mountains.

Procopius of Caesarea, *History of the Wars* (*The Persian War*), 8.9.6–30.

Trapezus, AD 69 – In the recently acquired Roman province of Pontus, Anicetus – a once-powerful subordinate of the former King Polemo II of Pontus – led an uprising against Roman authority. Ostensibly arousing a portion of the poorer population to arms in the name of the imperial contender Aulus Vitellius, he attacked the port of Trapezus (Trebizond) on the southeastern Black Sea coast and massacred an entire cohort of Pontic auxiliaries. He then set fire to the fleet in the harbour before escaping by sea. His license was further increased by the temporary absence of Roman naval patrols in the Pontus Euxinus (Black Sea), which were presently withdrawn to Byzantium. As a result, Anicetus' small, makeshift fleet roamed freely throughout the region in complete disregard of Roman authority. In due course, the loss of the cohort was brought to the attention of the Roman campaign general in Judaea, Titus Flavius Vespasianus, who dispatched a number of vexillations from his Syrian legions to resolve the developing situation. Commanded by Virdius Geminus, the forces caught up with Anicetus and his followers at the mouth of the Chobus (Khopi) River. The fugitives were protected for a time by a local king of the Sedochezi, but bribery and the threat of military action by Romans eventually compelled the barbarian ruler to surrender the rebel leader and his fellow refugees. The uprising ended with the capture of Anicetus.

Publius Cornelius Tacitus, *Histories*, 3.47–48.

Forum Trebonii, AD 251, see Abrittus, AD 251.

Treves, AD 70, see Augusta Treverorum, AD 70.

Trier, AD 70, see Augusta Treverorum, AD 70.

Tricamaron, AD 533, December (Vandal War, Wars of Justinian I) –
Emperor Justinian's senior general, Belisarius, invaded North Africa with
10,000 Roman infantry (*comitatenses* and *foederati*), 5,000 Roman cavalry (*comitatenses* and *foederati*), 1,000 mounted archers (400 Heruls and 600 Huns) and
his personal bodyguard of 1,400 *bucellarii*, all aboard 500 transport vessels.
Justinian provided a screen of ninety-two warships to protect the invasion
force from Vandal war fleets. The army landed at Caoutvada, 162 miles
(261km) south of Carthage. Once in North Africa, the Romans moved north,
defeated a Vandal force under King Gelimer at Ad Decimum 8 miles (13km)
from the Vandal capital and occupied Carthage without resistance the following day (September 15). Following his defeat and the occupation of the city,
the Vandal king and remnants of his force fled westward toward Numidia to
the plain of Bulla Regia. Hoping to quickly recover his capital, Gelimer summoned to Africa the main Vandal army under general Tzazo, currently suppressing a local rebellion in Sardina. The Vandal king and returning army
reunited for the march on Carthage in late autumn. The Roman and Vandal
armies collided 20 miles (32km) from the city at Tricamaron on the Mejerda
River. The engagement was largely a cavalry action, decided in Bellisarius'
favour after a series of charges by Roman *cataphracts*. Following repeated
Roman assaults, Tzazo's line broke and briefly rallied at the Vandal camp
before collapsing completely under a sustained attack. The Vandal defeat was
decisive. Tzazo died at Tricamaron and Gelimer fled to Numidia, but was
finally compelled to surrender in March 534. This victory permitted Emperor
Justinian to reorganize the region as a Roman province. For his efforts, Justinian permitted Bellisarius the first triumph by a Roman general in 500 years.

Procopius of Caesarea, *History of the Wars* (*The Vandalic War*), 4.3.1–15.

Turin, AD 312, see Augusta Taurinorum, AD 312.

Tzirallum, AD 313, see Campus Serenus, AD 313.

Urbicus River, AD 456, 5 October – On the banks of the Urbicus (Orbigo)
River, 12 miles (20km) from the Spanish town of Asturica Augusta, a force of
Roman *feoderati* led by the Gothic king, Theodoric II, defeated a sizeable
band of Suevians under King Rechiar. The Suevi were routed with heavy
losses, Rechiar himself being among the wounded.

Hydatius, *Chronicle*, 166 [Mom. 173].

Utriculum, AD 413, see Ocriculum, AD 413.

Utus River, AD 447 – An Eastern Roman army commanded by the general Arnegisclus fought a band of some 30,000 Huns led by King Attila near the Utus (Vit) River. The Romans were defeated after a fierce struggle that ended with heavy casualties on both sides. Counted among the Roman dead was Arnegisclus, who fell courageously in the struggle after being unhorsed. Following this victory, the Huns destroyed the city of Marcianopolis.

Marcellinus Comes, *Chronicle*, 15th indiction, Ardaburis et Calepii, in year 447 (Croke); Jordanes, *Romana*, 331. See also the seventh century *Paschel Chronicle*.

Vada, AD 70 (Revolt of Civilis, Batavian Revolt) – As part of a new tribal offensive against Roman forces in the province of *Germania Inferior* (Lower Germany), the Batavian leader Julius Civilis attacked a Roman encampment near the town of Vada. The detachment of *auxilia* stationed at the fort was insufficient to stop the German onslaught, but the timely arrival of a select force of Roman cavalry led by the general Quintus Petilius Cerialis capably checked the assault and drove the enemy into the Vacalis (Waal) River. In the resulting rout, Civilis briefly attempted to rally his men for a counter-attack, but was ultimately forced to abandon the struggle and swim across the river along with many of his fellow Germans.

Publius Cornelius Tacitus, *Histories*, 5.21.

Vagabanta, AD 371 – Near the city of Vagabanta in Mesopotamia, Roman legions under the command of the generals Trajanus and Vadomarius, former king of the Alamanni, engaged a mixed force of Parthian troops, including mercenaries, archers and *cataphracts*. An imperial prohibition against engaging the Persians in offensive operations initially compelled the legions to retreat when first attacked by enemy cavalry, but the persistent assaults finally compelled the Romans to respond in force. Finding Vagabanta a favourable location for the legions, Trajanus ordered the army to fully engage the Parthians. The Romans defeated the enemy in the resulting struggle, killing many of them during the course of the day's fighting. Afterwards, the armies entered into several inconclusive skirmishes before both sides elected to withdraw.

Ammianus Marcellinus, *Res Gestae*, 29.1.1–3.

Valeria, AD 374 – Angered by the murder of their king, Gabinius, at the hands of the Roman *dux Valeriarum* Marcellianus, the Quadi rose up with the Sarmatians and overran the Pannonian province of Valeria. The *Pannonica* and *Moesiaca* legions responded to the emergency but were defeated piecemeal after failing to coordinate their movements. The Sarmatians attacked the *Legio Moesiaca* before it was fully arrayed for battle, inflicted heavy casualties, and then turned on the remaining legion. After intense fighting, the Sarmatians succeeded in penetrating the line of the *Legio Pannonica*.

Subsequent assaults all but destroyed the two legions before the battle finally ended.

Ammianus Marcellinus, *Res Gestae*, 29.6.13–14.

Venetia, AD 549 (Gothic War, Wars of Justinian I) – Upon arriving in the north-eastern Italian region of Venetia, King Audouin and a Lombard army of 6,000 men routed a detachment of Roman troops commanded by Lazarus. The victorious army afterward abandoned all previous plans to unite with Gothic armies of the Ostrogothic king, Totila, and marched north in preparation for recrossing the Ister (Danube) River and returning to the lands of the Sclaveni peoples.

Procopius of Caesarea, *History of the Wars* (*The Gothic War*), 7.35.17–22.

Verona, AD 249, September – An army led by the usurper Caius Messius Decius, commander of Roman armies in Moesia and Pannonia, defeated the numerically superior forces of Emperor Philip near Verona. Both the emperor and his son, the appointed *Caesar* Philip the Younger, died in the struggle.

Zosimus, *New History*, 1.22; Anonymous (Sextus Aurelius Victor), *Epitome of the Emperors*, 28.10 (T. Banchich, trans.).

Verona, AD 285 – Soon after achieving military successes in Germania and Britannia, Emperor Carinus faced a threat from the rebellious governor Sabinus Julianus. Responding to the danger, Carinus moved his legions southward over the Alps and into northern Italy, where they clashed with the usurper's army near Verona. Carinus defeated Julianus in the struggle and then assumed command of his opponent's forces before moving against a second hostile army under the leadership of the pretender Diocles (later Emperor Diocletian).

Anonymous (Sextus Aurelius Victor), *Epitome of the Emperors*, 38.6; Sextus Aurelius Victor, *Liber de Caesaribus*, 39.

Verona, AD 312 (Wars of Constantine I) – Emboldened by his army's victories over Maxentius' *cataphracti* at Augusta Taurinorum (Turin) and Brixia (Brescia), Constantine marched against the city of Verona, presently defended by a substantial concentration of enemy troops led by the Praetorian prefect Ruricius Pompeianus. Constantine initiated a siege upon reaching the city, but could not fully circumvallate the community before Pompeianus attempted to rupture the lines in an effort to summon aid. The sally failed and his forces were driven back into Verona, having suffered heavy casualties. Constantine then resumed his assault with more vigour. While the investment progressed, Pompeianus managed at last to escape through the siege lines and rally a substantial army to relieve the beleaguered inhabitants of the city. The approach of these reinforcements compelled Constantine to divide his command, leaving a portion of the army to continue the attack on Verona while he personally led the remainder of his forces in a set-piece confrontation with Pompeianus. Constantine was immediately aware that he faced a numerically superior army, a circumstance which compelled him to abandon a double battle-line for a longer and necessarily thinner array in order to avoid envelopment. Once the fighting began, his more experienced force was able to take control of the contest and rout the enemy with significant losses. The prefect Pompeianus was among the dead. The defenders of Verona surrendered following the victory.

Anonymous Valesianus, Pars Prior, *The Lineage of the Emperor Constantine*, 4.12; Anonymous, *Panegyrici Latini* [AD 313], 12.8.1–11.2; Nazarius, *Panegyrici Latini*, 4.25–26.2; Zosimus, *New History*, 2.15; Sextus Aurelius Victor, *Liber De Caesaribus*, 40.

Verona, AD 403 – A Roman army led by the *magister militum* Flavius Stilicho defeated a Visigothic force under King Alaric outside the city of Verona in north-central Italy. The Goths then crossed the Alps into Illyricum.

Claudius Claudianus (Claudian), *Panegyric on the Sixth Consulship of the Emperor Honorius*, 201–209.

Vetera, AD 69, see Castra Vetera, AD 69.

Via Salaria, AD 69, 20–21 December (Year of the Four Emperors, Roman Civil Wars) – In preparation for marching his legions into Rome, Flavian general Marcus Antonius Primus sent an advance column of 1,000 cavalry along the Salarian Way with orders to enter the north-eastern part of the city and secure the Colline Gate. As the detachment of horsemen led by Quintus Petilius Cerialis approached their destination, they encountered a Vitellian force, consisting of both infantry and cavalry, blocking the *Via Salaria*. The resulting battle occurred in a developed area outside the city walls where the maze of buildings, gardens and winding streets proved a liability for Cerialis' troops. At the same time, the familiar surroundings permitted the Vitellians to exploit the situation to best tactical advantage and eventually put the enemy to flight. The subsequent pursuit by the victors lasted only as far as the town of Fidenae, some 5 miles (8km) north of Rome on the same highway.

Publius Cornelius Tacitus, *Histories*, 3.78–79.

Vicus Dolensis, AD 469 (Visigothic War, Gothic Wars) – The expansion of Visigothic authority into northern and central Gaul inevitably generated a military response from the Romans. The Bretons under King Riothamus challenged the Gothic invasion in the region of Armorica in north-western Gaul. Acting in their capacity as Roman *feoderati*, the Bretanii responded to an appeal for assistance from Roman Emperor Anthemius and engaged the Goths under King Euricus not far from the village of Dolensis (Deols,

Bourg-de-Deols). Riothamus attacked the enemy with 12,000 men near the Indre River, but was repulsed with heavy losses before Roman forces were able reach the theatre of fighting. Following this defeat, the king, together with the remnants of his army, sought refuge with the Burgundians, another Roman federate people. Euricus thereafter captured the city of Avaricum (Bourges) and threatened the northern reaches of Aquitainica Prima to the south.

Gallic Chronicle of 511, no. 649 *s.a.* 471; Jordanes, *The Origins and Deeds of the Goths*, 237–238.

Vicus Helenae, AD 428 – Aware of the declining Roman authority in some parts of Gaul, the Merovingian king, Chlodio, invaded territories of the Artebates. In response, Roman general Flavius Aetius moved against the Frankish invaders and defeated them at Vicus Helenae.

Sidonius Apollinaris, *Carmen*, 5. 212 sqq.

Vindonissa, AD 298 – The *Caesar* Constantius Chlorus defeated the Alamanni in a great battle.

Anonymous, *Panegyrici Latini* [AD 310], 6.3. For a discussion of the date and location of this event, see C.V.E. Nixon's comments in Nixon and Rodgers, *In Praise of the Later Roman Emperors: The Panegyric Latini* (University of California Press, 1995), footnote 25, pp. 225–26.

Visurgis River, AD 16 (German War) – Chief of the Cherusci and victor over Varus in AD 9, Arminius assembled a German army on the banks of the Visurgis (Weser) River in an effort to stop the legions of Germanicus Caesar, commander of Roman armies on the Rhine, from affecting a crossing. Unwilling to risk his legionary infantry in the face of such opposition, Germanicus ordered his cavalry to ford the river at several points so as to deny the Germans any opportunity to concentrate their forces. One detachment of cavalry, the Batavians under the leadership of Chariovalda, reached the far bank and was promptly drawn into a trap. The Cherusci, feigning retreat, compelled the Batavians to give chase and led their pursuers into an area of open ground surrounded by forest-covered hills. The Cherusci then surrounded Chariovalda's command and inflicted heavy casualties. Despite being hard-pressed by their attackers, the Batavians formed a circle and offered stout defence until the severity of their losses clearly revealed the location as untenable. Determined to extricate his men from the situation, Cheriovalda ordered his warriors to break through the Cheruscian formation en masse. The Batavian chieftain fell under intense missile fire in the resulting sally, but the action saved his force, which was spared any further enemy attacks by the timely arrival of Germanicus' cavalry.

Publius Cornelius Tacitus, *Annals*, 2.11.

Volandum, AD 58 (Parthian Wars) – War erupted in the spring of 58 after years of growing tensions between the Roman and Parthian empires over control of the kingdom of Armenia. Roman Emperor Nero responded to the crisis by dispatching an army under the command of Cnaeus Domitius Corbulo. The campaign began slowly and was initially characterized by a protracted period of skirmishing between opposing sides. After an aborted meeting between Corbulo and the Parthian-backed King Tiridates I of Armenia, the Romans moved against a number of enemy fortresses, the strongest of which was Volandum, located in eastern Anatolia south of the Aboras (Aras) River. Corbulo assigned the reduction of the minor strongholds to his *legatus*, Cornelius Flaccus, and the *praefectus castrorum*, Insteius Capito, while he concentrated the remaining legionary forces against Volandum itself. As some of his troops began the work of sapping the walls while protected by a *testudo*, others concentrated on scaling walls using ladders. Enemy opposition along the ramparts was at the same time suppressed by slingers, both *libritores* and *funditores*, and the army's *ballistae*. The assault proved irresistible. The fortress was captured and the entire adult population slain. Emboldened by this success, the Roman army next moved against the northern Armenian capital of Artaxata.

Publius Cornelius Tacitus, *Annals*, 13.39.

Volturno, AD 554, see Casilinus River, AD 554.

Volturno River, AD 554, see Casilinus River, AD 554.

Volturnus, AD 554, see Casilinus River, AD 554.

Watling Street, AD 61 (Revolt of Boudicca) – In Britannia, the death of the Icenian king, Prasutagus, was shortly followed by the Roman acquisition of his lands and the brutal treatment of his family: his household was pillaged, Queen Boudicca beaten and his daughters raped. Other members of the king's family were also poorly treated, and Roman authorities ordered the seizure of family estates belonging to leading men of the tribe. Such outrages quickly incited a rebellion led by Prasutagus' widow, and the fear of further violations likewise inspired the neighbouring Trinobantes to take up arms. Led by Boudicca, thousands of Celtic rebels soon overran and destroyed the Roman colony of Camulodunum (Colchester), sacked Londinium (London), massacred some 70,000 Romans and moved northward against the settlement of Verulamium (St Albans). All Roman efforts to suppress the uprising by military force failed until the rebels were challenged by an army led by the island's governor, Caius Suetonius Paulinus. Marching south-east from the Isle of Mona (Anglesey), the two armies clashed at a location somewhere along the length of Roman highway extending from Viroconium (Wroxeter) to Verulamium. In a narrow defile, enclosed by forest from behind and facing

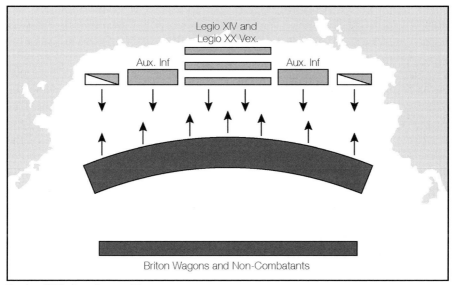

Battle of Watling Street, AD 61

a broad, uninterrupted plain, Paulinus assembled some 10,000 men in serried ranks. In the centre, he arrayed the *Legio XIV Gemina*, accompanied by a *vexillatio* of the *Legio XX Valeria Victrix* in a *triplex acies*. On each flank were stationed cohorts of auxiliary infantry, joined by cavalry on the wings. Across from the Roman formation were countless thousands of Celtic warriors, both infantry and horse, gathered in readiness to assault the enemy line. Boudicca's army swept forward while the legions stood motionless, awaiting their adversaries. When tribesmen had drawn to within yards of the Roman line, the legionaries discharged their *pila* to devastating effect and then charged the enemy in a wedge formation. The *auxilia* immediately followed, and then the cavalry. The counter-attack proved devastating and the dense mass of Britons suffered heavy casualties during the long struggle. Finally, in late afternoon, Celtic resistance completely collapsed under the inexorable pressure of the Roman assault. As the mass of fugitives streamed away from the battlefield, their flight was hindered by their own wagons which were assembled at the edge of the plain. Trapped between the advancing legions and the cordon of vehicles, the native army was largely destroyed. According to Tacitus, almost 80,000 Britons died. Roman losses were negligible.

Publius Cornelius Tacitus, *Annals*, 14.34–37; Dio Cassius, *Roman History*, 62.8–12.

Weser River, AD 16, see Idistavisus, AD 16

Westphalia, AD 9, see Teutoburg Forest, AD 9

Willows, AD 376, see Ad Salices, AD 376

Notes

CPL   Robert Cavenaile (ed.), *Corpus Papyrorum Latinarum* (Wiesbaden, 1958).

P. Oxy.   Bernard P. Grenfell, Arthur S. Hunt, et al. (eds), *The Oxyrhynchus Papyri* (London, 1898).

CIL   Theodor Mommsen, Hermann Dessau, et al. (eds), *Corpus Inscriptionum Latinarum* (Berlin, 1863).

FIRA   Salvatore Riccobono, et al. (eds), *Fontes Iuris Romani Anteiustiniani*, 2nd edition, 3 vols. (Florence, S.a.G. Barbèra, 1940–43).

ILS   Hermann Dessau (ed.), *Inscriptiones Latinae Selectae* (Berlin, 1892–1916).

1. *CPL* 102 (papyrus, Fayum, Egypt, in AD 92).
2. Lawrence Keppie, *Making of the Roman Army: From Republic to Empire* (New York, Barnes and Noble Books, 1994), 180; John Cecil Mann, *Legionary Recruitment and Veteran Settlement During the Principate*, Margaret Roxan (ed.), Occasional Publication No. 7. Institute of Archaeology. Whitestable (Kent, Whitestable Litho Ltd, 1983), 49–68; John Cecil Mann, 'The Raising of New Legions during the Principate' *Hermes*, 91 (1963), 483–89.
3. Candidates for military service were also expected to submit *litterae commendaticiae* (letters of introduction).
4. Approximately 5 feet 8.6 inches in modern measurement. Vegetius 1.5 (*Vegetius: Epitome of Military Science*, N.P. Milner (trans.), Liverpool, Liverpool University Press, 1993). The above stated height requirement was adjusted in the late fourth century AD to 5 feet 7 inches (approximately 5 feet 6 inches modern) in the Theodosian Code (*Codex Theod.* 7.13.3). For Vegetius' description of the physical expectations of the army recruit, see *Epitome* 1.6.
5. In *Epitome* 1.5 Vegetius notes that, 'if necessity demands, it is right to take account not so much of stature as of strength'. For additional discussion on this topic, see G.R. Watson, *The Roman Soldier* (Ithaca, Cornell University Press, 1995), 31–53.
6. In 13 BC, the period of legionary service was set at sixteen years (Cassius Dio, 54.25.6). Service was extended to twenty years in AD 6 (Cassius Dio, 55.23.1). In the second century AD, enlistment was raised to twenty-five years. See Alfred von Domaszewski, 'Die Rangordnung des romischen Heeres', *Bonner Jahrbucher*, 117, (1908), and H.M.D. Parker, *The Roman Legions* (New York, Dorset Press, 1992), 212–13.
7. Watson, *The Roman Soldier*, 72–74; *CPL 326/P.Dura 82*/Fink, *RMR 47* (papyrus from Dura Europus, early third century AD); *AE 1979.643* (ostracon from Bu-Njem, North Africa, third century AD, *Legio III Augusta*); Fink, *RMR 10* (papyrus from Egypt, late first century AD).
8. Parker, *The Roman Legions*, 221–22.
9. Parker, *The Roman Legions*, 218–19. Each cohort possessed a unit savings bank. Unlike soldiers of the early Empire, later Roman soldiers did not have to make payments for food, bedding and clothing.
10. Before the reign of Emperor Domitianus, legionaries were paid an annual income of 225 *denarii* and received a grant of 3,000 *denarii* upon retirement (Cassius Dio, 55.23; Watson, *The Roman Soldier*, 151). By the early third century AD, the discharge gratuity had risen to 5,000 *denarii* (Cassius Dio, 78.36).
11. *P. Oxy.* 39 (papyrus, Oxyrhynchus, Egypt, in AD 52).

12. Parker, *The Roman Legions*, 238–39.
13. Restrictions on marriage did not apply to officers with the rank of centurion or above; *CIL* 3.3271; *CIL* 7.229; *FIRA* 3.47; *ILS* 2389; *FIRA* 3.5; *FIRA* 3.19.
14. Polybius, vol. 4, *Histories IX–XV* (Loeb Classical Library, 1925), 11.33 and cf. 11.23.1; Sallust, vol. 1, *War with Jugurtha* (Loeb Classical Library), 49.
15. Sallust, *War with Jugurtha*, 49.6, 46.7.
16. For reference to Gallienus see: Yann Le Bohec, *Imperial Roman Army* (New York, Hippocrene Books, 1989), 24; Graham Webster, *The Roman Imperial Army of the First and Second Centuries AD*, 3rd edn (Totowa, New Jersey, Barnes and Noble Books, 1989), 111, ftn. 7; Pat Southern, *The Roman Army, A Social and Institutional History* (Santa Barbara, ABC-CLIO, 2006), 101–02; Josephus notes that 120 horsemen were attached to each legion.
17. Aurelius Victor, *De Caesaribus*, 33. For insight into the career of a Roman officer during the early Principate, see D.B. Saddington, 'An Augustan Officer on the Roman Army: *Militaria* in Velleius Paterculus and Some Inscriptions', in *Documenting the Roman Army, Essays in Honour of Margaret Roxan*, J.J. Wilkes (ed.) (London, Institute of Classical Studies, 2003), 19–29.
18. Le Bohec, *Imperial Roman Army*, 38; Parker, *The Roman Legions*, 51; Keppie, *Making of the Roman Army*, 40; Adrian Goldsworthy, *The Complete Roman Army* (London, Thames and Hudson Ltd, 2003), 48; Nigel Pollard and Joanne Berry, *The Complete Roman Legions* (London, Thames and Hudson Ltd, 2012), 38.
19. Parker, *The Roman Legions*, 187–88; Peter Connolly, *Greece and Rome at War* (London, MacDonald Phoebus, 1981), 222; Le Bohec, *Imperial Roman Army*, 38; Webster, *Roman Imperial Army*, 112; Alistair Scott Anderson, 'The Imperial Army', *Roman World*, vol. 1, John Wacher (ed.) (London, Routledge and Kegan Paul Ltd, 1987), 94.
20. Parker, *The Roman Legions*, 188–89; Connolly, *Greece and Rome at War*, 221; Le Bohec, *Imperial Roman Army*, 38–39; Webster, *Imperial Army*, 112–13; Anderson, 'The Imperial Army', 95.
21. Parker, *The Roman Legions*, 191–93; Connolly, *Greece and Rome at War*, 222; Le Bohec, *Imperial Roman Army*, 39; Webster, *Imperial Army*, 113; Anderson, 'The Imperial Army', 95; Jonathan Roth, *The Logistics of the Roman Army at War, 264 BC–AD 235* (Leiden, E.J. Brill, 1999), 272–73.
22. Parker, *The Roman Legions*, 189; Connolly, *Greece and Rome at War*, 221; Le Bohec, *Imperial Roman Army*, 39; Webster, *Imperial Army*, 113; Anderson, 'The Imperial Army', 95.
23. In *Epitoma rei militaris* the fourth century writer Vegetius confirms that during the Principate the first cohort was double the size of the remaining nine cohorts. Vegetius 2, 8; Hyginus 3, 4; *CIL* viii, 18072; David J. Breeze, 'The Organization of the Legion: The First Cohort and the *Equites Legionis*', *The Journal of Roman Studies*, 59 (1969), 50; Southern, *The Roman Army*, 100–01.
24. Despite the vast amount of historical material available to modern scholars about the Roman army of the early Empire, an exact figure for the full manpower complement of a typical cohortal legion of the Principate is still unknown. This uncertainty is due to the wide array of offices, staff positions and posts within a legion. Ancient sources record at least 154 different types of posts below the rank of centurion which existed in the legions during this period. Many of these positions have been identified as being more specifically related to the administrative or support services of the legion than to the tactical combat element, yet the duties assigned to numerous personnel also appear to have overlapped both areas of responsibility. To complicate this question further, for the vast majority of these posts, historians are uncertain as to how many men held one of these stations in a legion at any one time. For example, on an inscription dated around AD 20, there were twenty-two *librarii legionis* in the Legio III Augusta. Further inscriptions reveal that for the same legion, there were at least twelve *beneficiarii tribuni lacticlavi* in AD 198 and thirty-seven *cornicines* in AD 203 – Breeze, 'First Cohort and *Equites Legionis*', 50; *AE*, 1898, 108; *CIL*, viii, 2551,

2557. See also Alfred von Domaszewski, 'Die Rangordnung des romischen Heeres', *Bonner Jahrbucher*, 117 (1908), 48.

25. David Breeze, 'The organization of the career structure of the immunes and principales of the Roman army', *Bonner Jahrbucher*, 174 (1974), 245–92; Alistair Scott Anderson, 'The Imperial Army', 95; Parker, *The Roman Legions*, 205–06; Webster, *Imperial Army*, 117; Vegetius, 2.7.

26. Parker, *The Roman Legions*, 205–06; Connolly, *Greece and Rome at War*, 223.

27. *signifer CIL* viii: 2912, 18280, 2811, 2881, 2920, (A.E. 1957, 88), 3003, etc., *aquifer CIL* viii: 2794, 18311.

28. *optio CIL* viii: R.S.A.C. LVIII Lambaesis; *CIL* viii: 2531, 2790 18085, 2804 = 18142, 2994, 2858, 2879, 2947, etc.

29. *tesserarius CIL* viii: 2828, 2880 = 2996.

30. Webster, *Imperial Army*, 115, 117; Parker, *The Roman Legions*, 208; Connolly, *Greece and Rome at War*, 223; David J. Breeze, 'Pay Grades and Ranks Below the Centurionate', *The Journal of Roman Studies*, 61 (1971), 130–35.

31. Vegetius 2.21, *ILS* 2445, *ILS* 2446.

32. *custus armorum CIL* viii: 2902, 2918 and 2919, 4351 = 18531, 18320, etc.

33. Le Bohec, *The Imperial Roman Army*, 121; Webster, *Imperial Army*, 115, 117; Connolly, *Greece and Rome at War*, 223; Parker, *The Roman Legions*, 208. See also David J. Breeze, 'The Career Structure below the Centurionate during the Principate', *Aufstieg und Niedergang der romischen Welt* (1974), 435–51; *custus armorum CIL* viii: 2902, 2918, 1919, 4351 = 18531, 18320, etc.

34. Frank Graham, *Dictionary of Roman Military Terms* (Newcastle upon Tyne, Frank Graham, 1981), 12, 16, 19; Connolly, *Greece and Rome at War*, 223, 242; Webster, *Imperial Army*, 116–17; Le Bohec, *The Imperial Roman Army*, 53–55; *CIL* viii 18072, 18060; Anderson, 'The Imperial Army', 96.

35. Eric Sander ['Zur Rangordnung des römischen Heeres: die gradus ex caliga', *Historia* 3 (1954–55), 87–105] argues that the various posts below the rank of centurion were equal in rank but bore differing levels of prestige with them. Thus, the honour which accompanied a post offered the bearer greater status within the legion.

36. Watson, *The Roman Soldier*, 76; Frank Graham, *Dictionary of Roman Military Terms*, 4, 18–19; Justinian, *Corpus Iuris Civilis*, Editio Stereotypatertia Decima, vol. 1, Institutiones, recognovit Paulus Krueger; Digesta, recognovit Theodorus Mommsen; retractavit, Paulus Krueger (Berolini, Apud Weidmannos, 1920), *Digesta seu Pandectae* 50.6.7: dig., 50, 6, 7: quibusdam aliquam vacationem munerum graviorum condicio tribuit, ut sunt mensores, optio valetudinarii, medici, capsarii, et artifices qui fossam faciunt, veterinarii, architectus, gubernatores, naupegi, ballistrarii, specularii, fabri, sagittarii, aerarii, bucularum struc-tores, carpentarii, scandularii, gladiatores, aquilices, tubarii, cornuarii, arcuarii, plumbarii, ferrarii, lapidarii, et qui calcem cocunt, et qui silvam infindunt, quicarbonem caedunt ac torrent. In eodem numero haberi solent lani, venatores, victimarii, et optio fabricae, et qui aegris praesto sunt, librarii quoque qui docere possint, et horreorum librarii, et librarii depositorum, et librarii caducorum et adiutores corniculariorum, et stratores, et polliones, et custodes armorum, et praeco, et bucinator. Hi igitur omnes inter immunes habentur. Watson, *The Roman Soldier*, 181; Webster, *Imperial Army*, 119–20; Vegetius 2.7.

37. Connolly, *Greece and Rome at War*, 223–24; D.B. Saddington, 'The Roman Auxilia of Tacitus, Josephus and Other Early Imperial Writers', *Acta Classica*, Classical Association of South Africa, 13 (1970), 89–124; David S. Potter, *The Roman Empire at Bay, AD 180–395*, 2nd ed., Routledge History of the Ancient World (New York, Routledge, 2014), 129–30.

38. Connolly, *Greece and Rome at War*, 223–24; George Leonard Cheesman, *The Auxilia of the Roman Imperial Army* (Oxford, The Clarendon Press, 1971), 45–49. As an example, the title *cohors I Sebastenorum* indicates this auxiliary cohort was originally recruited in the com-munity of Sebaste in Samaria. Other examples of *cognomina* include *cohors I Gallorum, ala*

I Pannoniorum, and *cohors VI Commagenorum equitata*. Auxiliary units might also include the name of an emperor in their title, such as *Augusta* or *Flavia*.

39. See *Corpus Inscriptionum Latinarum*, viii 18122; and Tacitus, vol. 3, *Annals I–III*, John Jackson (trans.) (Loeb Classical Library, 1979), II.52; Roy W. Davies, 'Police Work in Roman Times', *History Today*, 18 (1968), 700–07; Brian Campbell and Lawrence A. Tritle, *The Oxford Handbook of Warfare in the Classical World* (Oxford, Oxford University Press, 2013), 354.
40. See the *adlocutio* delivered by the Emperor Hadrian in the summer of AD 128 to the numerous units stationed in Numidia. *CIL* viii 18042.
41. Cheesman, *Auxilia*, 64–101.
42. Pseudo-Hyginus (Polybius and Pseudo-Hyginus), *De Munitionibus Castrorum* (from *The Fortification of the Roman Camp*), M.C.J. Miller and J.G. DeVoto (trans. and ed.) (Chicago, Ares Publishers, Inc., 1944), 16, 26–27. A *turma* was a troop or squadron of cavalry containing thirty to thirty-two men.
43. A *cohors equitata* was also called upon when needed to provide mounted escort and other services for senior officers and officials such as *legatii* or proconsuls. Legionaries were not, however, exempt from such duties. *CIL* viii 18042Ab notes a detachment of soldiers from *Legio III Augusta* sent for duty at the *officuim* of the *pr[ocon]sulis*. *CIL* viii 18042Ab.
44. Rene Louis Victor Cagnat, *L'Armee romaine d'Afrique et l'occupation militaire de l'Afrique sous les empereurs*, Ernest Leroux (ed.) (Paris, Imprimerie Nationale, 1913. Reprint: New York, Arno Press Inc., 1975), 108; Roy W. Davies, 'Cohortes Equitatae' *Historie*, 20 (1971), 751–63; Cheesman, *Auxilia*, 29.
45. Pseudo-Hyginus, *De Munitionibus Castrorum*, 28.
46. Michael Speidel, 'The Pay of the auxilia', *The Journal of Roman Studies*, 63 (1973), 141–47; Webster, *Imperial Army*, 145–51.
47. Pseudo-Hyginus, *De Munitionibus Castrorum*, 16. Quick multiplication will arrive at a total figure of 512 men in each *ala quingenaria* and 768 in an *ala miliaria*. Such numerical discrepancies appear in all auxiliary units as well as the legions.
48. This individual more commonly bore the title *praefactus equitum* in the early Empire.
49. Keppie, *Making of the Roman Army*, 177–78.
50. The commanding officer of an *ala quingenaria*, *ala miliaria* or *cohors quingenaria peditata* were addressed as *praefectus*. The senior officer of a *cohors miliaria peditata* bore the title *tribunus*. Cheesman, *Auxilia*, 36; Keppie, *Making of the Roman Army*, 177–78; Eric Birley, 'The Equestrian officers of the Roman Army' *Roman Britain and the Roman Army* (1953), 133–53.
51. Connolly, *Greece and Rome at War*, 224.
52. 'The cavalry also, divided by troops [turmae] and armed, similarly traversed the same distance, performing equestrian manoeuvres, now pursuing, now retreating, and by some rally renewing the charge.' Vegetius (Flavius Vegetius Renatus), *De Roman empire Militari* (This work is also known by the titles *Rei miitaris instituta* and *Epitoma rei militaris*), Phillips (ed.), Milner (trans.), I.27.
53. Davies, 'Cohortes Equitatae', 760; see Josephus, *Bellum Judaicum*, Anr. XX.122, 160–61, 169–71, 188, XVIII.85–87; Josephus, *Jewish War*, II.236, 258–63, 296–332 where cavalry was used to deal with policing or crowd control; Pseudo-Hyginus, *De Munitionibus Castrorum*, 30.
54. Stéphane Gsell and Jerome Carcopino, 'La base de M. Sulpicuis Felix et les décurions de Sala', *Mel. D'Arch. Et d'Hist.* (Ecole franç. De Rome, 1931), 1–32; Jerome Carcopino, *Le Maroc Antique*, 9th ed. (Paris, Librairie Gallimard, 1943).
55. Le Bohec, *The Imperial Roman Army*, 31–32.
56. Nacera Benseddik, *Les troupes auxiliaries de l'armee romaine in Mauretanie Casarienne sous le Haut-Empire* (Alger, Societe nationale d'Edition et de Diffusion, 1979), 87–98.
57. Among these were the Pannonian revolt of AD 14 and the revolt of Civilis on the Rhine in 69–70.

58. Benseddik, *Les troupes auxiliarres*, 93–94.
59. Cheesman, *Auxilia*, 69–70.
60. Benseddik, *Les troupes auxiliarres*, 93–94.
61. Le Bohec, *Auxiliaries*, 164–65, 172–73.
62. *CIL* xi 5632; Cheesman, *Auxilia*, 128.
63. For a discussion of the overall size of the Late Roman Army, see Warren Treadgold, *Byzantium and Its Army, 284–1081* (Stanford, Stanford University Press, 1998); Peter Heather, *The Fall of the Roman Empire: A New History of Rome and the Barbarians* (Oxford, Oxford University Press, 2007); Richard Duncan-Jones, *Structure and Scale in the Roman Economy* (Cambridge, Cambridge University Press, 2002); Richard Duncan-Jones, *Money and Government in the Roman Empire* (Cambridge, Cambridge University Press, 1994).
64. Paul Elliott, *Legions in Crisis: The Transformation of the Roman Soldier, AD 192–284* (Stroud, UK, Fonthill Media Ltd, 2014), 28–31.
65. William Seston, *Diocletien et la tetrachie*, vol. I, *Guerres et reformes (284–300)*, Bibliotheque des Ecoles francaises d'Athenes et de Rome, facs. 162 (Paris, E. de Boccard, 1946), 246, 298; Arnold Hugh Martin Jones, *The Later Roman Empire, 284–602: A Social, Economic, and Administrative Survey*, vol. I (Norman, University of Oklahoma Press, 1964), 59–60; Pat Southern and Karen Dixon, *The Late Roman Army* (New Haven, Yale University Press, 1996), 31–32. For a sound discussion on the size of the Diocletianic legion, see Southern and Dixon, 31–32. Seston suggests the older pre-Diocletianic legions maintained their traditional size, and that the legions introduced by Diocletian possessed a manpower strength of approximately 1,000. Seston, *Diocletien et la tetrachie*, 299. Jones argues that the new legions raised by Diocletian were, like their earlier counterparts, about 6,000 strong. Jones, *The Later Roman Empire*, 56, 680.
66. Theodor Mommsen, 'Das romische Militarwesen seit Diocletian', *Hermes*, 24 (1889), 229, 254; Denis van Berchem, *L'Armee de Diocletien at La Reforme Constantienne* (Paris, Geuthner,1952), 110–11.
67. Jones, *The Later Roman Empire*, 56, 680; Seston, *Diocletien et la tetrachie*, 299.
68. Jones, *The Later Roman Empire*, 608. Jones writes, 'In Diocletian's day, when an important expeditionary force was required, it was formed in the manner habitual to the second century by assembling detachment[s] drawn from the frontier legions and auxiliary troops'. Jones, *The Later Roman Empire*, 54; Pat Southern, *The Roman Empire from Severus to Constantine* (New York, Routledge-Taylor Francis Group, 2007), 157–58; Edward Luttwak, *The Grand Strategy of the Roman Empire: From the First Century AD to the Third* (Baltimore, The Johns Hopkins University Press, 1976), 187–88; Arther Ferrill, *The Fall of the Roman Empire, the Military Explanation* (London, Thames and Hudson, 1988), 41–43. Vegetius (1.17) suggests that some of the legions under Diocletian retained their traditional size, but evidence is insufficient to determine the universality of this practice. See also Ammianus, 18.9.3–4.
69. Jones, *The Later Roman Empire*, 608; A.D. Lee suggests both Diocletian and Constantine shared in a more balanced realignment of the Roman army. A.D. Lee, *War in Late Antiquity, A Social History* (Malden, MA, Blackwell Publishing, 2007), 10–11. For further insight into the topic, see Martinus Johannes Nicasie, *Twilight of Empire: The Roman Army from the Reign of Diocletian until the Battle of Adrianople*, Dutch Monographs on Ancient History and Archaeology (Amsterdam, J.C. Gieben, 1998), 1–7.
70. Denis van Berchem supports the conclusion that the division of the Roman army into two parts, frontier army and field army, occurred during the reign of Constantine. Berchem, *L'Armee de Diocletien*, 87–88.
71. Jones, *The Later Roman Empire*, 606–611, 112; John Bagnell Bury, *History of the Later Roman Empire*, vol. I (New York, Dover Publications Inc., n.d.), 37. The *Scholae Palatinae* consisted of 3,500 men, and included the *protectores/domestici*, *scutarii*, *gentiles* and *armaturae*.

72. Jones, *The Later Roman Empire*, 612; Arther Ferrill, *Fall of the Roman Empire*, 129; Bury, *LRE*, vol. I, 42–43; Timo Stickler, 'The Foederati', in Paul Erdkamp (ed.), *A Companion to the Roman Army* (Malden, MA, Wiley-Blackwell Publishing Ltd, 2011), 495–514.

73. An officer with the rank of *comes* might possess authority over several *duces*, but for officers so titled the breadth of field and/or command responsibilities varied widely and in importance. Further, ancient sources provide no clear or uniform distinction between the authority and responsibilities of a *dux* and *comes* in command of frontier troops (Southern and Dixon, 58–60; L. Varaday, 'New evidence on some problems of the Late Roman military organization', *Acta Antiqua*, 9 (1961), 355; Robert Grosse, *Romische Miliargeschichte von Gallienus bis zum Beginn der Byzantinschen Themenverfassung* (Berlin, Weidmannsche Buchhandlung, 1920), 156.

74. Charles R. Whittaker, *Frontiers of the Roman Empire: A Social and Economic Study* (Baltimore, The Johns Hopkins University Press, 1994), 207; Ferrill, *Military Explanation*, 47; Bury, *LRE*, vol. I, 35; for discussion of the *limitanei* and *ripenses*, see Denis van Berchem, 'L'Annone militaire dans l'empire romain au IIIeme siècle' in *Memoires de la societe nationale des antiquaires de France*, vol. 80, ser. 8. Bk 10 (Paris, G. Klinckseick, 1937), 117–202; H.M.D. Parker, 'The Legions of Diocletian and Constantine', *The Journal of Roman Studies*, 23 (1933), 175–89.

75. Whittaker, *Frontiers of the Roman Empire*, 207; Jones, *The Later Roman Empire*, 651; for Jones' discussion regarding the *limitanei*, see pages 649–54; *Cod. Th.* 7.22.8.

76. Singular form, *cuneus*.

77. Jones, *The Later Roman Empire*, 681.

78. Southern and Dixon, *The Late Roman Army*, 36.

79. Jones, *The Later Roman Empire*, 649–54.

80. Jones, *The Later Roman Empire*, 651; see Jones, App. II, Tb. VII, 1435–1436; Hugh Elton, *Warfare in Roman Europe, AD 350–425* (Oxford, Clarendon Press, 2004), 212.

81. Jones, *The Later Roman Empire*, 608–10.

82. Jones, *The Later Roman Empire*, 610; R.S.O. Tomlin, 'The Army of the Late Empire', in *The Roman World*, Vol. I, John Wacher (ed.) (London, Routledge and Kegan Paul, Ltd, 1987), 113; Bury, *LRE*, vol. I, 35.

83. Jones, *The Later Roman Empire*, 608–09.

84. Jones, *The Later Roman Empire*, 682; Tomlin, 'The Army of the Late Empire', 113; Bury, *LRE*, vol. I, 35; John Lydus, *Mag* I.46

85. Pat Southern and Karen R. Dixon, *The Roman Cavalry, From the First to the Third Century AD* (New York, Routledge, 1997), 76.

86. See Ammianus, 16.10.8 for a description of a *clibanarius*.

87. Southern and Dixon, *The Late Roman Army*, 36; Southern and Dixon, *The Roman Cavalry*, 77.

88. Tomlin, 'The Army of the Late Empire', 111.

89. Southern and Dixon, *The Late Roman Army*, 19–20; Jones, *The Later Roman Empire*, 97–98, 681–682.

90. Philip De Souza, 'War at Sea' in *The Oxford Handbook of Warfare in the Classical World*, Brian Campbell and Lawrence A. Tritle (ed.) (Oxford, Oxford University Press, 2013), 386–87.

91. Olaf Höckmann, 'Late Roman Rhine Vessels from Mainz, Germany', *International Journal of Nautical Archaeology*, vol. 22, no. 2 (May 1993), 125–35.

92. 'And they [the Byzantines] had also ships of war prepared as for sea-fighting ... and they were single-banked ships covered with decks ... Such boats are called 'dromones' by those of the present time; for they are able to attain a great speed.' Procopius of Caesarea, *History of the Wars (Vandalic War)*, III, xi, 15–16.

93. The Greek δρόμων is derived from the word δρόμως meaning a 'race' or 'running'.

94. John H. Pryor and Elizabeth M. Jeffreys, *The Age of the Dromon: The Byzantine Navy ca 500–1204* (Boston, E.J. Brill, 2006), 123–29, 134–47.

95. Torsen Cumberland Jacobsen, *The Gothic War: Rome's Final Conflict in the West* (Yardley, PA, Westholme Publishing, 2009), 276–77.

96. R.W. Burgess, 'Principes sum Tyrannis: Two Studies on the Kaisergeschichte and Its Tradition' *The Classical Quarterly*, New Series, vol. 43, no. 2 (1993), 491–500. R.W. Burgess, 'A common source for Jerome, Eutropius, Festus, Ammianus, and the *Epitome de Caesaribus* between 358 and 378, along with further thoughts on the date and nature of the *Kaisergeschichte*,' *Classical Philology* 100 (2005), 166–92.

Bibliography

Modern Sources

Anderson, A.S., 'The Imperial Army', *Roman World*, 1, John Wacher (ed.). London, Routledge and Kegan Paul Ltd, 1987.

Benseddik, N., *Les troupes auxiliaries de l'armee romaine in Mauretanie Casarienne sous le Haut-Empire*. Alger, Societe nationale d'Edition et de Diffusion, 1979.

Birley, E., 'The Equestrian officers of the Roman Army', *Roman Britain and the Roman Army*, 133–53. Kendal, England, Titus Wilson, 1953.

Breeze, D.J., 'The Organization of the Legion: The First Cohort and the *Equites Legionis*', *The Journal of Roman Studies*, 59 (1969), 50–55.

Breeze, D.J., 'The organization of the career structure of the immunes and principales of the Roman army', *Bonner Jahrbucher*, 174 (1974), 245–92.

Breeze, D.J., 'Pay Grades and Ranks Below the Centurionate', *The Journal of Roman Studies*, 61 (1971), 130–35.

Breeze, D.J., 'The Career Structure below the Centurionate during the Principate', *Aufstieg und Niedergang der romischen Welt 2*, Principat, Band 1 (1974), 435–51.

Burgess, R.W., 'Principes sum Tyrannis: Two Studies on the Kaisergeschichte and its Tradition', *The Classical Quarterly*, 43 (2) (1993), 491–500.

Burgess, R.W., 'A common source for Jerome, Eutropius, Festus, Ammianus, and the *Epitome de Caesaribus* between 358 and 378, along with further thoughts on the date and nature of the *Kaisergeschichte*', *Classical Philology*, 100 (2005), 166–92.

Bury, J.B., *History of the Later Roman Empire*, 1. New York, Dover Publications, n.d.

Cagnat, R.L.V., *L'Armee romaine d'Afrique et l'occupation militaire de l'Afrique sous les empereurs*, E. Leroux (ed.). Paris, Imprimerie Nationale, 1913. Reprint, New York, Arno Press Inc., 1975.

Campbell, B. and Tritle, L.A. (eds), *The Oxford Handbook of Warfare in the Classical World*. Oxford, Oxford University Press, 2013.

Carcopino, J., *Le Maroc Antique*, 9th ed. Paris, Librairie Gallimard, 1943.

Cheesman, G.L., *The Auxilia of the Roman Imperial Army*. Oxford, The Clarendon Press, 1971.

Connolly, P., *Greece and Rome at War*. London, MacDonald Phoebus Ltd, 1981.

Davies, R.W., 'Police Work in Roman Times', *History Today*, 18 (1968), 700–07.

Davies, R.W., 'Cohortes Equitatae', *Historie*, 20 (1971), 751–63.

Elliott, P., *Legions in Crisis: The Transformation of the Roman Soldier, AD 192–284*. Stroud, UK, Fonthill Media, 2014.

Elton, H., *Warfare in Roman Europe: AD 350–425*. Oxford, Clarendon Press, 2004.

Erdkamp, P. (ed.), *A Companion to the Roman Army*. Malden, MA, Wiley-Blackwell Publishing Ltd, 2011.

Ferrill, A., *The Fall of the Roman Empire, the Military Explanation*. London, Thames and Hudson Ltd, 1988.

Goldsworthy, A., *The Complete Roman Army*. London, Thames and Hudson Ltd, 2003.

Graham, F., *Dictionary of Roman Military Terms*. Newcastle upon Tyne, Frank Graham, 1981.

Grosse, R., *Romische Miliargeschichte von Gallienus bis zum Beginn der Byzantinschen Themenverfassung*. Berlin, Weidmannsche Buchhandlung, 1920.

Gsell, S. and Carcopino, J., 'La base de M. Sulpicuis Felix et les décurions de Sala', *Melanges d'archeologie et d'histoire de l'Ecole française de Rome*, 47 (1931), 1–32.

Höckmann, O., 'Late Roman Rhine Vessels from Mainz, Germany', *International Journal of Nautical Archaeology*, 22 (1993), 125–35.

Jacobsen, T.C., *The Gothic War: Rome's Final Conflict in the West*. Yardley, Westholme Publishing, 2009.

Jones, A.H.M., *The Later Roman Empire, 284–602: A Social, Economic, and Administrative Survey*, 1. Norman, University of Oklahoma Press, 1964.

Keppie, L., *Making of the Roman Army: From Republic to Empire*. New York, Barnes and Noble Books, 1994.

Le Bohec, Y., *Imperial Roman Army*. New York, Hippocrene Books, 1989.

Le Bohec, Y., *Les unites auxiliaries de l'armee Romaine, en Afrique Proconsulaire et Numidie sous le Haut empire*, Etudes d'antiquites Africaines Series. Paris, Editions de Centre National de la Recherche Scientifique, 1989.

Lee, A.D., *War in Late Antiquity, a Social History*. Malden, MA, Blackwell Publishing, 2007.

Luttwak, E., *The Grand Strategy of the Roman Empire: From the First Century AD to the Third*. Baltimore, The Johns Hopkins University Press, 1976.

Mann, J.C., *Legionary Recruitment and Veteran Settlement During the Principate*, Margaret Roxan (ed.), Occasional Publication No. 7. Published by the Institute of Archaeology. Whitestable, UK, Whitestable Litho, 1983.

Mann, J.C., 'The Raising of New Legions during the Principate', *Hermes*, 91 (1963), 483–89.

Mommsen, T., 'Das romische Militarwesen seit Diocletian', *Hermes*, 24 (1889), 195–279.

Nicasie, M.J., *Twilight of Empire: The Roman Army from the Reign of Diocletian until the Battle of Adrianople*, Dutch Monographs on Ancient History and Archaeology. Amsterdam, J.C. Gieben, 1998.

Parker, H.M.D., *The Roman Legions*. New York, Dorset Press, 1992.

Parker, H.M.D., 'The Legions of Diocletian and Constantine', *The Journal of Roman Studies*, 23 (1933), 175–89.

Pollard, N. and Berry, J., *The Complete Roman Legions*. London, Thames and Hudson, 2012.

Potter, D.S., *The Roman Empire at Bay, AD 180–395*, 2nd edn, Routledge History of the Ancient World. New York, Routledge, 2014.

Pryor, J.H. and Jeffreys, E.M., *The Age of the Dromon: The Byzantine Navy ca 500–1204*. Boston, E.J. Brill, 2006.

Pseudo-Hyginus (Polybius and Pseudo-Hyginus), *De Munitionibus Castrorum* (from *The Fortification of the Roman Camp*). Translated and edited by M.C.J. Miller and J.G. DeVoto. Chicago, Ares Publishers, Inc., 1944.

Roth, J., *The Logistics of the Roman Army at War, 264 BC–AD 235*. Leiden, E.J. Brill, 1999.

Saddington, D.B., 'An Augustan Officer of the Roman Army: *Militaria* in Velleius Paterculus and Some Inscriptions', *Documenting the Roman Army, Essays in Honour of Margaret Roxan*, J.J. Wilkes (ed.). London, Institute of Classical Studies, 2003.

Saddington, D.B., 'The Roman Auxilia of Tacitus, Josephus and other Early Imperial Writers', *Acta Classica*, 13 (1970), 89–124.

Sander, E., 'Zur Rangordnung des römischen Heeres: die gradus ex caliga' *Historia*, 3 (1954–55), 87–105.

Seston, W., *Diocletien et la tetrachie*. vol 1. *Guerres et reformes (284–300), Bibliotheque des Ecoles francaises d'Athenes et de Rome*, facs. 162. Paris, E. de Boccard, 1946.

Southern, P., and Dixon, K.R., *The Late Roman Army*. New Haven, Yale University Press, 1996.

Southern, P., and Dixon, K.R., *The Roman Cavalry, From the First to the Third Century AD*. New York, Routledge, 1997.

Southern, P., *The Roman Army, a Social and Institutional History*. Santa Barbara, ABC-CLIO, 2006.

Southern, P., *The Roman Empire from Severus to Constantine*. New York, Routledge-Taylor Francis Group, 2007.

Speidel, M., 'The Pay of the Auxilia', *The Journal of Roman Studies*, 63 (1973), 141–47.

Stickler, T., 'The Foederati', *A Companion to the Roman Army*, P. Erdkamp (ed.). Malden, Wiley-Blackwell Publishing Ltd, 2011.

Tomlin, R.S.O., 'The Army of the Late Empire', *The Roman World*, 1, J. Wacher (ed.). London and New York, Routledge and Kegan Paul, 1987.

Van Berchem, D., *L'Armee de Diocletien et La Reforme Constantienne*. Paris, Geuthner, 1952.

Varaday, L., 'New evidence on some problems of the Late Roman military organization', *Acta Antiqua*, 9 (1961), 333–96.

Von Domaszewski, A., 'Die Rangordnung des romischen Heeres', *Bonner Jahrbucher*, 117 (1908), 1–275.

Watson, G.R., *The Roman Soldier*. Aspects of Greek and Roman Life Series, H. H. Scullard (ed.). Ithaca, Cornell University Press, 1995.

Webster, G., *The Roman Imperial Army of the First and Second Centuries AD*, 3rd ed., Totowa, Barnes and Noble Books, 1985.

Whittaker, C.R., *Frontiers of the Roman Empire: A Social and Economic Study*. Baltimore, The Johns Hopkins University Press, 1994.

Additional Sources Consulted for the Histories of the Ancient Authors

Bardenhewer, O., 'Lactantius', *Patrology: The Lives and Works of the Fathers of the Church*. Translated by T.J. Shahan. St Louis, MO, B. Herder Publisher, 1908.

Bowen, E.W., 'Claudian, the Last of the Classical Roman Poets', *Classical Journal* (May, 1954), 355–58.

Bowersock, G.W., 'Herodian and Elagabalus', *Studies in the Greek Historians: In Memory of Adam Perry*, D. Kagan (ed.). Yale Classical Studies, Vol. 34. New York, Cambridge University Press, 1975.

Brown, P., *St. Augustine of Hippo: A Biography*. Berkeley, University of California Press, 2000.

Burgess, R.W., 'Eutropius V.C. "Magister Memoriae?"', *Classical Philology*, 96 (Jan., 2001), 76–81.

Cameron, A., *Claudian. Poetry and Propaganda at the Court of Honorius*. Oxford, Clarendon Press, 1970.

Cameron, A., *Procopius and the Sixth Century*. New York, Routledge, 1996.

Clover, F.M., 'Flavius Merobaudes: a Translation and Commentary', *Transactions of the American Philosophical Society*, 61, 1 (1971), 1–78.

Croke, B., *Count Marcellinus and His Chronicle*. Oxford, Oxford University Press, 2001.

Croke, B., 'Cassiodorus and the *Getica* of Jordanes', *Classical Philology*, 82 (1987), 117–34.

Cross, F.L. and Livingstone, E.A., *The Oxford Dictionary of the Christian Church*. New York, Oxford University Press, 2005.

Den Boer, W., *Some Minor Roman Historians*. Leiden, E.J. Brill, 1972.

Drake, H.A., *Constantine and the Bishops: The Politics of Intolerance*. Ancient Society and History Series. Baltimore, The Johns Hopkins University Press, 2002.

Encyclopaedia Judaica.

Kaldellis, A., *Procopius of Caesarea: Tyranny, History, and Philosophy at the End of Antiquity*. Philadelphia, University of Pennsylvania Press, 2004.

Kazhdan, A. (ed.), *The Oxford Dictionary of Byzantium*. New York, Oxford University Press, 1991.

Kelly, G., 'The Roman World of Festus' Breviarium', *Cambridge Classical Journal*, Supp. 34 (2010), 72–91.

McLynn, N.B., *Ambrose of Milan: Church and Court in a Christian Capital*. Berkeley, University of California Press, 2014.

Matthews, J.F., 'Olympiodorus of Thebes and the History of the West', *The Journal of Roman Studies*, 60 (1970), 79–97.

Rohrbacher, D., 'Eutropius' *The Historians of Late Antiquity*. New York, Routledge, 2002.

Rohrbacher, D., 'Orosius' *The Historians of Late Antiquity*. New York, Routledge, 2002.

Rohrbacher, D., 'Socrates' *The Historians of Late Antiquity*. New York, Routledge, 2002.

Rohrbacher, D., 'Sozomen' *The Historians of Late Antiquity*. New York, Routledge, 2002.

Treadgold, W., 'The Diplomatic Career and Historical Work of Olympiodorus of Thebes', *International History Review*, 26 (2004), 709–33.

Van Nuffelen, P., *Orosius and the Rhetoric of History*. New York, Oxford University Press, 2012.

Van Nuffelen, P., 'John of Antioch, Inflated and Deflated. Or: How (not) to Collect Fragments of Early Byzantine Historians', *Byantion*, 82 (2012), 437–50.

Van Waarden, J.A. and Kelly, G. (eds), *New Approaches to Sidonius Appollinaris. Late Antique History and Religion*. Paris, Peeters, 2013.

Ancient Sources in Translation

The purpose of this list is to provide general readers with a reliable and user-friendly reference to ancient sources used in this work. I have cited almost exclusively from translations in the Loeb Classical Library for the compendium entries. When this was not possible, I necessarily consulted other translated works or scholarly publications. In such instances only a single modern translation for each ancient writer was used in this study. If more than one work by any single ancient author was employed, then only one translation of each work was referenced. The following is a list of modern English translations of ancient works used by the author that are not part of the LCL.

Ancient Sources used in this work which are not part of the LCL Corpus

Agathias, *The Histories*. Translated by Joseph D. Frendo. New York, De Gruyter, 1975.

Anonymous (sometimes ascribed to Aurelius Victor), *Epitome de Caesaribus* (*Epitome of the Emperors*). Translated as *Epitome de Caesaribus: A Booklet About the Style of Life and the Manners of the Imperatores* by Thomas M. Banchich. Canisius College Translated Texts, No. 1. Buffalo, Canisius College, 2009. Online at *De Imperatoribus Romanis*.

Aurelius Victor, Sextus, *De Caesaribus*. Translated by H.W. Bird. Liverpool, Liverpool University Press, 1994.

Banchich, T.M. and Lane, E.N. (trans.), *The History of Zonaras from Alexander Severus to the death of Theodosius the Great*. New York, Routledge, 2009.

Blockley, R.C. (trans.), *The Fragmentary Classicising Historians of the Later Roman Empire: Eunapius, Olympiodorus, Priscus and Malchus*. Vol. 2. Liverpool, Francis Cairns, 1983.

Burgess, R. (ed. and trans.), *The 'Chronicle' of Hydatius and the 'Consularia Constantinopolitana': Two Contemporary Accounts of the Final Years of the Roman Empire*. New York, Oxford University Press, 1993.

Burgess, R. (trans.), 'The Gallic Chronicle of 452: A New Critical Edition with a Brief Introduction' in Ralph Mathisen and Danuta Shanzer, *Society and Culture in Late Antique Gaul: Revisiting the Sources*. Aldershot, Ashgate Pub., 2001.

Burgess, R. (trans.), 'The Gallic Chronicle of 511: A New Critical Edition with a Brief Introduction' in Ralph Mathisen and Danuta Shanzer, *Society and Culture in Late Antique Gaul:
Revisiting the Sources*. Aldershot, Ashgate Pub., 2001.

Clover, F.M. (trans.), *Flavius Merobaudes: A Translation and Historical Commentary*. Transactions
of the American Philosophical Society, New Series, Vol. 61, No. 1 (1971), 1–78.

Dodgeon, M.H. (trans.) 'The Sons of Constantine: Libanius Or. LIX', in *From Constantine to
Julian: Pagan and Byzantine Views, A Source History*, S.N.C. Lieu and D.A.S. Montserrat (eds).
New York, Routledge, 1996.

Eusebius, *Life of Constantine*. Translated by A. Cameron and S. Hall. Clarendon Ancient
History. New York, Oxford University Press, 1999.

Eutropius, *Breviarium*. Translated by H.W. Bird. Liverpool, Liverpool University Press, 1993.

Festus, *Breviarium rerum gestarum populi Romani*. Translated as *Breviarium of the Accomplishments
of the Roman People* by T.M. Banchich and J.A. Meka. Canisius College Translated Texts,
No. 2. Buffalo, Canisius College, 2001. Online at *De Imperatoribus Romanis*.

George Synkellos, *The Chronography*. Translated by W. Adler and P. Tuffin. Oxford, Oxford
University Press, 2002.

Gregory of Tours, *The History of the Franks*. Translated by O.M. Dalton. Vols. 1–2. Oxford,
Clarendon Press, 1927.

Isadore of Seville, *History of the Kings of the Goths, Vandals, and Suevi*. Translated by G. Donini
and G. Ford Jr., Leiden, E.J. Brill, 1966.

Justinian, *Corpus Iuris Civilis*. 10th edn. Vol. 1. *Institutiones*, edited by P. Krueger; *Digesta*, edited
by T. Mommsen. Berlin, Weidman, 1920.

Lucan, *Pharsalia*. Translated by H.T. Riley. London, Henry G. Bohn, 1853.

Marcellinus, *Chronicle*. Translated by B. Croke. Sydney, Australian Association of Byzantine
Studies, 1995.

Milner, N.P. (trans.), *Vegetius: Epitome of Military Science*. Liverpool, Liverpool University Press,
1993.

Muhlberger, S., *The Fifth Century Chroniclers: Prosper, Hydatius, and the Gallic Chronicler of 452*.
Leeds, Francis Cairns, 1990.

Panegyrici Latini. Translated by C.E.V. Nixon and B.S. Rodgers. Berkeley, University of
California Press, 1995.

Paulus Orosius, *The Seven Books of History against the Pagans*. Translated by R.J. Deferrari.
Washington, D.C., The Catholic University of America Press, 2001.

Possidius, *Sancti Augustini Vita*. Translated by H.T. Weiskotten. Princeton, Princeton
University Press, 1919.

Prosper of Aquitaine, *Epitoma Chronicon*. From *Chronica Minora*, Vol. I, Monumenta Germaniae
Historica. Edited by T. Mommsen. Berlin, 1892. Reprint, 1961.

Pseudo-Zachariah Rhetor, *The Chronicle*. Translated by R.R. Phenix and C.B. Horn, with contributions by S.P. Brock and W. Witakowski. Liverpool, Liverpool University Press, 2011.

Rostovtzeff, M. I, 'Res Gestae Divi Saporis and Dura' *Berytus*, 8:1 (1943), 17–60.

Shea, G.W. (trans.), *The Iohannis or de Bellis Libycis of Flavius Cresconius Corippus* in *Studies in
Classics*, vol. 7. Lewiston, Edwin Mellen Press, 1998.

Shuckburgh, E.S. (trans.), *The Letters of Cicero*. Vol. 2. London, George Bell and Sons, 1899.

Sozomen, *Ecclesiastical History*. Translated by C.D. Hartranft. From *Nicene and Post-Nicene
fathers*. Second Series, Vol. 2, P. Schaff and H. Wace (eds). Buffalo, N.Y., Christian
Literature Publishing Co., 1890.

Vollmer, F. (ed.), *Fl. Merobaudis reliquiae, Monumenta Germaniae historica: Auctores antiquissimi*,
Vol. 14, 1905.

Zosimus, *New History*. Translated by R.T. Ridley. Sydney, Australian Association for Byzantine
Studies, 1982.

Index

People

Places